ROUTLEDGE LIBRARY EDITIONS: SLAVERY

Volume 11

SLAVERY

SLAVERY

C. W. W. GREENIDGE

Routledge
Taylor & Francis Group
LONDON AND NEW YORK

First published in 1958 by George Allen & Unwin Ltd.

This edition first published in 2023
by Routledge
4 Park Square, Milton Park, Abingdon, Oxon OX14 4RN

and by Routledge
605 Third Avenue, New York, NY 10158

Routledge is an imprint of the Taylor & Francis Group, an informa business

© 1958 George Allen & Unwin Ltd.

All rights reserved. No part of this book may be reprinted or reproduced or utilised in any form or by any electronic, mechanical, or other means, now known or hereafter invented, including photocopying and recording, or in any information storage or retrieval system, without permission in writing from the publishers.

Trademark notice: Product or corporate names may be trademarks or registered trademarks, and are used only for identification and explanation without intent to infringe.

British Library Cataloguing in Publication Data
A catalogue record for this book is available from the British Library

ISBN: 978-1-032-30942-2 (Set)
ISBN: 978-1-032-31331-3 (Volume 11) (hbk)
ISBN: 978-1-032-31334-4 (Volume 11) (pbk)
ISBN: 978-1-003-30922-2 (Volume 11) (ebk)

DOI: 10.4324/9781003309222

Publisher's Note
The publisher has gone to great lengths to ensure the quality of this reprint but points out that some imperfections in the original copies may be apparent.

Disclaimer
The publisher has made every effort to trace copyright holders and would welcome correspondence from those they have been unable to trace.

SLAVERY

BY

C. W. W. GREENIDGE

MA, LLB *(Cantab)*
Secretary of the Anti-Slavery Society (UK), 1941-1956
Director of the Anti-Slavery Society 1956 continuing
Member of the UN ad hoc Committee on
Slavery, 1950-51

Ruskin House
GEORGE ALLEN & UNWIN LTD
MUSEUM STREET LONDON

FIRST PUBLISHED IN 1958

This book is copyright under the Berne Convention. Apart from any fair dealing for the purpose of private study, research, criticism or review, as permitted under the Copyright Act, 1956, no portion may be reproduced by any process without written permission. Enquiry should be made to the publisher

© *George Allen & Unwin Ltd. 1958*

PRINTED IN GREAT BRITAIN
in 10 pt. Pilgrim type by
SIMSON SHAND LTD.
LONDON, HERTFORD AND HARLOW

PREFACE

ARE there still slaves in the world? Is there still a real need for an Anti-Slavery Society? I have been asked these questions so often during the past seventeen years, in which I have been first Secretary, then Director of the Anti-Slavery Society of the United Kingdom, that a book bringing the subject up to date seems called for.

Slavery is widely regarded as an ugly blot on the pages of history, but one which has been decently obscured by the passage of time. In most people's minds it came to an end a century or more ago, with the freeing of slaves in the colonies of European nations and in the United States of America.

But this is far from being true. Human bondage, in all its guises, is not a thing of the past. It is a pressing problem of our world today, and therefore of all its citizens, a problem which calls for fresh and determined action before the work so nobly begun by Clarkson, Wilberforce and Buxton in England, the Abbé Gregoire and Shoelcher in France, and Lincoln, Garrison and the Beechers in the United States of America, can be said to be completed.

Lincoln declared that a nation cannot be half free and half enslaved. Neither can the world in this era of 'total involvement', when improved communications have created a global consciousness. It is intolerable that while the basic human liberties are so widely acknowledged there should still be millions of men, women and children living in actual bondage. Yet such is the case: slavery continues to flourish in one or other of its four forms in Asia, Africa, and Latin America.

The truth once known demands action. In this book I shall endeavour to set out the facts, in the hope that those who read them may be stirred to give their support to the anti-slavery movement, either in the United Kingdom, which for more than a century and a half has taken the lead in anti-slavery endeavour, or in whatever country the reader may be. Our object is to keep constantly before the governments of the world the abiding need to bring slavery to an end.

Wilberforce and Buxton worked to convert public opinion to the view that slavery was an evil and unnecessary institution, and to secure a specific change in British law, i.e., to secure the abolition of the legal status of slavery in British colonies. The modern problem, however, is more international than national. As the late Viscount Simon wrote in 1929, in the preface to his wife's book on slavery, 'The new task is not to convince enlightened men and women that slavery is a monstrous thing, but that it still prevails over large portions of the earth, and that it can be swept away by the leadership and the pressure of the League of Nations. . . . And once the inhumanity of slavery as practised today in distant parts of the earth is, as the saying is, "brought home", the conscience of the world, working through the instrument of international action, will not rest until it be ended'.

Since then the United Nations has taken over the work of the League. Though its Charter does not specifically mention slavery, the incompatability of it with the principles of justice and humanity held by civilized peoples is clearly implied in Article 1. This states, among other things, that, 'The purposes of the United Nations are . . . (3) To achieve international co-operation in solving international problems of an economic, social, cultural or humanitarian character and in promoting and encouraging respect for human rights and for fundamental freedoms for all without distinction as to race, sex, language or religion. (4) To be a centre for harmonizing the actions of nations in the attainment of those ends'. Can there be a freedom more fundamental than personal liberty and the right to dispose of one's labour as one pleases, a right which slavery denies?

Another article of the Charter, Article 73 (a), also refers by implication to slavery. It enjoins on 'Members of the United Nations which have or assume responsibilities for the administration of territories whose people have not yet attained a full measure of self-government the duty to ensure, with due respect for the culture of the people concerned, their political, social and educational advancement, their just treatment and their protection against abuses'. Can there be an abuse more pernicious than slavery?

The first specific mention of slavery by the United Nations came in 1948, when on December 10th the General Assembly approved the Universal Declaration of Human Rights. Article 4 of this document states that, 'No one shall be held in slavery or servitude; slavery and the slave trade shall be prohibited in all their forms'. This marks the beginning of endeavour by the United Nations to bring slavery to an end.

Although many books on the history of slavery and the anti-slavery movement have been published in recent years, nothing on slavery as it exists in the world today has appeared since Lady Simon's book, *Slavery*, in 1929. Before Lady Simon died in 1955 I suggested that she might allow me to help her prepare a revised

Preface

edition of her book, and she expressed approval of the idea. But unfortunately she was never well enough. I have therefore attempted the task alone and dedicate the book to her memory

I express my gratitude to all those whose statements I have quoted in this book, as well as to Mr George Unwin, whose services have been invaluable in improving the literary style of this book.

CONTENTS

PREFACE 7

Part I. THE FACTS

1. Slavery, its Genesis and Definition — 15
2. The Treatment of Slaves — 27
3. Chattel Slavery Today — 36
4. Slaving Trading Today — 49
5. The Attitude of Islam — 58
6. Debt-bondage — 66
7. Serfdom or Peonage — 74
8. The Sale of Women into Marriage — 94
9. The Sham Adoption of Children — 105

Part II. THE FIGHT

10. Slave Charities — 119
11. The Anti-Slavery Movement: Slave Trading — 127
12. The Anti-Slavery Movement: Slavery Itself — 142
13. The Anti-Slavery Society — 159
14. International Action Before The League of Nations — 171
15. The League of Nations and After — 180
16. Action by The United Nations — 190
17. What Remains to be Done — 201

APPENDICES
 1. The Brussels Act of 1890 — 205
 2. The Slavery Convention of 1926 — 224
 3. The Supplementary Convention of 1956 — 228

INDEX 233

PART I
THE FACTS

CHAPTER I

SLAVERY, ITS GENESIS
AND DEFINITION

༄༅།

THE idea of personal freedom has become so well established in the West, that it seems incredible to many that slavery should still exist. The survival of a practice so universally condemned can only be understood if one remembers that it has had a place in every civilized society at some stage of its development, and may assume several different forms in the course of it. The complete abolition of slavery is therefore no easy matter. It is complicated on the one hand by the unequal development of human societies, and on the other by the legal problem of framing a suitable definition, one that would be internationally acceptable but at the same time cover the various degrees of restrictive freedom amounting to slavery that are known to exist.

Slavery arises from war and conquest, and could even be said to represent an advance upon a more primitive practice. For at first man simply killed his victims, and sometimes ate them. Only when he adopted a settled way of life did he find it more useful to spare their lives and enslave them, thus freeing himself from the burden of regular work. 'The greatest of all divisions,' writes Tyler, 'that between freemen and slaves, appears as soon as a barbaric warrior spares the life of his enemy, when he has him down, and brings him home to drudge for him and till the soil.'[1]

The history of slavery in Europe provides a complete picture of the way in which it can arise, become modified and die, through the growth of humanitarian ideas, only to revive with fresh conquests and the greed of exploiting them. In the ancient world slavery was already well established in Greece at the time of Homer, though probably not in a very harsh form. Later, it was accepted by Aristotle as necessary and natural; and also by Plato, though with some embarrassment.

With the rise of the Roman Empire slavery was more systematically developed, and its close connection with militarism became

[1] *Anthropology.*

Slavery

more evident. The victories of Roman arms secured a steady stream of vanquished and enslaved 'barbarians', who not only performed all the workaday tasks, but by doing so freed men for further conquest; a process attempted more recently by Hitler. The slave population of Rome, coming from Africa, Spain, Gaul (France), Britain, and Asia Minor, grew to equal the free population by the middle of the first century, and the risk of insurrection became dangerous. An elaborate code was therefore devised under which a slave could become a freedman. The poet Terence and the philosopher Epictetus were freedmen. So was the father of Horace.

But slavery remained an essential part of the social structure, and when the Roman conquests came to an end and the supply of slaves dwindled, fresh sources had to be found. In place of the old basis of enslavement by war there now developed a less justifiable commerce in slaves fed by piracy and kidnapping. In addition slaves were created internally by several methods. Citizens could be enslaved as a punishment for certain crimes and sentenced to work in public quarries and mines: debtors could become enslaved to their creditors; and a father could sell his children into slavery.

For their main supply of slaves, however, the later Romans had to resort to what Gibbon calls 'the milder but more tedious method of propagation'. The principle that the child of a slave woman, whoever the father may be, is a slave was established at an early date. In the changed conditions in Rome it was to the interest of each family to preserve its own hereditary slaves indefinitely, and this had the effect of eventually transmuting slavery into serfdom. The masters parted with their property in the persons of their slaves in return for only a determinate part of their services; while the slave, who had now become a serf, personally free, got the use of a piece of his master's land. To this, however, he was permanently attached (*adscriptus glebae*), an arrangement that became a hereditary fixity. 'The relationship between master and man,' as J. K. Ingram puts it, 'changed from a personal to a territorial one.'[1]

When the Teutonic races from Germany defeated the Romans about 300 A.D. there was nothing they did not know about enslaving their prisoners of war and weaker neighbours. The very word slave is but Slav, and a reminder of the large numbers of the great Slav people whom the Teutons captured in war and who made up the bulk of their slave population. But the Teutons had merciful ideas. It was their custom to encourage the better slaves to become free men and leaders. Wherever they settled they started the feudal system and raised their captives from complete slavery to serfdom.

[1] *History of Slavery.*

Slavery, its Genesis and Definition

In the British Isles slavery and serfdom had a long history going back to the Bronze Age, each successive wave of invaders enslaving those they conquered. It thus followed the same course as in other countries. Before the Romans came slaves were a British export, and after their coming and four hundred years' rule, education and civilization they still were. The Teutonic and Norman invaders that followed each had their accompaniment of enslavement and enserfment. But the net final result was that the slave became a serf, attached to the land and only vendible with it. He could, however, purchase his freedom; and in the course of time all the serfs in fact became free. In England the last deed of enfranchisement was enacted in 1574. In Scotland serfdom lingered a little longer, until the last vestiges of it were abolished by Act of Parliament in 1799.

Before this process came to its end, however, a fresh and wholly indefensible form of slavery grew up in the colonies of the western nations. If the ancient world could condone slavery as arising 'naturally' from war, there was no excuse for the merciless seizure and transportation of millions of negroes from West Africa to work on the plantations in America and in the West Indies. Yet this traffic, ironically enough, was begun on the advice of a compassionate Christian, Bartholemy de las Casas, the Bishop of Chiapas.

African slaves were first taken to Europe in 1442, in the time of Prince Henry, the Navigator, of Portugal. They worked in Portugal and Spain, and multiplied. Soon after the West Indies were discovered by Columbus in 1492, Nicolas de Ovando assumed the governorship of Hispaniola (now Haiti and San Domingo) and took some Spanish negroes with him. These withstood the ruthless treatment meted out to their labour force by the Spanish colonizers much better than the aboriginal inhabitants, the quiet and docile Arawak Indians, who were almost exterminated by it. It was his desire to save the Indians from extinction that prompted las Casas to give his fatal advice, which he came deeply to regret, to import negroes from West Africa to supply the labour needed. His suggestion was adopted and the African slave trade began, negroes being first imported to work in the gold mines of Hispaniola in 1510. Thereafter the traffic continued, and grew.

But though slavery waxed great in the Spanish colonies, exacting a rising toll of human misery, it was another century before the acquisition of colonies drew Britain into the business. And then the first British slaves were white. Slavery was chosen as a convenient way of disposing of political enemies. Cromwell sent many hundreds of Royalist prisoners to be sold in Bristol, and most of them were sent to the newly settled American colonies. Nor was there any com-

Slavery

passion for Irishmen who had massacred Englishmen and Protestants. The Council of State in the time of Cromwell ordered the Governor of Waterford to deliver to three Bristol merchants as many Irish prisoners as they might require as slaves for the West Indies. Later, after the Monmouth rebellion, the same punishment was meted out to hundreds of men and women from the west country of England.

Beginning with Sir John Hawkins in 1562 British seamen had taken a profitable part in the African slave trade supplying the Spanish colonies. But Britain's own share in its shame did not properly begin until 1620, when African slaves were offered for sale in the colony of Virginia, thus initiating the tragic history of slavery in the southern states of the USA. Slow at first the traffic into British colonies got under way in the latter half of the seventeenth century. Between 1680 and 1700 no less than 300,000 African slaves were imported into British colonies. Between 1700 and 1786 Jamaica alone imported 610,000. In the 106 years following 1680 the British colonies imported no less than 2,130,000 slaves. It is very difficult to arrive at a reasonably accurate idea of the total number affected by the African slave trade, but one estimate confidently states that some twelve million Africans were torn from their homes and taken overseas into slavery.

The first public signs of conscience about slave trading were long delayed, and when they did come one might say that it was mainly because the boot was on the other foot. The first treaty concerning slave trading was made in 1662; but it was between Britain and Tripoli, and prohibited the enslavement of His Britannic Majesty's subjects in Tripoli or any of its territories. It was an attempt to check the depredations of the Barbary and Turkish corsairs.

The name Barbary is derived from the Berbers (said to be of Teutonic origin), who were the principal inhabitants of the country known to the Romans, and for long afterwards, as Mauretania, the country of the Moors. When Islam let loose an Arab flood on the remnants of the older civilizations of North Africa the Mauretanian or Barbary states (Barka, Tripoli, Tunis, and Algeria) were never subjected, although the Moors and Berbers accepted the doctrines of the Koran and a caliph of the west, who has survived the Turkish caliph of the east, arose in what is now Morocco. The semi-independent Barbary rulers fostered, or certainly failed to control, piracy and slave-raiding in the middle and western Mediterranean, and are said to have secured a percentage of the corsairs' profits. For centuries the cities of the Mediterranean littoral struggled against this spoilation, and thousands of Europeans of all nations languished

Slavery, its Genesis and Definition

as slaves in North Africa. Not only were the crews of European ships enslaved but so also were their passengers, or else they were held to ransom at fantastic prices. Travel on the sea became a perilous venture and many a European woman was seized and sold to adorn the harem of the Sultan of Turkey or some lesser potentate.

The spread of the Turkish Empire into North Africa brought no mitigation. On the contrary, in the early sixteenth century the combination of the power of the Barbary corsairs with that of the Ottoman Turk increased the depredations and condemned to slavery tens of thousands of Europeans. At one time it was estimated that there were no less than 30,000 Christian slaves in Tunis alone. Of the Turkish corsairs the most famous and execrated was Khair ud Din, better known as Barbarossa (Redbeard). He was a Greek, born at Mitylene; but early in life he embraced Islam and worked his way up in the service of the Turkish Empire until he was able to attack and seize first Algeria and then Tunis. From there he soon became the terror of the seas and devastated the coasts of Europe, sacking and burning cities as far north as Baltimore in Ireland. Some suggest that the savagery of Barbary slave-raiding was a reprisal for the persecution and expulsion of the Moors from Spain. It has also been suggested that when European nations took to slave-raiding to supply their colonies with labour it would have been more equitable if they had drawn their supply of slaves from North instead of West Africa.

There is in Britain an interesting modern survival from this Mediterranean slave-raiding in the Slave Charities, which were created by testators in the Stuart period and later to redeem British victims of the corsairs. No serious attempt was made by the European states to check the menace, whether because they did not feel themselves a match for the corsairs in shipbuilding and naval warfare, or from some other cause. Instead they preferred to pay blackmail and maintained diplomatic emissaries and consuls in the Barbary states whose principal function was to ransom their countrymen; some of the barbary states also had envoys at the Court of St James and other European courts to facilitate arrangements. Inhuman cruelties were inflicted on the captives in the hope that this would encourage their ransom and redemption. The prospects of the rich were good, but the slave market was the fate of the poor. It was this state of affairs that prompted many charitable people in Britain to leave part of their estates on trust to be invested and the income devoted to the redemption of captives. An account of some of these charities and the manner in which their funds are applied today may be found in Chapter X.

Slavery

Though the iniquity of enslaving Christians was officially recognized with the Tripoli treaty of 1662, it was more than a hundred years before the iniquity of enslaving Africans began to receive similar recognition. The epoch-making decision of Lord Mansfield, the Lord Chief Justice, in the case of Somerset, the West Indian slave, came in 1772; and the Act of Parliament abolishing the slave trade in British possessions was not passed until 1807. Since then, however, the fight against slave-raiding, either by force or ruse, has been carried into the international sphere, until in 1925 the Temporary Slavery Commission of the League of Nations could say with truth that it had all but disappeared. Yet unhappily today it still blackens the record of some countries. These, as will appear in a later chapter, are in Arabia, where slavery is as old as time and still flourishes in this year of grace 1958. Recognized by the law, it is practised openly and holds some half a million people in its grip. The majority of these are born slaves, but in addition there is a flow of new slaves from neighbouring countries.

The slavery that arose from war, and subsequently from raiding, trading and dealing, and from birth, was what is known as 'classic' or chattel slavery, in which the slave was a piece of property. While this form still survives in Arabia, elsewhere slavery exists, as an exploitation of the weaker members of a society by the stronger, and frequently maintained by social sanction, in less straightforward guises. Debt-bondage, by which a debtor may enslave himself voluntarily, or someone under his control, as security for a debt is a major cause of practical enslavement; while the system of land tenure in several parts of the world keeps millions of people in a state of near slavery under such euphemistic terms as peonage. Finally, under the pressure of economic conditions there have developed such practices as the sale of daughters into marriage without their consent, an example of which is the vexed question of the African 'bride price', and the selling or giving of children to others who desire to exploit their labour under the guise of adoption, a practice particularly prevalent in the Far East. With the advent of international action to combat slavery definition of it and these analogous practices became a matter of some importance.

Until 1926, when the League of Nations framed its Convention on Slavery, definitions reposed upon the legislative enactments of the various nations or, more loosely, upon legal and philosophical opinion. L. T. Hobhouse, for instance, held that, 'The slave, properly regarded, is a man whom law and custom regard as the property of another. In extreme cases he is wholly without rights, a pure chattel. In other cases he may be protected in certain respects, but

Slavery, its Genesis and Definition

so may an ox or an ass. As long as he is for all ordinary purposes completely at his master's disposal, rendering to his master the fruits of his work, performing his work under orders, rewarded at his master's discretion, liable to punishment on his master's judgment, he may, though fairly protected in other relations, fairly be called a slave'.[1]

Another authority, Edward Westermark, emphasized a different aspect. 'According to a common definition of slavery, the slave is the property of his master, but this definition is hardly accurate. ... The owner's right over his property, even when not absolute, is at all events exclusive, that is, nobody but the owner has a right of disposal of it. Now the master's right of disposal of a slave is not necessarily exclusive: custom or law may grant the latter a certain amount of liberty, and in such a case his condition differs essentially from that of a piece of property. The chief characteristic of slavery is the compulsory nature of the slave's relation to the master.'[2]

This view is supported by Wharton's *Law Lexicon*, which defines slavery as 'the civil relation in which one person has absolute power over the liberty of another'; and by a judgment of the Supreme Court of the United States of America. In *United States* v *Ingalls* (73 Fed. Sur. 16 (1947)), a slave was defined as 'a person who is wholly subject to the will of another, one who has no freedom of action and whose person and services are wholly under the control of another and is in a state of compulsory service to another'.

A modern sociological writer, Bronislaw Malinowski, has described slavery as 'the denial of all biological freedom except in the self-interest not of the organism but of its master. The slave is also deprived of all satisfactions which culture guarantees to a man as the price paid for the trammels it imposes. The slave does not enjoy the protection of the law. His economic behaviour is not determined by profits and advantages. He cannot mate according to his choice. He remains outside the law of parentage and kinship. Even his conscience is not his own'.

The most exhaustive study of the meaning of slavery, however, was probably that made by H. J. Nieboer. After quoting seven well-known writers he agrees with them in concluding that, 'Slavery is the fact that one man is the property or possession of another beyond the limits of the family proper'.[3]

---

[1] *Morals in Evolution*, p. 27.
[2] *Origin and Development of Moral Ideas*, p. 670.
[3] *Slavery as an Industrial System*, p. 6 et seq.

Slavery

In 1926 when the League of Nations prepared its Slavery Convention it too followed this line of thought. Article I (1) of the Convention laid down the following definition: 'Slavery is a status or condition of a person over whom any or all of the powers attaching to the right of ownership are exercised.'

But this definition was at once criticized as being both inadequate and inaccurate. When the draft Convention was circulated to member states for comment before being submitted to the League's Assembly, it was criticized by Belgium and Germany. Belgium put forward no alternative proposals, but Germany suggested adding to the definition the following words: '. . . under private law by some other person or group of persons.' The German Government admitted that it was exceptionally difficult to harmonize the legal conceptions of highly civilized states and those of more backward peoples. Their suggestion was not adopted. The League's definition represented the greatest common measure of agreement that could be obtained at the time.

More serious criticism of it, in the light of practical experience in Africa, came some years later. Lord Lugard, an eminent authority on slavery and a member of the League's Slavery Commission of 1924-5, pointed out that, 'To an African the term "right of ownership" might not convey the precise meaning intended, namely, that of a chattel without human rights'.[1]

In 1930 an International Commission was appointed to enquire into the existence of slavery and forced labour in Liberia. It was charged to determine, amongst other things, 'whether slavery as defined in the Slavery Convention of 1926 in fact exists in the Republic of Liberia'.

The Commission began its report by stating that the League's definition left little room for distinguishing between degrees of restrictive freedom, a circumstance common in Africa, and that it was 'too inadequate in one sense and too comprehensive in another'.[2] On the basis of the evidence it collected the Commission made the following classification:

A. Common Slavery.
   1. Oppressive forms of slavery as practised inter-tribally, involving a commercialized traffic and transfer of slaves and their offspring by sale, gift or inheritance.
   2. Domestic slavery as practised inter-tribally, involving full proprietary rights and related to the social systems of the tribes involved.

[1] Article in *Africa* for January, 1933, p. 9.
[2] Publication No. 147. USA Govt. Printing Office, 1931.

Slavery, its Genesis and Definition

B. Oppressive practices, restrictive of the freedom of persons, constituting conditions analogous to slavery and tending to acquire the status of common or classic slavery.

Unfortunately the League's definition was widely interpreted by many States Parties to the 1926 Convention as embracing only chattel slavery, and as inapplicable to analogous forms of servitude. And this occurred in spite of the explanation of the definition given by Lord Cecil of Chelwood, the Rapporteur of the League of Nations Committee which drafted the Convention. Commenting on Article II of the Convention ('The High Contracting Parties undertake . . . (b) to bring about progressively and as soon as possible the complete abolition of slavery in all its forms') he wrote, 'A slight change has been made in the drafting of sub-paragraph (b) of this Article II; the words "notably in the case of domestic slavery and similar conditions" being now omitted. This modification was made because it was believed that such conditions came within the definition of slavery contained in the first Article and that no further prohibition of them in express terms was necessary. This applies not only to domestic slavery but to all the conditions mentioned by the Temporary Slavery Commission and to which I referred last year, that is, debt slavery, the enslaving of persons disguised as payment of dowry, etc. Even if, as is possible, these last practices do not come under the definition of slavery as it is given in Article I of this Convention, the Committee is unanimously of the opinion that they must be combated. In a more general way it interprets Article II as tending to bring about the disappearance from written legislation or from the custom of the country of everything which admits the maintenance by a private individual of rights over another person of the same nature as the rights which an individual can have over things.'[1]

However, the matter was put beyond doubt when the United Nations began its anti-slavery activities and set up an *ad hoc* committee to study the subject. The Committee found that 'there is not sufficient reason for discarding or amending the definition of slavery contained in Article I (1) of the Slavery Convention of 1926'. Nevertheless, it recommended the making of a 'Supplementary Convention on Slavery in which practices analogous to slavery should be defined and declared to be slavery, whether or not they are embraced by the definition of slavery in the Slavery Convention of 1926'.[2]

This was duly done. In August 1956 the United Nations convened

---
[1] League of Nations Doc. A.104.1926.VI, p. 2.
[2] UN Doc. E/1988. para. II.

Slavery

a conference at Geneva attended by the plenipotentiaries of forty-eight nations. The resulting Supplementary Convention on Slavery has since been signed by the representatives of thirty-three nations.[1]

Unfortunately, this Supplementary Convention included serfdom among the practices analogous to slavery. Yet serfdom is not slavery; it is a status intermediate between slavery and complete freedom. When the committee of the Economic and Social Council of the United Nations was preparing the preliminary draft of the Convention in January 1956, the distinction between the two was pointed out by the Anti-Slavery Society. Historically, as we have seen, slavery was not changed directly into a system of personal freedom; there was, as J. K. Ingram says, 'an intermediate step which has not always been sufficiently discriminated from slavery, though the confusion between the two leads to endless misconception. We mean serfdom'.[2]

Two other authorities make the same point. H. J. Nieboer writes that, 'As soon as the forced labourer is no longer entirely at the disposal of the lord, the latter being entitled to fixed services only, such a state of things is called serfdom but not slavery'.[3] And Sir George MacMunn: 'Serfdom is not slavery, in that speaking generally, the serf was bound to the land and went with it. He was "a bound tiller" who was compelled to live on the land, to till the owner's land for so many days a week, and for the remainder was free to work on his own holding. A serf could not be sold as an unattached slave.'[4]

This was also the conclusion reached by the League of Nations. The 1926 Convention made no attempt to define serfdom. The League's Advisory Committee of Experts on Slavery held that. 'The serf is not a slave because he is not the property of his master'.

Another borderline practice, in the words of the United Nations *ad hoc* Committee on Slavery, is 'the practice whereby an individual or group of individuals are obliged by customary or other law to perform services for another individual or for the collectivity and cannot commute those services'. The *ad hoc* Committee recommended that this should be included in the definition of practices analogous to slavery. The drafting Committee, however, wisely did not adopt their recommendation. As H. J. Nieboer says, 'We shall meet with instances of tribes, the members of which are bound to perform some kind of labour for other tribes. This is not slavery, for

[1] Up to October 3, 1956.
[2] *History of Slavery*, p. 71.
[3] *Slavery as an Industrial System*.
[4] *Slavery Through the Ages*.

Slavery, its Genesis and Definition

slavery is the subjection of one individual to another'. And he quotes Ingram as saying, 'The lowest caste may be a degraded and despised one, but its members are not in a state of slavery; they are in collective, not individual, subjection to the members of the higher classes'.

Herein also lies the distinction between slavery and forced labour, two institutions which are often confused. Slavery is the exaction of involuntary labour by one individual from another individual to whom the latter belongs, whereas forced labour is the exaction of involuntary labour from an individual to a government, i.e. a collectivity, to punish or discipline the person from whom the labour is exacted.

Both the League of Nations and the United Nations have distinguished between the two. The League dealt with them in separate conventions and each was assigned to the care of a different agency. The United Nations seems to have left forced labour in the care of the International Labour Office—but it has not yet assigned slavery to the care of any agency.

To conclude, we now have, whatever its imperfections, an internationally accepted definition of slavery which covers the whole field; and this must be our guide unless and until it is amended. It consists of Article I (1) of the Slavery Convention of 1926, which has been ratified by forty-four nations and is still in force, and Article I of the Supplementary Convention on Slavery of 1956, which defines practices analogous to slavery. Both these Conventions may be found in the Appendices of this book, but for convenience of reference the definitions from them are set out here.

Article I (1) of the Slavery Convention of 1926:
> Slavery is the status or condition of a person over whom any or all of the powers attaching to the right of ownership are exercised.

Article I of the Supplementary Convention on Slavery of 1956:
> Each of the States Parties to this Convention shall take all practicable and necessary legislative and other measures to bring about progressively and as soon as possible the complete abolition or abandonment of the following institutions and practices, where they still exist and whether or not they are covered by the definition of slavery contained in Article I of the Slavery Convention signed at Geneva on September 25, 1926:
>> (a) Debt bondage, that is to say, the status or condition arising from a pledge by a debtor of his personal services or those of a third person under his control as a security for a debt, where the value reasonably assessed of those ser-

Slavery

vices rendered is not applied towards the liquidation of the debt or the length and nature of those services are not respectively limited and defined;

(b) Serfdom, that is to say, the tenure of land whereby the tenant is by law, custom or agreement bound to live and labour on land belonging to another person and render some determinate services to such other person, whether for reward or not, and is not free to change his status;

(c) Any institution or practice whereby:
  (i) A woman, without the right to refuse, is promised or given in marriage on payment of a consideration in money or in kind to her parents, guardian, family or any other person or group;
  (ii) The husband of a woman, his family or his clan has the right to transfer her to another person for value received or otherwise; or
  (iii) The woman on the death of her husband is liable to be inherited by another person;

(d) Any institution or practice whereby a child or young person under the age of 18 years is delivered by either or both his natural parents or his guardian to another person, whether for reward or not, for the purpose of exploiting the child or young person or his or her labour.

CHAPTER II

THE TREATMENT OF SLAVES

∞

SINCE the slave is a piece of property his master's power over him is in principle unlimited. Though a certain amount of liberty has in fact been granted to slaves in all slave-owning countries, any checks imposed by law or custom are foreign to the nature of the institution, and the absolute power of the master has generally tended to corrupt and destroy self-control, leading to all manner of cruelties. The worst of these, and distinct from any particular instances of cruel treatment, are the practices that come under the general category of mutilation of the body.

Probably the most revolting concomitant of slavery from the earliest times has been the mutilation of male slaves by castration, that is the removal of the whole or part of the genital organs. This has been perpetrated on slave men and boys for thousands of years to fit them for certain duties, principally in the harems of orientals of high rank. Where many women are kept for the bed of a highly placed man and for him alone, there are among them many whose sexual appetites are rarely satisfied. To these the presence of an uncut male would inevitably be a stimulant. To protect the potentate's prerogative the harem is therefore guarded by emasculate males, who are charged under a head eunuch with the running of what is in many cases a large female establishment. Tradition has credited Semiramis, the legendary queen of ancient Babylon, with having originated the barbarous practice; but whether this is so or not, it is a very ancient custom, as is shown by references to it in the Old and New Testaments.

The majority of eunuchs are said to have had only the scrotum removed, but the operation may extend to the complete removal of the genital organs, both penis and scrotum, level with the belly; for unless this is done the eunuch may retain the ability to perform coitus. The operation is usually performed early in life, and it is part of the graveness of the charge against slavery in Arabia that slave mothers must submit to this mutilation of their sons for the eunuch market. Furthermore, since it is usually performed by an

Slavery

untrained surgeon, and without regard to antiseptics, the mortality is frightful. Cardinal Lavigerie states that of thirty boys operated on in Morocco to supply the harem of the Sultan with eunuchs, no less than twenty-eight died.[1] And there is little reason to believe that this staggering mortality has diminished with the passage of time; for the men who still perform the operation are for the most part not professional surgeons, though a small number are. In a letter to the Anti-Slavery Society of September 28, 1956, a doctor in Irak wrote that he had been a medical practitioner in Saudi-Arabia and that 'castration of slaves for use in harems was practised in hospitals by surgeons. In all cases a radical amputation of genitalia (penis and scrotum) was done on boys between ten and fourteen years old'.

The effects of the operation, if it is survived, need not necessarily be entirely adverse. Sir George MacMunn writes that, 'While the operation performed on the adult produces a feeble creature, that on the juvenile may direct the forces of growth into other channels and produce powerful men. . . . In men of education it has even produced men of action, for example, Narses, the Persian general. (However,) the organs of generation are more productive of the good than the evil elements in mankind, and the man thus deprived may lose all sense of the milk of human kindness. Most eastern executioners are deprived men'.[2]

A secondary but well-known effect of castration is to prevent the voice of an adolescent boy from breaking, and in the Middle Ages it was practised in Europe to preserve the boy sopranos of famous choirs. But this has long since ceased.

A further duty for which eunuchs are employed is to police the great mosque in Mecca. Squabbling women sometimes have to be ejected from it, and in Moslem countries no man is supposed to touch a woman who is not his wife or closely related to him. But since a eunuch is not classed as a man in the proper sense of the word he can deal with them. These eunuchs, called 'aghas', were first established in the mosque in the eighth century, and have often been presented by Mohammedan princes. There are now about fifty of them in Mecca, usually tall negroes wearing immense turbans, of whom twenty or so are usually to be seen standing or walking near the mosque.

Besides castration, other types of mutilation are practised in Arabia as a punishment for crime. The Koran states that 'If a man or woman steal, cut off their hands in retribution for that which

[1] *Document on the Foundation of the Anti-Slavery Movement*, p. 394, quoting from a Blue Book of 1888.
[2] *Slavery Through the Ages*, p. 14.

The Treatment of Slaves

they have committed, this is an exemplary punishment appointed by God and God is mighty and wise. But whoever shall repent after his iniquity, verily God will be turned unto to him, for God is inclined to be forgiving and be merciful'. (Ch. 5.) This punishment applies to the free as well as to slaves, but it is not inflicted unless the value of the goods stolen exceeds four dinars, or about two pounds. However, a member of an International Locust Control Commission, who had worked in Arabia, informed the Anti-Slavery Society that although he had seen many Arabians, including slaves, whose toes or ears had been cut off as a punishment for stealing, he had not seen any who had lost fingers or hands; presumably because it would decrease their capacity for work. Slaves are also branded with identifying marks like cattle, in order to trace them if they escape.

That the mutilation of slaves was not originally a Moslem practice, is made clear by Syed Ameer Ali, a distinguished writer on Islam from Pakistan, who says, 'The mutilation of the human body was also explicitly forbidden by Mohammed, and the institution which flourished both in the Persian and the Byzantine empires was denounced in severe terms . . . but with the accession of the usurping house of Ommeyya a change came over the spirit of Islam. Muawiyah was the first sovereign who introduced into the Moslem world the practice of acquiring slaves by purchase. He was also the first to adopt the Byzantine custom of guarding his women by eunuchs'.[1]

Little attempt was made to check mutilation until the General Act of Brussels for the Repression of the Slave Trade of 1890. Article V of this required the contracting parties to enact laws in their territories making mutilation of male adults and children a criminal offence. There was some doubt whether this most effective convention was still in force, or whether it had been abrogated by the Convention of St Germain-en-Laye of 1919, but on November 1, 1956, the British Foreign Minister stated in the House of Commons that it is still in operation, although it has fallen into disuse.

But more recently the Supplementary Convention on Slavery of 1956 has made similar provisions. Article IV states that, 'In a country where the abolition or abandonment of slavery or of the institutions mentioned in Article I of this Convention is not yet complete, the act of mutilating, branding or otherwise marking a slave or person of servile status in order to indicate that status or as a punishment or for any other reason or of being accessory therefore, shall be a criminal offence under the laws of the States

[1] *Spirit of Islam*, p. 267.

Slavery

Parties to this Convention and persons convicted thereof shall be liable to punishment'.

There is a further form of mutilation practised in some Moslem countries which has had an important indirect bearing on slavery. It is practised not on slaves but on free women and is called in English, for want of a better term, female circumcision. It is really clitordectomy. The clitoris, the part of the female genital organs which gives pleasure to her during sexual relations, is removed, so that women, and especially married women, may not be tempted to indulge in extra-marital relations. But by this attempt to ensure fidelity the Moslem husband usually succeeds in providing himself with one or more, not exceeding four, frigid wives, who are unresponsive to his affections; and this leads to a demand among men for women who find pleasure in love-making, a demand met by slave women. A Moslem man is forbidden to have relations with another man's female slave but he may lie with as many of his own women slaves as he likes.

Such a custom, with its vicious consequences, is an additional powerful obstacle in the way of getting slave-owning Arabs to accept abolition of slavery. As an explorer noted throughout Asia Minor writes, under the *nom de plume* of John Lewis Carver, 'It will be extremely difficult for any agency to control this traffic, particularly in girls. For traffic in women trained to make love is an essential element in the battle of the sexes peculiar to Arabia. No wives are more embittered and frigid than the Arab wives. Female frigidity is a vital element in the Arab culture pattern. The Arab males, whose sexual appetites are keen, are without doubt the world's unhappiest husbands. Here then is the explanation of the prevalence of concubinage and for the survival of slavery in this part of the world. Most women slaves combine the functions of servant and concubine in any Arab home that can afford a slave'.[1] This is also borne out by Hughes, who says, 'There is no limit to the number of slave girls with whom the Arab may cohabit and it is the consecration of this indulgence which so popularizes slavery amongst Arab nations'.[2]

Apart from these deliberate mutilating practices for particular purposes, the general treatment of slaves and the amount of liberty permitted to them has depended through the ages on the social climate of the time and on the degree of local isolation from the influence of more enlightened ideas, where these have existed.

In biblical times, the Jews made some attempt to ameliorate the

[1] *The United Nations World*, 1948.
[2] *Notes on Mohammedanism*.

The Treatment of Slaves

lot of a slave. Mosaic law provided that all slaves should be freed in the year of Jubilee, which recurred once every fifty years. It also gave the debt-bondsman the right to redeem himself, or to be redeemed by his relatives, and equitable rates of redemption were laid down, having regard to the proximity of the year of Jubilee.

The Greeks went much further and regulated the position of their slaves with some care and benevolence. Domestic slaves, i.e. slaves in the home, were admitted to the family circle with a service of dedication, which implied that both master and slave had mutual obligations. They were not entirely excluded from public amusements and rejoicings, and the position of a slave might often be a confidential one. Although the lash was in use as a punishment for refractoriness, serious crime had to be judged and punished as it would be in the case of a free man; the slave was not the pure chattel of the master that he became in the early days of Rome. Masters could not kill their slaves with impunity, and a slave constantly ill-treated could apply to be sold to another master in the hope of finding better treatment. A Greek slave could purchase his freedom with his savings, which usually took five years according to Cicero, if he was industrious. On manumission, however, a slave was not entitled to citizenship *ipso facto*, but could be elected to it by a vote in a general assembly, as in the case of foreigners.

In Rome, as one might expect in the course of its history, the treatment of the slave ran the whole gamut from severity to final semi-freedom. Originally Roman law gave the master absolute ownership over his slave, even to the power of life and death; the Roman slave could not own property, all he acquired being legally the property of his master; and the union of a male slave with a female slave was not recognized by law, cohabitation between slaves being terminable by the master. But as Rome expanded into the Empire many laws were passed, largely in the interests of humanity, controlling the slave status, and in the later days of Rome no slave need despair of becoming a free man and a citizen. A slave was given the right of ownership of his savings, called his *peculium*, and he was also given the right to buy himself out of slavery under certain conditions. Finally the slave became more and more a part of the family, rarely being sold, and with the change into serfdom Rome reached the half-way house between slavery and freedom.

The influence of Christianity on the course of slavery and serfdom was considerable, both as a moral force suffusing the relationship between master and slave and also as an institution working to improve the lot of slaves. Sundays and Holy days were secured as days of rest for them, and the sale of children over the age of seven

Slavery

was forbidden. Murder of a slave also met with the condemnation of the Church, and the clergy taught that manumission of slaves by will was a deed which would help the Christian soul on death.

But the blackest of all slave stories, for inhumanity and cruelty inspired by greed, is undoubtedly that which began in 1510 with the importation of slaves from West Africa into Hispaniola. For no less than three and a half centuries African chiefs, egged on by European agents, kidnapped men, women and children of their own race and sold them to European slave traders, who packed them into ships like sardines and took them across the seas. The toll of human life was terrific. Over and above losses in the slave raids and before embarkation on the slave ships, twelve and a half per cent died during the crossing and four and a half per cent in harbour before sale. Some captains of slavers on the other hand made many voyages without losing a slave. Once in the West Indies appalling cruelties were inflicted on the slaves. Since the European population in all the colonies was heavily outnumbered by the slave population, fear of slave uprisings bred a ferocity which impelled them to brutalize the slaves to a degree unknown elsewhere, in the hope of thus cowing them into everlasting submission. Slaves would be harnessed and driven by the whip, flogged ruthlessly by a special estates flogger. Even women were beaten on the bare buttocks in the fields as a matter of routine for any dallying, and beaten with a lash that tore flesh from them. When emancipation came to the West Indian colonies the degree of hatred engendered between the two races made the transition from slavery to freedom all the more difficult. It took nearly a century for it to fade from memory.

The similar barbarities practised in the southern states of the USA have been vividly portrayed by Harriet Beecher Stowe in *Uncle Tom's Cabin*. Today cases of ill-treatment of black people by white people still come to light, survivals of the relations between the two races in the days of slavery.

The general treatment of slaves in the patriarchal Arabian countries, which until very recently were secluded from the outer world, and where domestic slaves are part of an ancient system, is usually good. It appeals to the Arab to have large numbers of slaves to rule. They are often kindly ruled, but definitely ruled; fed, clothed and maintained, but unpaid. The head of the Arab family likes to have his slaves awaiting his orders, and since the slave is usually friendless, he has no other niche in life but service to his master. Good and fair treatment of slaves is enjoined by the Koran, and their liberation is recommended as meritorious. As long as slaves are tractable and obedient to their masters, they usually meet with

The Treatment of Slaves

kindness; but woe betide the slave who has a will of his own. If he attempts to escape and is recaptured, he will be beaten within an inch of his life, if not to death. Sometimes he is decapitated.

But even the relatively benevolent domestic slavery of the Arab is basically a heartless institution, ever open to abuse. Eldon Rutter has written, 'Now I shall have to show that slaving in Arabia is in its physical aspect a slight thing. Regarded in a material way only, the lot of a slave in Arabia is quite as happy as that of thousands of human beings in the most advanced countries in the world. This is because social conditions are still in, not exactly a primitive state, but an old-fashioned state. Such conditions make for contentment simply because the essential difference between the life lived by prominent citizens and that lived by the less fortunate, even by servants and slaves, is not very great. In the more advanced countries the difference between the life lived by the rich and that lived by the poor has now for several centuries been enormous. In mediaeval times it was not so; a rich man did not live in a pauper-proof mansion. He was accessible to everybody. This is the position in Arabia today, and there the levelling influence of Islam has preserved one set of manners for rich and poor alike. Moreover, the many injunctions to release slaves which are contained in the Koran have certainly given rise to a feeling among the more pious Mohammedans that they hold their slaves on sufferance. They treat them kindly, even affectionately. And that is precisely why I regard the slavery of the easy-going Mohammedan kind as the worst of all kinds of slavery'.[1]

He then described how heartless and hypocritical slave-owners liberate their slaves when they are too old to work and too old to sell. 'As we moved along in the cloisters (of the Mosque),' he said, 'we saw two or three very old men and women, who looked like dreary skeletons. If we go to the Mosque at sunrise we shall see some of them. If we go at sunset they will be there too. And if we pass by at midnight we shall see them there still, sleeping on the stones in their rags. They are manumitted slaves, free men and women. They have no home but the Mosque, and no food but what they receive in alms, turned out "to seek the bounty of Allah" as their masters would say. So much for even a benevolent slave system; though it is but fair to say that good masters maintain their old slaves till they die. There is yet another repulsive blot on human manners which is rendered possible by Arab slavery. Mecca is always full of students who settle in the city for years to study theology. Some of these marry slave women belonging to the Arabs. Any child of these so-

[1] Lecture to the Royal Asian Society, London, 1933.

Slavery

called marriages is born into slavery, and becomes the property of the women's owner. The father is usually too poor to buy the woman's freedom. I do not think I have anything more barbarous than that to report out of all I have seen and heard of Arab slavery.'[1] Eldon Rutter believes that slavery in Arabia could be brought to an end by the pressure of the hundreds of millions of Moslems in the world to whom Mecca is the Holy of Holies.

An account of the kindness shown to slaves in the average Arabian home is given by Colonel Gerald de Gaury in his book, *Arabian Journey*. Dr Paul Harrison,[2] an American medical missionary, also agrees with this general estimate, until he comes to the treatment of slaves in the pearl fisheries on the north coast of Oman. There slaves are made to dive for oysters without any diving apparatus, with the result that their ears and organs of respiration are injured. Their diving moreover is often into waters infested by man-eating fish, and they may return to the surface maimed—if they return alive at all. Nor must one forget, of course, the mutilations described earlier in this chapter. Dr Harrison writes that the mere thought of the cruelties to be inflicted on a slave awaiting punishment will cause him to lose his reason.

An attempt to regulate the condition of the slave in Saudi-Arabia was made by the late King Ibn Saud of Saudi-Arabia. On October 2, 1936 he issued a Decree entitled *Instructions Concerning Traffic in Slaves*, Part II of which was concerned with their treatment. The second Article of this Part gives the slave certain rights, to be fed, clothed and housed, to medical attention, and to be treated well, as well as any other member of the household. Article III prescribes the remedies a slave has if he is persistently ill-treated. Article IV gives the slave who was born free the right of emancipation. Article V prohibits the separation of a slave husband from his wife, and Article VI prohibits the separation of the slave mother from her child. Article VII gives the slave the right to buy his freedom, and Articles VIII-XI inclusive require the registration of slaves within a year of the making of the Decree, in default of which any slave not so registered may apply for his freedom. But in view of the tendency for anything designed to improve the lot of the slave in Arabia to be ignored, it is permissible to wonder to what extnt this code is implemented.

In the Far East, children who have been 'adopted' for the sake of exploiting their labour are probably well treated on the whole but, as is so often the case in any form of slavery, there is also much

[1] Lecture to the Royal Asian Society, London, 1933.
[2] Author of *Doctor In Arabia*, published in 1943.

The Treatment of Slaves

evidence of cruelty. C. H. Coates has described their plight as follows: 'The trodden misery of these children is hidden away in back rooms of castigated drudgery in the Chinese home, voiceless, unseen, unchampioned and without hope.'[1] Cases have come to light in which it was proved that a child had been suspended by a rope fastened around her wrists and ankles for a whole night, so that both hands and feet had to be amputated. In other instances it has been proved that children have been branded and burnt, and that boiling oil has been poured over their hands. This is, of course, in addition to those who are regularly beaten and whose lives are made a daily hell of misery too fearful to contemplate.

Enough has surely been said to show that whatever mitigations of the condition of slavery may have existed at different times and places, the fundamental nature of the relationship between master and slave has always held the temptation of abuse. Slavery is the negation of civil liberty, and is in its very nature evil. It is bad for the slave because it tends to make him harsh, sensual and cruel, and to grow to despise the work in which he is engaged, and to shirk it. It is bad for the master because the habit of absolute rule is corrupting. It offers constant facilities for libertinism, and the morality of the slave-owner and his sons is undermined by intimate contact with a despised and degraded class. Cruelty and lust have been its shadows wherever it has existed.

---

[1] *The Red Theology in the Far East*, p. 152.

CHAPTER III

CHATTEL SLAVERY TODAY

EFFORTS to abolish slavery were first directed at slave-trading, partly because its horrors were more evident and because Europeans had such a direct share in it, and partly because by cutting off an importance source of fresh enslavement it was hoped to check the practice itself. Today, however, it is more logical to consider slavery first; for without an established institution to feed, slave trading cannot exist.

Of all the forms slavery can assume, classic or chattel slavery is manifestly the most pernicious, and though it is to be regretted that the League of Nations definition has often been too narrowly interpreted in the past, it is in the abolition of this traditional type of slavery that the greatest progress has been made. During the past fifty years the number of countries in which it still flourishes has steadily been reduced, until now only a handful remain. But that it still flourishes in these with undiminished vigour cannot be doubted in the face of the evidence, both official and unofficial.

In 1925 the Temporary Slavery Commission of the League of Nations could report that, 'The legality of the status of slavery is not recognized in any Christian State (mother country, colonial dependency or mandated territory) except Abyssinia (Ethiopia). ... The great independent States of the Far East have enacted laws forbidding or abolishing slavery. This institution has been forbidden in China since 1909. ... In Siam an Act of 1905 definitely abolished slavery. Japan has extended the prohibition of slavery to its mandated territories. The status of slavery is recognized today by law only in certain Asiatic countries such as Tibet and Nepal and in most of the Mohammedan States of the East, such as Afghanistan, the Hejaz and other Arabian States'.[1]

Seven years later further progress was reported. Six more countries had taken decisive action. The League's Committee of Experts on Slavery of 1932 recorded that Afghanistan had abolished the legal status of slavery in 1923, Iraq in 1924, Nepal and Kelat in

[1] League of Nations Doc. A.19.1925.VI, paras. 3-6.

Chattel Slavery Today

1926, and Trans-Jordania (Hashemite Jordan) and Iran in 1929. It added that, 'unless slavery is still a legal institution in Tibet and Central Asia, countries of which the Committee had no information, slavery is now recognized only in the Hejaz (now a part of Saudi-Arabia), in the Yemen, in the Sultanates of the Hadramaut, in the Sultanate of Kuwait and in Assam'.[1]

Besides Tibet and Central Asia the League was also unable to get information about Spanish Morocco. Though Spain has adhered to the Slavery Convention of 1926, when doing so she made a reservation that it did not apply to her protectorate in Morocco. In 1935 the League Advisory Committee of Experts on Slavery reported that efforts to get information on slavery in Spanish Morocco had failed to produce a reply from the Spanish Government.[2]

Since then the legal status of slavery has been abolished in Bahrain (1938), Ethiopia (1942), Kuwait (1949), and Qatar (1952). It only survives therefore in the rest of Arabia, with the exception of the British colony of Aden; that is to say, in Saudi-Arabia, the Yemen, the Sultanate of Oman, and the Aden Protectorate, which is made up of the small sultanates and sheikhdoms of the Hadramaut under British military protection; and it must be presumed to survive in the former Spanish Protectorate of Morocco.

Until very recently the peoples of Arabia lived aloof from the outer world and our knowledge of conditions in their countries, particularly concerning the existence of slavery, has largely depended upon the unofficial accounts of travellers. Critics have been quick to seize upon this and point out the lack of official confirmation. But such confirmation is by no means lacking. In the absence of any pronouncement abolishing the legal status of slavery, in common with other countries of the world, its existence could in any case be reasonably inferred. But in addition, the United Nations has addressed to the Government of Saudi-Arabia no less than eight requests for information on slavery in its territories, in terms identical with requests addressed to the Governments of other member states, and no reply has ever been received to any one of them. The silence of the Government of Saudi-Arabia on this subject cannot but be construed as an admission that slavery exists in the country.

There is also official internal evidence in the Decree of the late King Ibn Saud of October 2, 1936, entitled *Instructions Concerning Traffic in Slaves*. Part II, as we have seen, dealt with the treatment and rights of slaves; Parts I and III were concerned with slave

[1] League of Nations Doc. C.618.1932.VI, para 2.
[2] League of Nations Doc. C.189.M.145.1936.VI, Ch. II.

Slavery

trading. This Decree is still in force. Is it conceivable that any Government would legislate in such detail to protect slaves if there were no slaves in the country to protect?

Turning to our travellers' tales, we find that many of the writers have in fact lived long in Arabia and are sympathetic to the Arab way of life; but their testimony to the existence of slavery in Arabia remains unanimous. Eldon Rutter, who has spent most of his life in the country, has stated categorically, 'Slavery exists in every part of Arabia as a normal social institution, with the exception of (the colony of) Aden, but I have seen only one slave market where slaves are displayed in a public place, like merchandise. That is in Mecca. In all other towns and villages, including the Persian Gulf towns, the slaves are sold privately. In some places there are dealers who keep a definite stock of slaves; in others there are merely agents who dispose of any whom a person may wish to sell'.[1]

Another long-standing resident in the Near East and an extensive traveller in Arabia since 1917 is H. St John Philby, the author of *The Heart of Arabia* and *Arabia*. In these he mentions seeing slaves in the countries of Arabia, though he makes no comment on the institution.

A particularly inhuman aspect of Arabian slavery was pointed out by G. E. de Jong in 1934. 'It is little known,' he wrote, 'that in Arabia, in Mecca and in the Yemen corps of slave men and women are maintained and bred like cattle in order that their children may swell the slave markets',[2] and he cites Eldon Rutter[3] in support of his statement.

The deep-rooted character of slavery in Arabia adds greatly to the difficulties in the way of its abolition. Bertram Thomas, who was for many years Adviser to the Sultan of Oman, writes of this with understanding and authority. 'Within Arabia itself slavery flourishes with the full support of public opinion and any extraneous authority interfering becomes odious, in the eyes of the people. It is a vested interest of immemorial respectability.' And he continues, 'Most enlightened Arab rulers, though they doubtless consider privately that it would be a good thing if slavery were no more, dare not affront influential subjects who favour slavery and possess slaves. And short of coercive measures, which no one is likely to take, only a change of opinion, a new general attitude of mind, will ensure permanent abolition. Today King Ibn Saud is tackling this very difficult problem sympathetically and wisely. Changes in the social system

---
[1] Lecture to Royal Asian Society, London, 1933.
[2] Article in *Moslem World*, April, 1934.
[3] *The Holy Cities of Arabia*, Vol. II, p. 113.

Chattel Slavery Today

have to be gradual if an upheaval is to be avoided. The answer to the question "Why do the Arabs want slaves?" is in part sociological and in part economic. Slavery is a traditional part of the social structure. It is congenial. The peninsular Arabs are in the mass far to proud to work as servants, far too independent in spirit to obey a master, so that the well-to-do have either to do their work themselves or resort to slaves. That is why among a poor people, having little more than a subsistence agriculture, all attempts at suppression of slavery have failed.'[1]

There is also no lack of evidence of slave dealing in Arabia, including details of the prevailing market prices, though these have since risen considerably. Colonel Gerald de Gaury, who has lived long in Saudi-Arabia and in Iraq and received high honours from the late King Ibn Saud, writes in his book *Arabian Journey*, published in 1950, that, 'Slaves are still sold in Saudi-Arabia, in spite of the Convention whereby slavery was abolished by Ibn Saud and the practice of manumission was given up by the British. The chief market is in the Sug-al-Suwaigua in Mecca[2] and the main route for them is to Mecca from the Yemen, to which they are brought by sailing boats from the opposite coast of Africa. In 1941 the price of a small boy was about £20, for a stronger male £50, for a Somali rather more, and for a small girl £12, which is considerably less than the price of a good horse and a little less than that of a camel'. He mentions that he had heard on good authority that cargoes of boys were still arriving on the Oman coast in 1947 from the Mokran coast of Baluchistan, and that in 1949 two shipwrecked sailors had been sold in Saudi-Arabia. Girls are brought from Aleppo in Syria and sold; being fair they are favourites. He added that, 'slavery is not so hateful to the slaves as might be supposed. Being a valuable property they are well cared for and are often fully trusted by their masters. . . . Slavery in the East is not as cruel as it was in the West'.[3]

Finally, and confirming the above, in 1956 a regular traveller between India and Arabia informed the Anti-Slavery Society that Baluchis were being taken to Arabia and sold into slavery as late as 1953 to his certain knowledge.

Concerning the Yemen, the ancient land of the Sabaeans in the

---

[1] *The Arabs*, p. 267.
[2] Described by Eldon Rutter in *The Holy Cities of Arabia*.
[3] *Arabian Journey*, published 1950. The Convention referred to by Colonel de Gaury is no doubt the Treaty of Friendship between His Britannic Majesty and H.M. the King of Saudi-Arabia made at Djedda on May 20, 1927, by which Britain surrendered the right of manumission of slaves in Saudi-Arabia and Saudi-Arabia agreed to co-operate in abolishing the slave trade, but not slavery.

Slavery

south-west of the Arabian peninsula, evidence of the existence of slavery is less plentiful, but still fairly conclusive, especially about the passage of slaves through the country on their way to Saudi-Arabia. The theocratic dynasty which rules the Yemen has pursued a deliberate policy of isolating it from the rest of the world in order to keep out any alien influence. To enter the country requires a special permit from the Imam (ruler) himself, and few are granted. However, although there have been less numerous observers of what is going on in the Yemen, there have been some.

The significance of the Yemen in the slave trade was pointed out in 1934 by Mr G. Percival Kaye, who was from 1917-19 second-in-command of HMS *Susetta*, a vessel patrolling the Red Sea and the Persian Gulf. He wrote, 'The nearest point to which slave craft from Africa can gain the shelter of the Arabian reefs is the land of the Yemen.... I visited Sanaa (the capital) in the interior. The first day I travelled over the desert-like plain of Timba and then nine days in the hills. The passing of slaves over this huge area is never seen near the Post road from Hodeida (the port) to Sanaa, 160 miles. You must traverse the lesser known camel tracks leading to the Hejaz (now part of Saudi-Arabia) and to the Hadramaut, or visit border villages, where contact with Europeans is non-existent. I stayed at Sok-al-Khamis and on the second day my friend, a Sanaa merchant, took me out a half day's journey to Musa-Chid, a hill village a score of miles away. The attached photograph shows some women labourers who had come from Africa and were ostensibly free but were in reality slaves. We interrogated one and discovered that she had been to a Mission School in Africa and could read and write'.[1]

A French mission in 1930 also found evidence of the passage of slaves through the Yemen, though not of slavery itself. The mission, sent by *Le Matin* of France and led by Mr Joseph Kessel, was to enquire into slavery conditions in Arabia and Ethiopia. One of its members was Mr Henry de Monfried, who had spent much time among the pearl fishers on the Persian Gulf and amongst the inland tribes of Ethiopia. The mission reported, 'In the Yemen we found no slaves. From what we were told we expected more than in any other Arab country, yet in the whole month we passed there we saw none. The porters loading the sambouks were miserably paid, but they were not slaves. Every kind of interdiction exists but still the Jews of the Yemen, although they are considered as an inferior race by the warriors of the mountains, are not slaves'.[2] Cruising along the

---

[1] From a series of articles entitled 'The Middle Passage Slavery Today', published in *The Slave Market News*, Oct. 1935 to Jan. 1935.
Le Matin, May-June, 1930.

Chattel Slavery Today

Yemenite coast, however, the mission learned from the fishermen in the little creeks that groups of men, women and children were landed on that coast from time to time and were at once despatched to Saudi-Arabia.

Though the amount of actual slavery present in the Yemen may be hard to assess from the testimony of outside observers, more than one of its dark aspects has been revealed by an eminent Moslem. In a conversation with Eldon Rutter the following exchanges took place:

'Had I but two or three hundred guineas,' said Shafig, 'I could profit much from slaves, I know a place of slaves.'

'Where it is?' I enquired.

'Above El Gunfuda,' he replied, 'on the coast between Birk and El Hodeida (Yemen) to the South.'

'And those slaves, are they Yemenis or Habashis (i.e. Ethiopians)?'

'Yemenis,' replied Shafig. 'They are said to be children stolen from their parents in the inner wilderness of the Yemen. And Allah is more knowing. There are Habashis also.'

'But when they bring the Habashis from Africa, O my uncle,' I said, 'do they land them at El Gunfuda?'

'No,' said he, 'they land them more to the southward, near El Hodeida, for there the distance between Arabia and Africa is not great. Their desire is to pass the sea quickly.'

'They say that some of the people of the Yemen sell their own children,' said Hassan.

'I take refuge in God!' exclaimed Shafig. 'But there are people who own men slaves and women slaves; so they let them breed that they may profit by selling the children.'[1]

More recently evidence has been collected by M. Emmanuel La Graviere, a member of the Assembly of the French Union. In 1955 he published his report after investigating the rumoured revival of the slave trade into Arabia, which will be studied in the next chapter. Several passages of it refer to the Yemen. He wrote that, 'Authoritative evidence from civil servants, from men of learning, and from military officers confirms that the slave trade (from Africa) is directed towards Saudi-Arabia and the Yemen, where slavery exists with public approval and with the century-old characteristics of such an institution'.[2]

However, he also drew attention to the views of Dr Claude

[1] *The Holy Cities of Arabia.*
[2] Document No. 75 of the Assembly of the French Union, Session of 1955-56, p. 32.

Slavery

Fayein,[1] who was a medical practitioner in the Yemen for eighteen months. During that time she attended two slaves, and two only. One was a girl of fifteen belonging to a brother of the king, whom a visitor from Saudi-Arabia wished to buy as a present for one of the royal family in Saudi-Arabia. Completion of the sale was made subject to Dr Fayein's giving a medical certificate that the girl was in perfect health. When Dr Fayein was informed of the purpose for which the certificate was desired she withheld it, and the sale fell through. The other was a woman of about thirty-four, who was a slave of one of the princesses, a sister of the king. Dr Fayein advised her to marry; but she replied, 'That is impossible, for I am a slave'. Dr Fayein did not agree that a permanent state of slavery gripped all of the people of the Yemen, as was stated by Dr Abdel Aziz Khaldi in a letter to *Le Monde*.

M. La Graviere was also informed by another French lady doctor that she had given medical attention to slaves in the Yemen This was Dr Serin, who was a medical practitioner in the Yemen.

When slavery was debated by the United Nations, in the General Assembly in Paris in 1948, the delegate from the Yemen rose and said: 'There is no slavery in the Yemen.' But unfortunately such statements cannot always be accepted at their face value. A year earlier an equally categorical statement to the contrary effect was made by an American organization named 'The Nation Associates'. In 1947 it submitted a memorandum to the General Assembly of the UN in which it stated: 'Slavery flourishes in the Yemen as it does in Saudi-Arabia.' In 1950, moreover, an officer of a Jewish organization engaged in repatriating Jews from the Yemen to Israel informed the UN *ad hoc* Committee on Slavery that he had seen many slaves in the Yemen.

That the legal status of slavery has not been abolished in the Yemen is certain. Eldon Rutter in his lecture to the Royal Asian Society in 1933 said that he had been told by the Iman that it could not be abolished because public opinion in the country desired slavery. That it is actually practised is also clear from the evidence, though in the absence of any reliable figures its extent must remain a matter of conjecture. Less open to doubt is its major rôle in supplying Saudi-Arabia with slaves, both from Africa and from within its own borders.

In the Oman promontory of Arabia, made up of the Sultanate of Oman, with its date plantations, and the Trucial States, or Pirate Coast, on the Persian Gulf, with its fishing and pearl-diving industries, slavery not only exists but presents some sharp contrasts.

[1] Author of *French Woman Doctor in the Yemen*.

Chattel Slavery Today

Dr Paul Harrison, an American medical missionary who spent close on thirty years in Oman, has described a trip he made in the Bottina district among the date plantations. It was, he says, 'my first introduction to slavery. It was a slave economy; but the slaves were obviously contented and extremely well fed. Some of them needed treatment for obesity'.[1]

Later, however, he made another trip, on the Pirate Coast among the pearl divers. Of this he wrote, 'I had seen a great deal of slavery in the plantations back of Muscat and it is a pleasure to testify to the good treatment those slaves received and their evident contentment with their lot. But on the Pirate Coast the situation was very different. Thousands of slaves were there, and with them hundreds of pearl-diving boats were manned. The dark places of the earth are full of cruelty. While I was in Abu Dhubai three slaves tried to escape to Bahrain. Fortune refused to smile on their desperate venture and they were recaptured. They were beaten so severely that one of them died. . . . The Baluchi slaves were the most pathetic, they rebelled bitterly against their bonds. All slaves were miserably treated, but the Africans were the most patient. Their souls were manacled with their bodies, but still they could sing'.[2]

But in the Sultanate of Oman at all events there appears to have been a further improvement. In May 1950 Dr Harrison wrote to the UN *ad hoc* Committee on Slavery. He reported that since the demand for dates had shrunk and slave labour no longer needed for the plantations in such numbers as in the past, Oman now had relatively few slaves. Bahrain and Kuwait, he added, had never had many.

Further evidence about slavery in Oman, including the furtiveness surrounding the markets, has come from Raymond O'Shea, an officer of an air line stationed at Shargah in Oman. 'It must not be assumed that slavery has been entirely abolished in Arabia,' he writes. 'It is known to flourish in the dominions of King Ibn Saud and in the Yemen. Negro slaves may still be seen in the houses of the Sheikhs and of the merchants of the Trucial Oman coast, whilst a great many are employed in the fishing and pearl-diving industries. Once I was talking to a young slave of a pearl merchant of Dhubai. I said to him, I suppose your father was an ex-slave here? To my surprise he said that he had been with his present master only four years, and had been born in Zanzibar, from which he had been abducted by Arab merchants when four years old, smuggled into the Hadramaut and sold in the slave market at Buraimi for

[1] *Doctor in Arabia*, published 1943, p. 39.
[2] Ibid.

Slavery

500 rupees.'[1] He also describes the case of a Persian who told him that he had been travelling in Arabia in 1939 when he was seized and sold into slavery, in which condition he remained until 1945, when he succeeded in reaching the British authorities, who secured his release.

Raymond O'Shea made an unsuccessful attempt to visit a slave market. 'I have been informed that a regular slave market exists at the small town of Harfit, as well as at Baraimi. Several official delegations have been despatched to Baraimi and Harfit to investigate the slave trade, but the Bedouins, who are the principal slave-dealers, concealed the slaves and closed the market long before the approach of any foreigner.' He then describes a visit he himself made to Baraimi. 'Among the crowd we did see several negroes whose legs bore the marks of iron chains and the healed scars of a lash, but they were quickly hurried out of sight at our approach and we were not allowed to question them. When we attempted to enter the door of the fort (where the slave market was) the crowd's attitude became threatening and I thought they would attack us.'[2]

As in the Yemen, many of the slaves of Oman eventually find their way into Saudi-Arabia. In 1956 the Anti-Slavery Society was informed by Major W. O. Little, the British officer commanding the Oman levies in the Buraimi oasis during most of 1955, that Saudi-Arabians paid high prices for slaves from Oman.

In Kuwait, the situation as far as slavery is concerned, according to H. R. P. Dickson, 'is a comparatively happy one. . . . Masters in Kuwait town are as a general rule kind to domestic slaves born in their families'.[3] Mr Dickson was British Political Agent in Kuwait for seven years, and still resides there. On the subject of slavery in Arabia as a whole he has this to say: 'Almost every desert sheikh or well-to-do member of a tribe has his male slaves, whether born in the family or bought, and their womenfolk have female slaves. Speaking generally bought slaves are the rule. . . . The Nejd and Northern Bedouins treat their bought slaves better than the slave-owning public generally.'[4] The legal status of slavery was abolished in Kuwait in 1949, which of course is not to say that it has yet ceased entirely.

The abolition of slavery in the Aden Protectorate, in spite of British influence in the area, has not yet proved possible. It does not exist in the colony of Aden itself, but this is only a small area of

---
[1] *Sand Kings of Arabia*, published 1947, p. 175.
[2] Ibid.
[3] *The Arabs of the Desert*, published 1949, p. 498.
[4] Ibid., p 502.

Chattel Slavery Today

seventy-five square miles. In what is often described as the British Protectorate of Aden it still exists, though on a steadily diminishing scale. The so-called Protectorate is not a Protectorate but a British Protected State; that is to say, the many sultanates and sheikhdoms of which it is made up are under British military protection. as is the Sultanate of Oman, and while this implies some influence in their foreign policy, it does not include any control over their internal administration.

In 1951 the United Nations was informed by the British Government that, 'the complete abolition of slavery in the Aden Protectorate is a matter of some difficulty. The majority of the slaves who still exist enjoy a certain measure of security under the relatively humane provisions of the Moslem law, and the harsh environment of the country renders them unwilling to change their status. In the western half of the Aden Protectorate there is comparatively little slavery and in the Quaiti and Kathiri States of the Hadramaut the selling of slaves is forbidden and any slave has the right of manumission on application. The importation of slaves from Africa appears to have completely stopped. Of persons remaining in a state of slavery in the Protectorate only a very small number can have been born outside of Arabia. It is the constant aim of Her Majesty's Government to assist the Rulers to bring about the complete abolition of slavery'.

How many slaves there are in the whole of Arabia is impossible to know precisely, particularly since no census of the population of any country in Arabia has ever been made. But an approximate estimate can be arrived at. The total population of Arabia is believed to be ten million, and slave populations are usually estimated to be ten per cent of the whole, which would give a figure of one million. But since much of Arabia consists of uninhabitable desert the ten per cent should in this case be halved. The most reliable estimate of the slave population would thus be 500,000.

The existence of slavery in Spanish Morocco was presumed from the silence of the Spanish Government in 1935. Since then, in 1956, Morocco has gained her independence. It is to be hoped that the national government will do its utmost to bring slavery to an end. There have been no declarations on the subject as yet, however, nor is there any further information on slavery in the territory.

Ethiopia, the last Christian country to abolish slavery, took this step on the restoration of the Emperor Haile Selassie II in 1942. But as recently as 1955 disquieting reports suggest that the abolition of the legal status has not been fully implemented in practice. Slaves from the Province of Wallega in Ethiopia were still seeking refuge

Slavery

in the Sudan at the end of 1955. The long history of slavery in the country, and hence the difficulty in ending it, has been described by Margery Perham. She writes: 'Slavery has been an institution in Ethiopia from the earliest days of which we have record. It was an important feature of the social and economic organization of the country. Christianity, through most of its history, was not felt by the nations which professed it to be incompatible with slavery. Ethiopian Christianity was especially deeply imbued with Hebraic precepts which recognized slavery. From the earliest times the Ethiopians have considered it their right to enslave other races, on the grounds that according to Mosaic law they were entitled to reduce to bondage the negro or Hamitic tribes which were said to be descended from Ham, upon whom Noah bestowed a curse. The Old Testament laid down: "Both thy bondmen and thy bondmaids, which thou shalt have, shall be of the heathen that are round about you, of them shall ye buy bondmen and bondmaids." ' She added that 'it has certainly been a custom which persisted through the reign of the Emperor Menelik (1889-1913) for Ethiopians to enslave their prisoners of war, and when he conquered the kingdom of Walamo in 1894 he brought back 1,800 slaves. Merab, Menelik's physician, estimated that in 1929 one quarter to one third of the total population of Ethiopia were slaves'.[1]

When Ethiopia was admitted to membership of the League of Nations in 1923 she undertook to make particular efforts to ensure the suppression of slavery in all its forms, and also 'trading in negroes on land and sea'; and she further promised to 'furnish the Council (of the League) with all information desired'. A year later a first step was taken with a Decree declaring that all children of slaves born after the date of the Decree were to be free, and granting slaves their freedom under specified conditions. In 1932, when the Emperor Haile Selassie received a delegation from the Anti-Slavery Society, he assured them that he would abolish slavery within fifteen or at most twenty years. But within three years Ethiopia was conquered by Italy. A Decree abolishing the legal status of slavery was made at once, and the Italians claim to have freed 420,000 slaves.

Since Haile Selassie's restoration and Decree in 1942 the Government of Ethiopia has informed the United Nations that there is no slavery in Ethiopia. But right up to 1955, when the British left the Sudan, officials reported that slaves were seeking refuge there, crossing the frontier into Sudan from the province of Wallega in Ethiopia. They were often followed by other Ethiopians who said

[1] *The Government of Ethiopia*, p. 217.

Chattel Slavery Today

they had come to retrieve their slaves. Legal abolition is thus often only the first, though most necessary, step in the fight against slavery.

Another country in which this measure has been taken—as long ago as 1909—is China. But that slavery survived for a great many years after that date is evident from what Sir John Harris wrote in 1933. 'The actual marketing of slaves is probably carried on to a greater extent in China than anywhere else. . . . The systems of slave-owning are indeed numerous. . . . First come systems of admitted slavery, and this is where ownership is clearly and frankly recognized. . . . It was the late Archbishop of Canterbury who first drew public attention to this in a debate in the House of Lords. Dr Davidson recounted a conversation which had taken place between an eminent Chinaman and himself. He stated that in the conversation he himself drew a dark picture of the state of China, as it appeared to him, and said that the picture seemed so dark that he hardly liked to put it to this eminent Chinaman as being true, but emphasized that he was speaking of Western China where slavery is rife; but he presumed that it was not possible to buy slaves in the great cities of the East. His Chinese friend replied, " Oh, yes it is. I could buy them in half an hour. There is not the slightest difficulty in buying girls; I could buy them anywhere".'[1] Under the name Mui Tsai, or Little Sister, the system of child adoption long practised in China developed into a regular trafficking in girls in spite of the supposed legal abolition of slavery. An account of this will be found in Chapter IX. It is believed to be diminishing today.

More news of progress in China has recently come from Mr Basil Davidson, who returned from a long journey in Chinese Central Asia in 1956. He writes, 'As all previous authorities on this area have confirmed this was an area of intensive slavery or near-slavery in a form of peonage called Chakar. It would interest you to know that this form of near-slavery is now entirely at an end. The Chinese assert—although now I am speaking from hearsay—that slavery among the Yi people of Yunnan and Western Szechwan will also end this year (1958). This minority—which is several million strong—was certainly using slaves and taking slaves until 1949. There seems every reason to believe that they have continued to do so on a reduced scale; the reason being that the Chinese Government has, it seems, deliberately not imposed political or economic reforms. There seems to have been a good deal of trouble with the hereditary chieftains of the Yi and of some of the other of these wild hill tribes, but they say that most of these troubles are

[1] *A Century of Emancipation*, p. 256.

Slavery

now over and that slavery among the Yi will end this year'.[1]

In the world as a whole, chattel slavery, the degradation of a human being into a thing possessed by another, is thus happily declining. But it cannot be too often stated that its final eradication can only be achieved—and maintained—by the steady pressure of public opinion and international action and vigilance. Even in countries in which legal abolition has already been secured the powerful forces of long-standing custom are not easily overcome. And there remains one region, one black spot, as yet scarcely touched: Arabia, in which there flourishes not merely slavery but also its more hateful attendant evil, slave-trading.

---

[1] Letter to the author dated September 18, 1956.

CHAPTER IV

SLAVE TRADING TODAY

THE traffic in human beings which finally roused the world to action was, of course, the African slave trade to the West Indies and America; and it was Britain, driven by the fervour and energy of such men as Clarkson and Wilberforce, who led the way in seeking to end it. From January 1, 1808, it became illegal in British possessions, and in the following hundred years British governments concluded nearly six hundred treaties and international instruments designed to check or abolish it, not only in the west, but also in the east, to Arabia.[1] With the emancipation of slaves in the west, that branch of the trade ceased. But that in the east remained, and still remains today.

For a brief period, however, it was almost abolished. Though most of the treaties proved fruitless, one, the General Act for the Repression of the Slave Trade made at Brussels on July 2, 1890, was effective. And it was effective because for the first time its detailed provisions, to which the contracting parties were bound, established efficient machinery of control. Under it a Slavery Bureau was set up and the seas around Arabia were subject to naval patrolling, with the right to stop ships suspected of carrying slaves. In the twenty-four years from its enactment in 1890 until the outbreak of the First World War, more was done to abolish the slave trade than at any other time, and by 1925 it had all but disappeared.

But unfortunately, after the First World War, the peacemakers of Versailles in their enthusiasm to build a new world executed a fresh convention, the Convention of St Germain-en-Laye of 1919, one of the Articles of which purported to have abrogated the Brussels Act of 1890. Whether or not this Convention really abrogated the powerful Brussels Act is still open to doubt. That it was not abrogated received official recognition on November 1, 1956, when the British Foreign Minister stated that it was not abrogated, although it had fallen into disuse, but its effect was to weaken it disastrously, until today all its machinery has ceased to function.

[1] *A Century of Emancipation*, by Sir John Harris, p. 217.

Slavery

In the disturbed period of the Second World War, when vigilance had inevitably to be relaxed, the slave trade between Africa and Arabia began to increase, as was announced by the British Foreign Minister (then Mr Anthony Eden) in Parliament on September 22, 1943. Since the war the naval patrols have not been resumed.

For several years disquieting rumours reached Europe of the revival of the slave trade between Africa and Arabia on the one side and between Arabia and other countries in Asia on the other. Then, in 1954, M. Emanuel La Graviere, a member of the Assembly of the French Union, drew the Assembly's attention to them. As a result he was appointed to go to Africa and investigate, and report whether the rumours were true or false. He spent several months of 1955 in Africa collecting evidence and in November of that year submitted his report to the French Legislature. He found that the rumours were substantially true

The most impressive evidence included by M. La Graviere in his report was a despatch from the French Ambassador in Saudi-Arabia. Written to the French Foreign Office on November 7, 1953, this stated that although it was well known that slavery existed in Saudi-Arabia, and that there was a trade in Africans, induced by various ruses to leave their native land and go to Arabia, there to be sold to the wealthy inhabitants of Mecca, Riyadh and Djedda, it was not easy to get evidence of it because the traffic was clandestine. The Ambassador had been able to collect evidence in Djedda, however, and the details of it, coupled with the agreement among the witnesses, established its authenticity. The method was for slave merchants in Mecca and Djedda to send Africans back to Africa to recruit slaves. These go to villages in the French Sudan, in the High Volta and Niger Provinces of French West Africa, and to the region of Timbuctoo, where they pose as Moslem missionaries and persuade Africans to accompany them on pilgrimages to the Holy Places of Islam in Saudi-Arabia. Many Africans fall into the trap and are conducted by their 'benevolent' guides to the coast of the Red Sea at Port Sudan or Suakin. From there they are taken across the Red Sea to Lith, a port in Saudi-Arabia south of Djedda. On arrival at Lith they are declared by the Government of Saudi-Arabia to be unauthorized immigrants because they have entered the country without visas, and are put into prison. Soon after they are delivered to slave-traders, who sell them into slavery. The Ambassador gave the names of ten men engaged in this trade, and added that the number of people disposed of in this way was a few hundred a year.

Saudi-Arabia has tried to deny the existence of this trade. In April

Slave Trading Today

1956 when the information was brought to the notice of the United Nations by the Anti-Slavery Society, the delegate for Saudi-Arabia stated that his country had laws prohibiting slave-trading, and claimed that these were enforced. It was pointed out in reply that while it was true that Saudi-Arabia had a law prohibiting the importation of slaves by sea, Article 12 of the same Decree authorizes the Minister of the Interior to license slave-traders. There was, furthermore, the statement of the French Ambassador, who must be regarded as a credible witness. The arrest of pilgrims to the Holy Places of Islam and the handing over of them to slave-traders, together with the licensing of traders, amounts at the very least to complicity in slave-trading.

Neither is evidence of slave-trading on the other side of Arabia lacking. Cargoes of boys were being brought from the Mekran coast of Iran and Baluchistan to Saudi-Arabia and sold into slavery as late as 1947, according to Colonel Gerald de Gaury. This traffic was confirmed in 1956 by a regular traveller between India and Arabia, who informed the Anti-Slavery Society that he could say with certainty that people were being brought from Baluchistan to Arabia up to 1953, to be sold into slavery.

One particular case was reported in the Iraqi Press. A certain Mohammad Husain was reported to be supplying highly-placed persons in Saudi-Arabia with under-age male and female slaves brought from Iraq and Iran. In September 1953 he was caught by the Iraqi police with more than fifty under-age girls in his possession, destined to be sold into slavery in Saudi-Arabia. He was tried and convicted, and sentenced to ten years' imprisonment. The girls were restored to their families.

Within Arabia itself the traffic of slaves into Saudi-Arabia from its southern periphery, the Yemen, the Aden Protectorate and Oman, is well attested. The geographical position of the Yemen has made it for many years a convenient route for African slaves destined for Saudi-Arabia; while in the east the Buraimi oasis was found in 1954 to be a main centre of the Saudi-Arabian slave trade. The Anti-Slavery Society has received information from an unimpeachable source that members of certain tribes operating in this region, and in the southern desert of Saudi-Arabia, bring slaves from Muscat and Dhubai in Oman and sell them to slave-traders from Saudi-Arabia, who take them to Riyadh and re-sell them. Prior to being seized the victims of this traffic are often decoyed to dances organized by the slave-traders. Musicians and other entertainers are employed to provide amusement in a village, to which the local inhabitants are attracted, little knowing it is a ruse leading them into slavery.

Slavery

In a recent case of a boy sold at Buraimi the British Embassy in Djedda made an unsuccessful attempt to recover him for his stepfather. In November 1951 this man, a resident of Shargah in Oman named Mubarakbin Obaid, informed the British Agency in Shargah that three years previously his stepson, Swayab bin Khamis, then aged fourteen, had been kidnapped by bandits. Learning later that the boy was in Saudi-Arabia he went to Riyadh, where he found him serving as a slave and he named the house in which he was serving. On asking for the boy to be delivered to him he was told by the Saudi-Arabian authorities that he had been purchased legally. Obaid was able to see his stepson, who told him that his kidnappers had taken him to Buraimi and sold him to a slave-trader. The British Embassy in Djedda then made representations to the Saudi-Arabian Foreign Office and asked that the boy be restored to his family. But the Embassy was told that he could not be traced. This in spite of the fact that his stepfather had not only said that he had seen him in Riyadh, but also in whose house he had seen him.

In another case, however, British action proved effective. A female native of the Eastern Aden Protectorate, Sulayim bint Khaviullah, in servitude in Saudi-Arabia, was released on January 20, 1952, after six months' pressure by the British Embassy. But her two children could not be found.

It is probable that in the absence of the close control exercised under the Brussels Act the slave trade around Arabia would have revived in any case after the Second World War. But there is a further reason. Since the status of a man in Arabia is determined largely by the number of slaves he has, any increase in wealth is inevitably reflected in a demand for more slaves. For many years now large sums of money have been pouring into Arabia in the form of oil royalties, and a great deal of it has undoubtedly been invested in slaves. As a result the demand has risen, and with it prices. Where formerly an able-bodied male slave sold for about £50, now an able-bodied man fetches about £150 and an attractive girl anything from £400 to £700. This has naturally increased the profitability of the slave trade enormously.

The traffic discussed so far has been an active one employing force or ruse, but there is a further way in which the slave markets of Arabia are fed. This is through the sale by pilgrims to Mecca of their servants or children, who are sometimes used virtually as living travellers' cheques. Every faithful Moslem endeavours to make a pilgrimage to the Holy Places in Islam, Mecca and Medina, both in Saudi-Arabia, once in his lifetime, and every year some half-a-million pilgrims converge on it from Pakistan, India, Malaya, Indonesia,

Slave Trading Today

Africa—from all over the Moslem world. Of the pilgrims from Africa many make the journey on foot, and two or three years may elapse before they return home. They therefore take with them their wives, children and servants. Furthermore, in view of its sacred nature the cost of the pilgrimage is not taken into account by many who make it, and they may thus arrive in Mecca almost at the end of their financial resources. There, on top of everything else, they are faced with the toll levied on faith by the local inhabitants. It is to meet these demands that they sometimes sell their servants and even their children into slavery.

When it discovered the existence of the practice the League of Nations was able to do something so check it. Governments of countries with a large Moslem population were recommended to exercise vigilance over the travel papers of pilgrims and their entourages to ensure that of those who set out all either returned or were satisfactorily accounted for. The most thorough system of inspection of travel documents was instituted by the Dutch, from whose Indonesian possessions large numbers made pilgrimages. Other nations took similar steps, even if their methods were less efficient, and by this means the traffic was almost checked. In the course of time, however, and in the absence of the watchful interest of an international organization, vigilance has been relaxed, and this source of recruiting slaves is once more in full vigour.

The story of an African who was enslaved in this manner was included by M. La Graviere in his report. He had accompanied his master to Mecca and had been sold by him into slavery; but he had managed to escape and make his way back to his village in Africa, where M. La Graviere met him. A native of Bamako in French West Africa, Awad el Joud was a servant of Mohamed Ali ag Attaher, Chief of the Kel Antessar tribe, which lives in the region of Bamako. In 1949 his master decided to make a pilgrimage to Mecca and set out accompanied by his wife, his three children, six servants, the wife of one of them, and her child. Their journey occupied a year. On arrival in Mecca his master bought a house, and for a while all went well. Then one day his master told Awad that he had found work for him with one of his friends, a prince, who lived in Djeddah. Awad went to the prince in 1951. But he soon found out that he was a slave, one of forty owned by the prince, some of whom were Yemenites, and others Eritreans. They were well treated, provided they obeyed their master implicitly; but Awad once saw one of the slaves beaten to death because, being suspected of theft, he had tried to run away and been recaptured. In May 1953 the prince sent Awad to the slave market in Djeddah to be sold. But from there he escaped

Slavery

and went to the French Embassy. He related how he came to be in Djeddah, but was told that the Embassy could not intervene. He therefore returned to the prince, who forgave him and took him back. After his return he saw the prince buy a girl eight years old and give her to his chauffeur, who had come from Kano in Nigeria. On another occasion the prince bought five girls and gave them to his sons. At the end of 1953 the prince went to France. During his absence Awad asked for a few days' leave in order to make a pilgrimage to Mecca. It was granted and he went. But on his return to Djeddah he stowed away on a ship bound for Port Sudan. On landing there he worked his way back to his village, Bamako, where he arrived on April 15, 1954. Awad told M. La Graviere that four other servants were also sold into slavery by Mohamed Ali ag Attaher.

Concerning the slave trade in Arabia, Awad said that there are slave markets at Djeddah, Mecca, Taif and Riyadh, and that slaves are now sold at high prices. The slaves are brought from everywhere, but the African ones come chiefly from the French Sudan and Mauritania. He added that slaves also come from Kuwait and from a country under British influence north of Arabia. But this is presumably a mistake, for there is no such country. He must have meant to the south of Arabia, and this would indicate the Hadramaut and Oman.

Awad's story has received confirmation from the French Ambassador in Saudi-Arabia. In a letter to the Governor-General of French West Africa dated October 13, 1953, the Ambassador stated that a certain Mohamed Ali ag Attaher born at Goundam, but residing at Bamako, formerly Chief of the Kel Antessar tribe, had visited the French Embassy and had got passports for his three sons who had hitherto been on his passport; and that he had learnt later that Mohamed Ali ag Attaher had sold five slaves in Arabia, of whom two were women. He did not mention the names of the slaves sold. Mohamed Ali ag Attaher has not returned to Bamako.

And so the slave trade goes on, from Africa through the Sudan and the Yemen, from Iran and Baluchistan, and from Oman and the Hadramaut. And it continues in spite of treaties and declarations and even a resolution denouncing slavery by a Moslem World Conference held in Mecca itself in 1926, where for centuries the trade has prayed on pilgrims. The recent history of Arabia is full of promises but very little action.

In 1927 a treaty was made between Britain and the newly-created Saudi-Arabia in which Saudi-Arabia undertook to co-operate in the suppression of the slave trade. This promise arose out of previous attempts to end slavery in the Hejaz.

Slave Trading Today

In its day the Turkish Empire claimed sovereignty over most if not all of Arabia. Though it is doubtful whether its rule was effective in all that was claimed, it was in the Hejaz; and when slavery was abolished in the Turkish Empire in 1889, the law was applied there with some success. By the time of Turkey's defeat in the First World War slavery as a legal institution and as an open and publicly declared practice had almost ceased to exist in the Hejaz. After the war, however, it returned in full force. By the Treaty of Lausanne Turkey ceded all her colonies to the Principal Allied Powers. Some were placed under mandate to Britain and France and have since become independent states, but the Hejaz was set up as an independent kingdom at once, with King Husein as its first ruler. Shortly after he ascended his throne he abrogated the Turkish law abolishing slavery and restored the legal status of slavery in the Hejaz. He even imposed an *ad valorem* duty on the sale of slaves as a revenue measure.

Nevertheless, Britain was able to extract a concession from Husein. By a treaty she was granted the right to emancipate slaves in the Hejaz who presented themselves to the British Embassy and applied for their freedom. Husein's reign was not a long one, however. In 1925 he was defeated in battle by Ibn Saud of the Nejd; whereupon he fled the country and was granted asylum in Cyprus, where he later died. The Hejaz was annexed by Ibn Saud and added to the Nejd and Saudi-Arabia came into existence.

It was Britain's right to manumit slaves in the Hejaz that secured from Ibn Saud his promise of co-operation. The treaty with him was made at Djeddah on May 20, 1927. By it Britain agreed to surrender the right of manumission, receiving in exchange Article 7 of the Treaty. This read, 'His Majesty the King of Hejaz and Nejd and its Dependencies undertakes to co-operate by all the means at his disposal with His Britannic Majesty in the suppression of the Slave trade.' The Treaty was ratified on September 17, 1927. Attached to it is a letter from the British Plenipotentiary saying that Britain felt it her duty to humanity 'to abstain from renouncing the right of manumitting slaves' until it became clear that the co-operation stipulated in Article 7 of the Treaty resulted in such practical measures as would render the right of manumission unnecessary. This was acknowledged the same day, May 19, 1927, by King Ibn Saud himself. Since the British later refrained from manumitting slaves effective measures must have been employed by Saudi-Arabia. But the co-operation seems more recently to have fallen into desuetude.

Britain also has a treaty with the Yemen, a Treaty of Friendship and Mutual Co-operation, made at Sanaa, the capital of the Yemen,

Slavery

on February 11, 1934, and ratified on September 4th of that year. Annexed to the Treaty are Notes which were exchanged between the two parties. The British Note recited the 'common desire of all enlightened nations to co-operate in the suppression of the slave trade', and asked for an 'Assurance that you (the King of the Yemen) will by every possible means assist them (the British) in their endeavours to prevent the African slave trade by sea'. The King of the Yemen replied that, 'we agree to the prohibition of the African slave trade and we will command all our Amils (Governors) to do their utmost to prevent it in all the Yemen country and ports'. But their current efforts can scarcely be considered very successful.

Then there is the Decree made in 1936 by the late King Ibn Saud entitled *Instructions Concerning Traffic in Slaves*. Part I of this prohibited importation of slaves by sea and the importation of slaves by land who had been free in their own country, and also prohibited the enslavement of free persons in Saudi-Arabia. Though technically still in force, practically it is not enforced.

Above all there is the United Nations. Both the Yemen and Saudi-Arabia are member states, and therefore bound by its Articles to promote and encourage 'respect for human rights and for fundamental freedoms'. Both sit at the United Nations in an odour of sanctity with other nations which have long ago abolished slavery, yet they make a mockery of its basic principles and ignore its requests. No less than eight times the United Nations has asked them for information on slavery in their territories, in common with other member states, and on each occasion the request has gone unanswered.

That none of these treaties and public declarations has proved successful only demonstrates the strength of the hold that slavery has in Arabia, and in her present prosperity, the strength of the demand for new slaves. It is unlikely that this hold can be broken without great and prolonged effort by all the nations and organizations that can bring any pressure to bear. Britain and France and other nations from whose territories in Africa and Asia people are carried off and sold into slavery have a duty to their citizens in those territories, and a right, to take whatever steps they can to bring the iniquitous slave trade to an end. Britain may surely press, and continue to press, for a more effective measure of co-operation, as promised under her treaties with the Yemen and Saudi-Arabia. As for the United Nations, it cannot afford to let its requests be ignored. Ethiopia and Liberia, when asked by the League of Nations to give pledges that slavery would be abolished in their territories, both complied and took steps to carry them out. The United Nations

Slave Trading Today

must keep the matter in the full light of international publicity until some action or firm undertaking is forthcoming.

Finally, what is the attitude of Islam? As long ago as 1926 a resolution denouncing slavery was adopted by a Moslem World Conference. Was this only one more hollow, easily-made declaration, or does it represent the true feelings of Moslems? If it does, the religious faith of Arabia may be, as Eldon Rutter has suggested, the best means by which to bring about the end of slavery and the trade in human beings in Arabia.

CHAPTER V

THE ATTITUDE OF ISLAM

ಣಿ

SINCE chattel slavery flourishes still only in Moslem countries, that is to say, in countries whose inhabitants profess the Moslem faith and which are ruled by the law of Islam, non-Moslems may be forgiven for wondering whether there is not some supposed religious justification for it; whether the Koran, the Holy Book of Islam, does not give its blessing to the practice. There are critics of Islam who have maintained that it does. One of them, Mishkat, states that 'Slavery is in complete harmony with the spirit of Islam, whilst it is abhorrent to Christianity. That Mohammed ameliorated the condition of the slaves as it existed under the heathen laws of Arabia we cannot doubt, but it is equally certain that the Arabian legislator intended it to be a perpetual institution'.[1]

It must be borne in mind, of course, that at the time the Koran was written, in the seventh century, slavery was still an almost universally accepted institution. As the Rev E. J. Bolus has written, 'Just as Greece and Rome deemed slavery sufficiently sanctioned by the Law of Nature, so the Moslems, taking their cue from their Prophet, have rarely discovered in it an immoral or irreligious element'. But he adds, 'History tells of no general movement against this institution in any Mohammedan country'.[2]

Two critical authorities on the Koran have also emphasized its negative teaching on the subject of slavery. Roberts writes, 'Whether the Prophet of Islam could have abolished slavery altogether among his followers is very doubtful; and his prescriptions regarding the just and humane treatment of this unfortunate class, taken all in all, are praiseworthy. On the other hand there is nothing whatever in Islam to the abolition of this curse'.[3] The other authority, Sir William Muir, has neatly summed up this point of view: 'Rather, while lightening, he rivetted the fetter. . . . There is no obligation on a Moslem to release his slaves. The strongest state-

[1] Book XII, Ch. XX, Pt. I.
[2] *The Influence of Islam*, p. 121.
[3] *The Social Laws of the Koran*.

The Attitude of Islam

ment made by the Prophet in favour of freeing slaves was when he ruled that the punishment for certain sins should be manumission of slaves, "than which there is not an act more acceptable to God".[1]

But the Koran, like the Bible on other matters, does not speak with an unequivocal voice, and it is open to different interpretations. In spite of the above views, the majority of writers on Islam hold that slavery is contrary to its spirit, and that its attitude even compares favourably with that of Christianity. Challenging the statement that the Koran permits slavery, Sir George Maxwell, Vice-Chairman of the League of Nations' Standing Advisory Committee of Experts on Slavery, has written, 'That is not so, the Koran merely recognizes the existence of the system. The Prophet Mohammed saw that system as an integral part of the life of the pagan people of Arabia, and it was as such that he accepted it in teaching the Mohammedan religion. For many centuries before the birth of the Prophet the practice of employing negro slaves had been prevalent, not only in Arabia but in Europe. Immediate prohibition of slavery would not only have entirely disorganized the social and economic system of Arabia but, as experience in many other countries had subsequently proved, might well have caused real hardship to the slaves themselves. . . . The wisdom of the Prophet was shown in permitting slavery to continue and in making provision for their liberation in many way'.[2]

The views of an English Moslem, Lord Headley, are even more emphatic, not to say enthusiastic. After discussing the place of slavery in Greece, Rome and India, he writes, 'Turning to Islam, we recognize in it the first religion that dealt a death-blow to the very roots of this ignoble institution of slavery, which would have been completely abolished through its influence but for its being so deeply rooted in all nations. Islam, however, laid down principles which cannot fail to approximate towards a vastly improved state of affairs. In the early days of his ministry, Mohammed could not command enough wealth to purchase the freedom of the slaves. He, however, preached the religion of liberating slaves and made their emancipation a virtue of great merit. "And what will make you comprehend what the uphill road is? It is the setting free of the slaves or the giving food in the day of hunger to an orphan." (Koran Ch. XC. 11-16) . . . No other revealed book says anything on the subject, and no other Prophet, including Jesus, inspired his fol-

---

[1] *The Koran: Its Composition and Teaching*, p. 58.
[2] 'Slavery in Mohammedan Countries', article in *The Contemporary Review*, July, 1938.

Slavery

lowers to emancipate those they held in bondage or to mitigate their sufferings. . . . The farewell address of Mohammed is a great charter of liberty. It runs thus: "As to your slaves, male and female, feed them with what you eat yourself and clothe them with what you wear. If you cannot keep them or they commit any fault, discharge them. They are God's people like unto you and be kind to them." [1]

It is in the nature of religious teachings that there should be a considerable gap between the teaching and the practice. But the Arabs have on the whole carried out their Prophet's injunction to be kind to their slaves. What remains is to convince them that Mohammed also aimed at the complete abolition of slavery Lord Headley writes, 'All European scholars who have studied Islam with an unbiased mind have come to the conclusion that Islamic teachings do condemn slavery and aim at its abolition, and the only legal cause of bringing others into bondage is prisonership of war; and as long as war continues in the world the system must continue'. And again, 'The Koran abolished all kinds of slavery, with the sole exception of bondage that resulted from fighting, provided that the fighting was in self-defence'.[2]

With regard to enslavement by war, Islam has certainly been active enough in the past, and not only in self-defence; the Jehad was carried far beyond any ethnographical boundaries. As Eldon Rutter has written, 'Under Islamic law unbelievers who commit an act of aggression against Moslems are offered the alternative of embracing Islam, of paying tribute and retaining their religion and property, or of fighting to the death. Under the second destitute enemies are often enslaved in default of payment. Under the third they were often captured and enslaved instead of being massacred'.[3] However, this form of enslavement is unlikely to revive, unless indeed our international arrangements suffer a wholesale breakdown.

Lord Headley also explains how the Koran, far from condoning a perpetuation of slavery, is actively concerned with the practical difficulties of its abolition. 'The task of Islam was not only to secure freedom for those already in slavery but to make them useful members of society. . . . Immediate emancipation of the slaves would have brought more harm to them than benefit, seeing that under the conditions under which the class throughout the world then laboured, slaves neither owned any property nor had any skill in any handicraft which would afford them a means of livelihood. It

[1] Pamphlet, *Islam on Slavery*, p. 4.
[2] Ibid, pp. 9, 19.
[3] *Holy Cities of Arabia*.

The Attitude of Islam

was necessary that they should be taught some method of getting a living, and upon this vital necessity the Prophet laid special stress. Masters were enjoined to give good breeding and good education to their slaves; and if any slave demanded manumission, the master must yield to that demand under certain conditions. On this point the Koran says: " And to those of your slaves who desire a deed of manumission, execute it for them, if you know good is in them, and give them the property which God has given you." (Koran Ch. XXV, 33.) The words "if you know good is in them" were explained by the Holy Prophet to mean, "If you know they are good in some handicraft, by which they can gain their subsistence, so that they are not left to be a burden upon society". The execution of a deed of manumission was compulsory when the slave applied for it.'[1]

Another European writer, Professor Snouck Hurgronje of Leyden University, has made a valuable assessment of the whole rôle of slavery in Islam, putting it into admirable perspective. He writes, 'The law of Islam regulated the position of slaves with much equity; there is a great body of testimony from people who have spent a part of their lives among Mohammedan nations which does justice to the benevolent treatment which bondsmen received from their masters there. Besides that we are bound to state that in many Western countries, or countries under Western domination, whole groups of the population live under circumstances with which those of Mohammedan slavery may be compared with advantage. The only cause of enslavement is prisonership of war or birth from slave parents. The captivity of enemies of Islam has not at all necessarily the effect of enslaving them; for the competent authorities may dispose of them in any other way, also in the way prescribed by modern international law or custom. In proportion to the political ideal of Islam, the number of its enemies must diminish and the possibility of enslaving men consequently decrease. Setting slaves free is one of the most meritorious works and at the same time the regular atonement for certain transgressions of the sacred law. According to the Mohammedan principle slavery is an institution destined to disappear'.[2]

But the fact remains that it has not yet been abolished in all Moslem countries, whereas it has in Christian ones. This has occurred in spite of the plentiful references to slavery in the Koran and their scarcity in Christian scriptures; an interesting commentary on the spirit in which the two faiths have hitherto been inter-

[1] *Islam on Slavery.*
[2] *Mohammedanism*, p. 150.

Slavery

preted in practice. On the religious ethic of Islam towards slavery *The Encyclopaedia of Islam* has this to say, 'Islam, like its two parent monotheisms, Judaism and Christianity, has never preached the abolition of slavery as a doctrine but it has followed their example (though in a very different fashion) in endeavouring to moderate the institution and mitigate its evil and moral effects. . . . The Koran regards the discrimination between human being as in accordance with the divinely-established order of things (Koran Ch. XVI, 71, 75, and Ch. XXX, 28). But over and again, from beginning to end of the Preaching, it makes the emancipation of slaves a meritorious act, a work of charity (Koran II, 177, XC 13), or a deed of expiation for certain felonies, such as unintentional homicide. The unemancipated is mentioned among those who should be treated kindly. . . . Tradition delights in asserting that the slave's lot was among the latest preoccupations of the Prophet. . . . If the Koran and Tradition show a certain favouritism towards such as are Moslems, another direction is taken in the *hadiths* forbidding the keeping of male Arabs in slavery; they invoke a decision to this effect, said to have been given by the Caliph Umar in favour of disposing of instances of slavery against the payment of a ransom where these were the result of pre-Islamic practices'.[1]

For a most penetrating analysis of the attitude of Islam towards slavery, and a thorough-going critical comparison of it with other religions, Syed Ameer Ali, a Moslem writer of high authority from Pakistan, is worth quoting at some length. The late Mr Ali was also a member of Her Majesty's Privy Council. He writes, 'The practice of slavery is coeval with human existence. Historically its traces are visible in every age and in every nation. Its germs were developed in a savage state of society and it continued to flourish even when the progress of material civilization had done away with its necessity. The Jews, the Greeks, the Romans and the ancient Germans—people whose legal and social institutions have most affected modern manners and customs—recognized and practised both kinds of slavery, praedial servitude as well as household slavery. Among the Hebrews from the commencement of their existence as a nation two forms of slavery were practised (enslavement for debt and enslavement of vanquished enemies, or slaves acquired by slave-raiding or purchase). Christianity as a system and a creed raised no protest against slavery, enforced no rule, inculcated no principle for the mitigation of the evil. Except for a few remarks on the disobedience of slaves (I Tim. VI, 1-2) and a

[1] *Encyclopaedia of Islam*, Vol. 1, p. 25.

The Attitude of Islam

general advice to masters to give servants their due, the teaching of Jesus, as portrayed in the Christian traditions, contained nothing expressive of disapproval of bondage'.[1]

Of slavery imposed by Europeans, and maintained up till only a century ago, he writes, all too truly, 'Christianity failed utterly in abolishing slavery or alleviating its evils. Under its influence the greatest civilians of Europe upheld slavery. . . . And it was under the same influences that the highly cultured Christians of the southern states of North America practised the cruellist inhumanities upon the unfortunate beings whom they held as slaves, many of them their own kith, and shed torrents of blood for the maintenance of the curse of slavery in their midst'.[2]

He then makes out a strong case for Islam. 'The Islamic teachings dealt a blow at the institution of slavery which, had it not been for the deep root it had taken among the surrounding nations and the natural obliquity of the human mind, would have been completely extinguished as soon as the generation which then practised it had passed away. It has been justly contended that as the promulgation of the laws, precepts and teachings of Islam extended over twenty years, it is naturally to be expected that many of the pre-Islamic institutions, which were eventually abolished, were at first tacitly permitted or expressly recognized. In one of these categories stood slavery. The evil was intertwined with the innermost relations of the people among whom Mohammed flourished. Its extinction was only to be achieved by the continued agency of wise and humane laws and not by sudden and entire emancipation of the existing slaves, which was morally and economically impossible. Numberless provisions, negative and positive, were accordingly introduced in order to promote and accomplish a gradual enfranchisement. A contrary policy would have produced an utter collapse of the infant commonwealth. The Prophet exhorted his followers repeatedly in the name of God to enfranchise slaves, "Than which there is not an act more acceptable to God". He ruled that for certain sins of omission the penalty should be manumission of slaves. He ordered that slaves should be allowed to purchase their liberty by the wages of their service; and that in case they had no present means of gain and wanted to earn in some other employment enough for that purpose, they should be allowed to leave their masters on an agreement to that effect. He also provided that sums should be advanced to the slaves from the public treasury to purchase their liberty. In certain contingencies, it was provided that the slaves should become

[1] *The Spirit of Islam*, p. 259.
Ibid.

Slavery

enfranchised without the interference and even against the will of his master.'[1]

A point he emphasizes particularly is the restricted nature of the type of enslavement condoned by the Koran. 'From all that we have said it is abundantly clear that the Legislator himself looked upon the custom as temporary in its nature and held that its extinction was sure to be achieved by the progress of ideas and change of circumstances. . . . The Koran recognized in fact only one kind of slavery, the servitude of men made captives in *bona fide* lawful warfare. Among all barbarous nations the captives are spared from a motive of selfishness alone, in order to add to the wealth of the individual captor or of the collective nation by their sale money or their labour. Like other nations of antiquity the Arab of pre-Islamic period spared the lives of his captives for the sake of profiting by them. Mohammed found this custom existing among his people and laid down strict rules for their guidance, enjoining that only those may be held in bondage who were taken in *bona fide* war, until they were ransomed or the captive bought his or her own liberty by the wages of service. Slave-lifting and slave-dealing, patronized by dominant Christianity (e.g. the sale of Irish men and women after the massacre of Drogheda by Cromwell, and the sale of rebels after the Monmouth rebellion to colonists in the North American colonies) and sanctified by Judaism, were utterly reprobated and condemned. It was forbidden in absolute terms to reduce Moslems to slavery. . . . It will be seen, therefore, that Islam did not "consecrate" slavery, as has been maliciously affirmed, but provided in every way for its abolition and extinction by circumscribing the means of possession within the narrowest limits.'[2]

Finally, he reaches a conclusion with which nobody is likely to disagree. 'The time is now arrived when humanity at large should raise its voice against the practice of servitude, in whatever shape or under whatever denomination it may be disguised. Moslems especially, for the honour of the great Prophet, should try to efface that dark page from their history. It remains for Moslems to show the falseness of the aspersions cast on the memory of their Prophet by proclaiming in explicit terms that slavery is reprobated by their faith and discountenanced by their code.'[3]

This view, whatever critics of Islam may say, seizing upon only a single facet of the Prophet's teaching, has the weight of responsible opinion behind it, both Moslem and non-Moslem. It certainly repre-

[1] *The Spirit of Islam.*
[2] Ibid.
[3] Ibid.

The Attitude of Islam

sents the view of modern interpreters of Islamic teaching. Eldon Rutter has written, 'The Koran rightly practised would soon bring about the complete cessation of slavery'.[1] And Bertram Thomas, another sympathetic authority on Arabia, 'In the unabatement of slavery Arabia has been false to her Prophet'.[2]

A distinguished Moslem of our time, the Imam Dr H. Ghoraba, spoke of slavery in a sermon he delivered in London in 1955. In it he quoted with approval 'a great Moslem scholar, who claimed that meditation upon the policy of Islam would prove that Islam came to abolish slavery in spite of its recognition of it'. He said that, 'Slavery before Islam was like a river flowing from many sources into a reservoir which, by constant supply, grew bigger and bigger. Islam aims at drying this up and dispersing the water in the reservoir by opening up ways of escape. . . . Therefore it can be claimed that although Islam admitted (recognized) slavery in one form, it aimed undoubtedly to abolish it, and the means by which this was brought about were many and wise'.

It is clear then that slavery as a permanent institution is by no means sanctioned by the teachings of the Holy Prophet of Islam. That it still thrives in Arabia is due, in Syed Ameer Ali's words, to 'the natural obliquity of the human mind', coupled with an interpretation of the Koran that is limited by self-interest. The majority of Moslem states have followed a truer, more progressive, interpretation and have abolished slavery — to their benefit. It remains for this view to gain acceptance among the faithful in Arabia. Since this is a religious matter, responsibility for convincing them rests primarily with their co-religionists. Efforts by the non-Moslem world inevitably tend to arouse some degree of resentment It is for fellow Moslems to exert every effort to convince their recalcitrant brothers-in-faith that the good name of their religion is being tarnished in the eyes of the world by the continuance of slavery in the countries of Arabia. Only the Moslem states which have already abolished slavery are in a position to exert this form of influence. The world may surely ask them to use it.

---

[1] *The Holy Cities of Arabia.*
[2] *The Arabs.*

CHAPTER VI

DEBT-BONDAGE

SECOND only to war and conquest the great imposer of servitude is economic pressure. Debt-bondage, as its name implies, is a form of slavery created by indebtedness, and it approaches chattel slavery most closely in the degree of power it enables one person to exercise over another.

It arises chiefly under primitive economic conditions, in countries which have not yet reached a money economy, i.e. where money does not circulate freely. In such a country ownership of immovable property is usually communal and movable property is of little value. A poor man who incurs a debt or who wishes to raise credit frequently has nothing to pledge as security for it except his services, or those of someone under his control. When he does this he, or his pawn, enters a state of debt-bondage to the creditor, for whom he must work, in exchange for maintenance, until the debt is repaid, and the value of the services rendered is not credited towards the extinction of the debt.

Like chattel slavery it is a very ancient custom, and there are references to it in the Bible. The Jews recognized the practice, and their law regulated it. Debtors and their families could be sold into debt-bondage, though the permanent enslavement of a Hebrew was forbidden. A Hebrew could only be sold into debt-bondage for a period of six years; at the end of that time he was free, whether the debt was repaid or not. If, however, at the end of the six years the debtor-bondsman wished to remain in servitude, as he might under certain circumstances, he and his master could appear before a judge, who could make an order to that effect. His master would then bore a hole in the lobe of his ear, and he would remain a slave for ever.

The evil of debt-bondage lies in the opportunities it presents to the unscrupulous landlord or moneylender to use his power to obtain an unbreakable hold over the debtor, which can amount to permanent slavery, either for the debtor himself, or, even worse, for his hapless pawn. At the same time, it has been recognized that it can-

Debt-Bondage

not be entirely eliminated in backward countries, since it is the only way a poor man can raise credit. Efforts have therefore been directed mainly at regulating and limiting it. Though the majority of countries have legislated against it, cases still come to light in several regions; while in India it remains a major problem.

A particularly compelling reason why even the humblest Indian is sometimes driven to raise money is for the celebration of the marriage of a child. Marriage and procreation, as the practical manifestation of eternity, have always had an important place in Indian thinking; so important that even the most impoverished families will spend far beyond their means to provide what is considered the appropriate ceremony and entertainment. In Southern India especially a system of debt-bondage has existed for centuries and become a permanent part of the social structure. Employers, landlords, and others have always been ready to lend money if the borrower will assign himself and his children to work as bond-slaves for their keep till the principal is repaid. But since, under the contract, the bondsman has parted with the possibility of earning money himself, and since he is working solely for his keep, it means that the debt will never be repaid, unless it is repaid by a third person, which is a remote contingency. The debtor-bondsman is therefore usually enslaved for life. The creditor, however, maintains him and his family, thus assuring them of subsistence until the debt is paid.

The system is not entirely without advantages for the bondsman. It is not uncommon for traders and moneylenders to lend money to humble labourers, usually on the occasion of a marriage, on condition that the lender takes all the debtor's earnings when he is in work, until the debt is repaid. In exchange the lender maintains the debtor and his family, even to the extent of keeping them when the debtor is not working. In a country in which there is no unemployment relief or other social security, and where poverty is acute, this system at least has the merit of making the debtor carefree, even though poorly nourished and dependent. But he is content; his children have been married with the pomp decreed by custom.

In recent times, with the development of modern industry, the ancient system of debt-bondage in India has been given an extra exploitative twist. A full report has recently been made by Bruno Lasker, a member of the UN *ad hoc* Committee on Slavery. He writes: 'It is on the Indian sub-continent that bondage for debt as part of an inherited class system has found its largest and socially most devastating development in Asia. The system is variously known as kamiauti, khamberi, goti; in some parts of Southern India as marichetti and casigallu, and in Hyderabad as baghela. In addition

Slavery

to servile relations arising from debt that go back to pre-colonial days, there are to be found also modern forms of debt-bondage designed to secure labour on the cheapest possible terms and resembling customs that have similarly grown up, as already shown, on the margins of modern industry in China and Japan. Indeed, the labour recruiter and the factory-moneylender have taken advantage of earlier customs, so that it is often difficult in a given instance to decide whether the debt-bondage arises from new uses found for the exploitation of population groups traditionally of low status, or whether certain branches of business and industry have created for their own ends new methods of subjecting formerly free and self-directing persons to a regime little short of slavery.'[1]

But it is not looked upon as slavery. The desire of the employer to exploit cheap labour is matched by the willingness of the lowest classes to bind themselves for the sake of the modern goods they desire. Bruno Lasker goes on: 'Action taken by the Central and Provincial Governments of India to scale rural indebtedness by the appointment of Debt Adjustment Boards acting under the provisions of Agricultural Debt Relief Acts shows that the existence of such indebtedness in itself, even though the debts may be large in relation to income, is not regarded as a form of servitude for if that were the case it would be covered by the legal provisions for the punishment of slavery. However, indebtedness in India often is a characteristic condition of an ethnic group which for generations has in one way or another been held down to a status of involuntary servitude. It is a form of bondage in the case of millions of aborigines who have been brought into contact, directly or indirectly, with the modern economy. Although both their means of livelihood and their standards of living still are relatively primitive, they have come to desire modern articles of consumption: they resort to credit when the rent charges of the landlord or the assessments of the government absorb all their income above that required for bare subsistence. The most frequent cause for indebtedness here as elsewhere is the necessity of the cultivator to pay his rent in advance of the harvest, so that he must either sell his crop in advance at much less than it would bring later, or borrow money at a high rate of interest. In any case, there is little likelihood, unless the Government intervenes with restrictive regulations, that he will ever be free of debt again, whether on the landlord's books or on those of the professional moneylender. And from the standpoint of these persons this is as it should be; they are more interested in being able to command the

[1] *Forms of Involuntary Servitude in Asia, Oceania and Australasia*, UN Doc. E/AC.33R.11.

Debt-Bondage

debtor's services or his produce (on their own terms) than in a direct return on their investment.'[1]

The magnitude and depth of the problem obviously preclude any easy solution; it is intimately bound up with India's whole development. 'A considerable body of recent legislation notwithstanding,' writes Mr Lasker, 'bondage for debt is still the lot of millions of people in India. A spiritual apathy has developed, which these measures, unless accompanied by comprehensive programmes of social rehabilitation, cannot remove. Thus, one of the papers presented at the Asia Relations Conference at New Delhi in 1947 states that when members of population groups which have long been held down to a servile status are enabled to earn good wages, they are liable to spend a large part of their earnings on extravagant living instead of paying their debts and building up modest capital resources of their own. Such conditions as these are not, of course, typical of all of Indian industry but occur in its margins, where the transition from traditional rural social relations to modern industrial relations is as yet in an early stage. Among the laws adopted in recent times — partly as a result of the Royal Commission on Labour in India (Cd. 3383. 1931), the so-called Witney Commission — the first place is taken by Agriculturalists or Debtor Relief Acts and Moneylenders Regulation Acts, some of them designed to reduce the power not only of the professional moneylender, but also of the landlord and merchant who operates on a credit basis, by licensing systems and by placing ceilings on interest rates of unsecured debts, also by setting up tribunals for scaling down debts. Several of the governments have prescribed legal maximum amounts that may be spent on marriages and funerals. In several provinces comprehensive programmes have been adopted to raise the social level of aboriginal and other depressed classes.'[2]

Much time and sustained effort will clearly be needed before these measures can succeed.

While India is undoubtedly the country in which debt-bondage is most prevalent and hard to eradicate, it is also known to exist elsewhere in Asia, in Burma, Siam and Indo-China. Bruno Lasker has again described its course. In Burma, before the British took over the administration of the country, debt-bondage was widespread. Chattyar moneylenders had come over from Southern India and gained a considerable hold over the small farmers who owned the land. By lending money to them at rates of interest equivalent to

---
[1] *Forms of Involuntary Servitude in Asia, Oceania and Australasia*, UN Doc. E/AC.33R.11.
[2] Ibid.

Slavery

45 per cent per annum they gradually took away much of the land and converted the Burmese debtors into tenant farmers, perpetually in debt. The British Government passed various laws, and so has the Burmese Government since the country became independent. But debt-bondage unhappily continues. And similar conditions prevail in Siam and Indo-China, according to Mr Lasker.

Another part of the world where economic conditions are relatively primitive is Africa; and there too the pledging of persons for debt is far from unknown. But since the enactment of laws making it illegal, and with the improvement of living standards, it has fortunately been reduced to negligible proportions in most parts. In 1950 Britain was able to report to the United Nations that 'the practice of pawning of persons for debt has been associated with the Gold Coast, Nigeria and Sierra Leone, but that in recent years only two cases have come to light in the Gold Coast. It is still known to occur in Nigeria but is on the decline. In Sierra Leone it is of rare occurrence. It is a criminal offence "to place or receive any person in servitude as a pledge or a security for a debt".' In Nigeria thirty-four persons were convicted in the years 1945-1947; but only six in 1948, and six again in 1949.

According to a similar report from the French Government debt-bondage is no longer practised in French Africa, with the exception of Togoland. There people still pledge themselves as security for debt, although it is illegal. Two people were convicted in 1949.

In the Belgian Congo, however, there is still a regular system of debt-bondage. It has been described by Madame Jane Vialle. 'In the Belgian Congo the custom of pledging oneself or a third person in payment of a debt is known as Kivi. A Kivi is an insolvent debtor who gives himself up to a member of another clan on condition that the latter pays his debt. The Kivi becomes a slave, subject however to the restriction that he cannot be sold without the members of his clan having first been invited to set their clansman free by re-imbursing his owner.' But there is little information on its extent and social consequences.

So strong is the temptation for an indigent person to pledge his services for the sake of credit, and the tendency for the creditor to tighten his hold, that cases of debt-bondage still crop up even in the advanced economic conditions of the west. In the USA in recent years a few cases have been dealt with by the Supreme Court. Rural poverty, especially among a despised or submerged class, is usually the cause. In South America, where the native Indians are in this position, there is, as a legacy of the Spanish conquests, a well-established form of debt-bondage of particular severity. But as it is closely

Debt-Bondage

connected with the system of land tenure it has more in common with serfdom, and will therefore be discussed in the next chapter.

The precise status of the debtor-bondsman, whether he is actually a slave, or a serf, or neither, has been thoroughly argued by H. J. Nieboer. He writes: 'Among some peoples a debtor, unable to pay a debt he has contracted, becomes the slave of his creditor. Sometimes such persons are ordinary slaves; but pawns or debtor-slaves in the restricted sense are a class whose slave-state is conditional; they become free as soon as the debt is paid by or for them; the creditor cannot refuse to accept the money . . . a pawn is a person placed in temporary bondage to another by the head of the family, either to pay a debt or to obtain a loan. When a person is pawned on account of a debt, the services of the pawn, even should they extend over a considerable number of years, count for nothing towards the liquidation of the debt. . . . As long as the debt remains unpaid, the pawn is in the same condition as a slave. He has to perform not a fixed amount of work but to serve his master without any limitation. The master has over him a power, which in principle is unlimited. Is this pawn a slave, i.e. is he the property of his master? . . . We for our purpose may classify the pawns among slaves, if we can prove that sociologically a system of pawning performs the same function as a slave system. And this certainly is the case. The same system of compulsory labour, the same subjection of the entire person exists, whether the subjected are perpetually slaves or temporary pawns, viz. in those cases where the master's power is in principle unlimited. Where pawns have a fixed amount of work to do, they are temporary serfs, but where (as in most cases) no limit is put to the amount of work the master may exact from them, they are temporary slaves, and as long as they are slaves, take the same place as other slaves in the social system.'[1]

When the League of Nations began to study the matter and gather information it found that most nations agreed that debt-bondage was indeed slavery, and in most the pledging of persons had been made illegal. Only a few argued that it was permissible for an individual to pledge his services as security for a loan. The majority of governments believed that it could be abolished through the enforcement of their existing laws against slavery offences. But the League found that debt-bondage often survived, supported by custom, in various disguised forms. It therefore recommended that in any countries in which debt-bondage existed the government should consider a 'revision of the contracts between creditor and debtor in conformity with the requirements of justice'.

[1] *Slavery as an Industrial System*, p. 39.

Slavery

The objectionable feature of debt-bondage is that the value of the services rendered by the pawn do not count towards liquidation of the debt. Yet at the same time the pawn has no means of earning money to pay the debt. This is the crux of the matter, as was recognized by the ancient Jewish law which limited the period of bondage. It is not the pledging of services that is in itself evil; it is the lack of any limits to them that leads to a state of unqualified servitude.

Modern legislation to regulate debt-bondage has followed a regular pattern, creating a framework to protect the weak and needy. The earliest was enacted in 1859, in the Netherlands East Indies. This required the debt to be registered and fixed a time limit on the services of the pawn. It also determined the value of the services and required that it should be applied to liquidate the debt. In the Portuguese colonies too all agreements for repayments of debt by performance of service are limited by law to a period of three years

The first British law of this type was made in 1910. This was the Debt-Bondage Enactment for the state of Kedah in Malaya, which required that all agreements for labour in consideration of a debt should be reduced to writing and registered. It also fixed a limit of two years to such agreements, determined the value of the services, and provided that the value should be applied for the liquidation of the debt. The Act was later extended to other states of Malaya.

Similar legislation was passed in Cambodia in 1934, and in Hyderabad in 1936.

The impossibility of preventing a person from pledging his services, and hence the need to concentrate on regulating it, was recognized by the League of Nations in 1934. The Advisory Committee of Experts on Slavery in its report recommended that: 'Pledging of the debtor himself should not be done away with but should be developed in a way to deprive it of any objectionable features. In backward countries it is the only known method of obtaining credit for the penniless and may be a necessary condition of development, but it should be regulated. It should be modified so that:

(1) constraint of the debtor should take place only by order of a competent court and the person under constraint should no longer be kept under detention by his creditor but should be under the guardianship of the public authorities;
(2) the duration of the constraint should be reduced to a limited time; and
(3) it should be strictly prohibited to subject to constraint any person other than the debtor himself.'

This was following in 1939 by the International Labour Office Convention on Minimum Standards of Social Policy in Dependent

Debt-Bondage

Territories, which fixed a maximum period of service for all contracts of indigenous workers. It has since been ratified by Britain.

The international view of debt-bondage is today unequivocal. Although the 1926 Convention of the League of Nations was intended to embrace it in its definition of slavery, many countries which subscribed to the Convention succeeded in evading their responsibilities by interpreting it narrowly to refer to chattel slavery only. But this loophole has now been closed. Debt-bondage has been included in the Supplementary Convention of 1956, and has been declared to be slavery.

These two international declarations, the ILO Convention of 1939 and the UN Convention of 1956, provide an ample basis for bringing about the abolition of debt-bondage, if they could only be applied throughout the world. The economic problems underlying it such as those of India, cannot of course be readily solved; but the pressure of international concern is an invaluable bulwark against apathy.

CHAPTER VII

SERFDOM OR PEONAGE

ಣಿ

THE intermediate state between slavery and complete liberty, known in Europe as serfdom, still exists in many parts of the world, usually as a survival from some earlier subjugation of a people. It may take several different forms, according to the type of service or tribute exacted, and it has received various names. In South America, where it has long been established, and where some ten million indigenous Indians struggle through life in most depressed circumstances, it is known as peonage.

The essential difference between slavery and serfdom is that the serf or peon is not the property of his master, with the absolute power that this implies; the master is entitled to fixed services and tributes only. A serf is bound to the land and compelled to live on it. He must till its owner's fields, or render other services, for so many days a week without payment. But for the remainder he is free to work on his own holding. Unlike the slave, therefore, he is not entirely deprived of rights by his very birth. He has some means of acquiring property, and he may marry and have legitimate descendants to inherit his goods. His share in the fruits of the soil gives him a personal interest in its cultivation; and he may even dispute the tribute he has to pay. He cannot be sold apart from the land, and the owner of the soil has no rights over his person, or the females of his family, except for such customs as the *jus primae noctis* or *le droit du seigneur*, which have existed in certain countries. On the other hand, his status is usually hereditary, and economic forces have tended to keep his life at a miserable level.

Though most serfs have been predial, that is to say, attached to the soil, there are also records of domestic serfs. In India, even today, there is still a form of hereditary domestic serfdom. Under the caste system, and subject to no legal compulsion, certain castes gladly serve the family to which they are attached in a hereditary menial capacity.

The part played by serfdom in the development of human socie-

Serfdom or Peonage

ties is one of extraordinary interest. It seems to have existed in some form throughout the world from the earliest times, both contemporary with and after the slave-holding periods. In Europe it was often a development from slavery. J. K. Ingram writes, 'The transition to serfdom took place in civic communities when the master parted with or was deprived of the property in the person of the slave and became entitled only to his services of a determinate part of them. In rural life, where the march of development was slower, the corresponding stage was reached when, in accordance with the fundamental principles of feudalism, the relation between the lord and the serf, from being personal, became territorial'.[1]

But, like slavery, serfdom can also arise directly from war, as it frequently did under the Teutonic conquests. The difference is this: the slaves of a conqueror were actual prisoners of war, whereas the serfs were usually the folk of the conquered race. The conquerors desired land to own and control, but not to work on. The local inhabitants were therefore usually allowed to remain, to act as hewers of wood and drawers of water, as ploughmen, herdsmen and tillers of the soil. It seems to have been the rule of the world that less powerful or less developed races go down before the more powerful or the more virile, though not necessarily the most civilized. Throughout the ages, too, the debt-ridden freeman has sold himself into bondage for the sake of sustenance for himself and his family, a system as modern as it is old, as we have seen in India.

In South America these two age-old burdens of life, tilling the soil and debt, come together in the type of serfdom still imposed there under the name of peonage; for the peon is bound to the land not so much by status as by debt. The Spanish word peon means literally a foot soldier, but it has been applied for centuries to American-Indian and mestizo labourers in Latin-America and the Philippine Islands; for the peonage system is a legacy of Spanish colonization.

When Spain conquered these lands, the idigenous people were forced to work for their masters under the institution known as repartimientos and encomiendas, by which a number of American-Indians, with or without the land they occupied, were assigned to a Spaniard, who was entitled to exact service from them. The encomiendas were abolished by law in 1811; but the Spanish settlers in Latin-America and the Philippines contrived to keep their labourers in a state of involuntary servitude. One of the methods by

[1] *History of Slavery*, p. 262.

Slavery

which this was done was for the Spanish landlord to let the peon have a small parcel of land on his estate provided he agreed to work for him for a stipulated number of days a week, usually without payment. As the peon was landless, his agreement was readily secured; he had no alternative.

On the face of it such contracts were not inequitable; they amounted to no more than a payment of rent by service. But in practice they became transformed into enslavement, or rather enserfdom, for life. To rivet the shackle more firmly the landlord kept a shop on the estate, which would be the only shop within reach. There the peon would buy whatever he needed which he was unable to produce himself; and he would be given credit. Little by little the debt would grow until it reached such proportions that it could never be repaid. Care was taken to ensure that the peon's debt was never extinguished, but was increased beyond the limit he could bear.

Arising from a system of forced labour imposed by a conquering people, peonage is thus a distinctive form of serfdom. The peon is not a slave like the debtor-bondsman. As Prof. G. M. McBride has written, 'In ancient and certain primitive societies non-payment of debt frequently resulted in the enslavement of the debtor to the creditor. The status of the debtor under such circumstances was one of slavery, whereas the peon is not legally a slave. Peonage is found exclusively in a capitalistic society, where the law protects the creditor and where employer-employee relationships prevail. Its development has been relatively recent, and chiefly in regions where other types of forced labour are not permitted, not infrequently after other forms of servitude, such as slavery, have been abolished'.[1] As the peon was unable to leave his holding unless his debt was paid, he became in effect a serf. On a change of ownership he was sold with the land. Indebtedness is the chief attribute of peonage, where as it is not necessarily a feature of slavery or pure serfdom.

Two court cases in the United States of America have also clarified the status of the peon. In Clyatt v United States (197 US 207, 1905), before the Supreme Court, peonage was defined as 'a status or condition of compulsory service based on the indebtedness of the peon to the master. The basic fact is indebtedness'. And in Bailey v Alabama (219 US 219, 1911), also before the Supreme Court, Chief Justice Hughes gave the following definition: 'The essence of the thing is compulsory service in payment of a debt. A peon is one who is compelled to work for his creditor.'

[1] *Encyclopaedia of Social Services*, Vol. 12, 12.70, article on Peonage.

Serfdom or Peonage

In theory free, the peon is in practice bound, unable to break his yoke of debt. On his death it passes to his children, and so the status becomes hereditary. When the Spanish colonies evolved into republics slavery was prohibited in all their constitutions. But in many of them the peonage system still survives, and until relatively recently little attempt has been made to abolish it.

This state of affairs was noted by the League of Nations when it made its survey. In 1925 the Temporary Slavery Commission reported: 'There is reliable information that many pathetic forms of debtor-pledging exist in some countries in America, where they constitute a system called "peonage". Under this system the debtor agrees to work for the creditor until the labour supplied is considered equivalent to the value of the land allotted to him or of any advance made to him. It often happens that the creditor so arranges that his debtors get more and more into debt, with the result that what was in the beginning only an apparently equitable contract is transformed finally into enslavement for life. The Governments of the countries where these practices are said still to exist have not given any information in this point in their replies to the request for information sent to them by the Secretary General of the League of Nations. On the other hand, the Commission has not yet had time to communicate to the Governments concerned the information on this subject which it has received from private sources.'[1]

The Commission was concerned with the social consequences of peonage, which it considered, with good reason, to be worse than debt-bondage. 'The abuses of the system known in certain parts of the world as peonage may lead, in the opinion of the Commission, to a form of debt slavery even graver in its social effects than those practices which arise out of native custom. The latter, for the most part, are methods of redeeming debt owed by one native to another of approximately equal status; they affect individuals only, and they are usually well understood by both parties. The obligations resulting from peonage are, on the other hand, imposed by persons of a more privileged position upon others less favoured; they result in a class of permanently enslaved debtors who, when entering into the arrangement in question, do not apparently understand its consequences. The Commission consider that this form of debt slavery, whenever it exists, calls for immediate action. Legislation might be adopted which would only recognize as valid the arrangement by which the debtor pledges his services in payment of his original debt and provides that this original debt shall be extinguished after a fixed time proportional to the original amount.

[1] Report A19, 1925 vi, para. 69.

Slavery

It may be recalled in this connection, that by Article 58 of the Portuguese Law of October 14, 1914, relating to labour in the colonies, all debts of this class are considered to be annulled at the expiration of 600 days of effective work, the debtor being held to have redeemed his debt by his labour.'[1]

The fundamental cause of peonage was pinned down when the League of Nations returned to the subject in 1936. The Advisory Committee of Experts on Slavery reported: 'The problem of the agricultural debt-slaves is exceptionally difficult. The root of the trouble lies in the system of land tenure, under which a few favoured persons own most of the land, and the peasantry are landless folk dependent upon them for permission to cultivate the soil. In some places it may well be that the system is almost indistinguishable from serfdom, and in such cases it may be difficult to say whether the persons are in debt because they are serfs, or whether they are serfs because they are in debt.[2] Prompted by a report of the ILO on American-Indians it concluded, 'It is possible that there is more human misery as a result of debt slavery than there is anywhere as the result of domestic slavery'.

In 1949 a close analysis of the systems of land tenure in South American countries was made by the ILO, at a conference it held in Montevideo on 'Conditions of Life and Work of Indigenous Populations of Latin-American Countries'. Its report stated, 'The type of tenancy that is most common in Latin-American indigenous areas is a mixed system under which the Indian is both tenant of a parcel of land and peon. The estate gives him the usufruct of a parcel of land, the payment for which consists of (a) part of the harvest handed over direct to the land-owner at the price he fixes; and/or (b) a specified number of days' work in the field, to which is sometimes added the payment of tithe or the compulsory performance of unpaid personal or domestic services in the landowner's house or on his estate. Although the two forms of payment described above are considered to be the essential features of this mixed system of land tenure, there is a third in certain areas, which should be mentioned here. According to this method the landowner provides the tenant peon with seed, fertilizer, tools and an advance of cash to cover his needs, in return for which payment is due in kind at a fixed rate by the owner. An "account in kind" is opened, which produces a position of dependence through the accumulation of debt, which often compels the Indian to remain indefinitely in the owner's service. Frequently the parcel of land which the indigenous peon-tenant

[1] Report A.19, 1925 vi, para. 75.
[2] Report C.189 (i) M.145, 1936 vi, p. 25.

Serfdom or Peonage

received is a stony mountainside, and usually the crop is insufficient to meet his needs. Various names are given to this mixed system of tenancy and peonage and to the parcel of land. In Ecuador it is known as huasi-pungo, and the occupant as huasi-pungero; in Peru the tenant-peon is normally known as the yahacona, and the practice as yahaconago; in Bolivia the parcel of land is called ponguea je or parcela; in Venezuala it is known as conuco, and the occupant as conuquero'.[1]

There is no lack of national legislation against oppressive practices; the difficult is to secure their enforcement in the absence of any real will to do so. In all the South American republics slavery as such is prohibited; and serfdom has been included in the UN definition of slavery. But in addition, a Peruvian law of 1916 declared that Indians living on a hacienda could not be held by indebtedness to the landowner; the Mexican constitution of 1917 abolished all forms of involuntary servitude, except as a punishment for crime; Ecuador in 1918 withdrew legal enforcement of the practice of peonage; and Bolivia in 1945 prohibited peonage by law, subject to certain conditions.

How hypocritical such laws may be has been indicated by Prof. Miguel Bonifaz. About the Bolivian law, he pointed out that it served a purely demagogic purpose, because subsequent provisions in it require the tenant-peons to transport the produce from the estates to the towns or the ports, and require named officials to intervene to compel them to do so. 'Farewell the free consent of the contracting parties,' he adds, 'armed force is allowed to secure compliance.'[2]

Similarly, the 1949 ILO report remarks, 'Nevertheless, it should be pointed out that in many cases such protection is insufficient for the Indian, especially in rural areas, where supervision of its application is slight or non-existent'.[3] And again, 'In spite of legal prohibition, the Indian tenant or peon in various regions of Latin-America is still required to give services free of charge in the landlord's house or on his estate'.[4]

This discrepancy between theory and practice became very evident when the United Nations gathered information on slavery. In many cases its inquiries received an official answer from the governments concerned denying that any form of servitude existed: but a later ILO report disclosed a different picture.

[1] Report 11, p. 25.
[2] *El Problema Agrario-Indigeno en Bolivia.*
[3] Report 11, p. 53.
[4] Ibid, p. 94.

Slavery

Ecuador made such a denial, but the ILO's report showed how an apparently innocuous system actually operates. It first described the system: 'The huasi-pungo of the mountain region of Ecuador is a small piece of land which the estate owner makes available to the Indian worker, and on which he is entitled to build a hut, cultivate a garden and keep a few head of cattle. In exchange the Indian is required to work on the estate as a labourer for a small wage during a specified number of days in each week, and also to take his turn as a domestic servant in the employer's house. The Labour Code provides that the number of days in question may not exceed four in the week, and that the wage may not be less than half the minimum rate laid down for an agricultural labourer in the locality. Despite these and other protective measures, the system lends itself to a number of abuses, as will be seen below. Some have sought to define the huasi-pungero as a type of tenant who pays his rent in the form of work for the landlord; in fact he is a special type of labourer, part of whose pay takes the form of the right to use a plot of land; and it is precisely in this way that the Labour Code defines the term. Section 244 of the Labour Code defines a huasi-pungero as a "person who works on an estate for remuneration which he receives partly in cash, as wages, and partly in the right to use a piece of land made available to him by the employer".'[1]

Drawing for information on a comparatively recent official publication, the report continued by describing conditions in one of the principal provinces of the plateau. 'On some estates the pay is nominal only; on others it amounts to ten sucres a month; as a rule it ranges from forty-five centavos to three sucres a working day (usually of twelve hours). Very often the huasi-pungero has to wait for months before he receives his pay. This obliges him frequently to request the favour of a suplido, or advance in cash. At the end of the year the employer checks the advances received and the number of days worked, with the result that the labourer is in debt to him. This system of piling up debts serves to retain the Indians on the estate for an indefinite period. When the father dies, the huasi-pungo passes to the wife or to an elder son, if there is one. Before a man may leave his huasi-pungo he has to pay off his debt. Apparently the payment of tenant-labourers in cash has disappeared altogether in some districts. The huasi-pungo is an institution typical of the plateau region.'[2]

So too with Peru. The Peruvian Government denied the existence

[1] *Indigenous Workers in Independent Countries*, ILO Doc. CEIL/1/3, of January 1951, pp. 115-118.
[2] Ibid.

Serfdom or Peonage

of serfdom or peonage in Peru.[1] It added that yanaconazgo had been abolished by an act of March 1947,[2] though some parts of it sanctioned vestiges of this traditional tenancy, which had 'practically disappeared'. It said that the term yanaconazgo is disliked, and that a Bill had been drafted to replace the 1947 Act, with the title 'Law on Small Leases', and that it would eliminate 'any vestige or formula which might resemble serfdom'.

The ILO, however, was less optimistic. It described the types of tenancy and service obligations of the Indian under the following heads: 'Colonato: the differences between this system and that of a tenancy for rent have been described as follows: In the case of tenancy for rent, the contract is for a specified time and is the result of agreement between two equal parties. In the case of colonato, the contract is for an unspecified period and very frequently results from a situation of fact in which previous agreement has had no part. The Indian was born on the estate and is obliged to accept conditions established in the past by custom or tradition. As a rule, in exchange for the use of a piece of land allotted to him, or for the right to graze his animals on the estate, he is obliged to give the land-owner part of his crop and/or to work on the estate as a labourer. Colonato is a double contract of hire, in which the tenant is lessee of the land and at the same time lessor of his own services. In some districts of the Sierra, the relationship between landlord and colon takes a special form, which may be described as follows: the owner provides the tenant with seed, fertilizer, farm tools and cash to meet his immediate requirements. These advances must be paid off at a rate of exchange determined by the landowner. The operation takes the form of a "goods account", which often obliges the Indian to remain indefinitely in the landowner's service. The whole situation is expressed on the credit and debit sides of a very long and very old account, which is handed down from father to son; some tenants owe for advances made to their grandfathers.

'Other forms of tenancy: Apart from the simple form, in which rent is paid in cash, several other types of tenancy resembling the yanacona and colonato systems appear to exist in some parts of the Sierra. The following have been mentioned: rent expressed in terms of labour; rent expressed in terms of produce (compania); and mixed tenancy. According to the first of these the rent may be paid in the form of a special number of days' work without wages, or in the form of a specified quantity of work per year, payable at a

[1] UN Doc. E/AC.33/10, Add. 52.
[2] Act No. 10,885.

Slavery

yearly rate based either on the current daily wages or on an agreed figure. Under the second system rent takes the form of part of the crop; the proportion is, however, not agreed in advance but depends on the value of the crop.

'Personal Services: Despite legislation prohibiting the practice in various parts of the Sierra and the coast, Indian tenant-labourers and members of their families are still obliged to render personal services on the landlord's estate or in his house, usually without pay or for a very low wage. That the system of personal services is still extant in various parts of the plateau region proceeds from a study of reports published between 1944 and 1948.'[1]

Bolivia made a very full reply to the United Nations request for information; but until very recently her efforts to improve the condition of the Indian have not got at the root of the problem. The Government of Bolivia said that slavery and any form of servitude are prohibited in the Bolivian Constitution, as well as unpaid personal service. It explained that the aborigines of Bolivia belong to three groups: 1 Originarios, who own land over which they exercise unlimited control; 2 Communarios, who own and cultivate land collectively, which they cannot alienate without the consent of a prescribed authority; and 3 Colonos, who work on fixed days of the week on the estate of a landowner in return for the usufruct of land granted to them by the landowner. To protect the colonos the Government had taken steps to make adjustments where it was found that the value of their labour exceeded in value the profit they got from the land they held. It denied that there was debt-bondage in Bolivia, but added, 'In agreements freely entered into by the parties, one party may receive advances of money, goods or a loan, the performance of work being a condition of payment.' A copy of the Labour Code was attached to the reply; but it does not cover agricultural workers.

The services known as pongueaje were prohibited, according to the Bolivian Government, by a decree of 1945.[2] The Preamble to this decree admits that in spite of the prohibition contained in Article 50 of the Constitution, tenant-labourers are still subject to exactions of a kind that have been imposed ever since the colonial age. The decree then provides that tenants shall not be required to do work for their landlord not connected with agriculture and stock-raising unless they consent and receive a fair wage.

But the exactions continue. Several reports confirm this, the most authoritative being again that of the ILO, which describes in

[1] ILO Doc. CEIL/1/3, pp. 160, 168-71.
[2] Decree No. 318, May 15, 1945.

Serfdom or Peonage

detail the feudal position of the colonato. 'Colonato: the essential feature of this system is that the indigenous tenant-labourers must furnish certain services to the owner of the estate in exchange for the right to live there and to cultivate their plots. The allotment is usually tiny and insufficient for the most modest livelihood. The character and extent of the tenant-labourer's rights and obligations are governed by custom, which varies from place to place and in some cases is not easily distinguishable from the owner's personal whim. The Labour Code expressly excludes agricultural workers from the scope of its provisions. It was announced that special regulations for agriculture would be issued, but this has not yet been done and only a few special isolated provisions in certain matters have so far been adopted. The general characteristics of the tenant-labourer may be summarized as follows:

'Rights: The tenant is allotted a plot of land on which to build his house and receives an additional plot alongside the fields of the estate for cultivation purposes. The extent and quality of the tenant's allotment may vary considerably; it may be small, indeed barely sufficient, in regions where there is a large supply of labour; on the big marginal estates, where the problem is to attract manpower, the tenant is usually free to cultivate whatever extent of land he pleases; in this case there is no problem of dearth of land, but the fact that the cultivation has to be carried out in the tenant's spare time and the great distance to the market limit the scope of his possibilities. Local custom determines the extent to which the tenant is entitled to the use of streams, woodlands, etc. As a rule only animals employed on the work of the estate (ploughing oxen, mules) are admitted free to the pasture lands, and the tenant has to pay "grass money" for his other stock.

'Obligations: Tenant-labourers are placed under foremen or bosses appointed by the employer from among those who have his confidence; tenant-labourers work the estate land together, as ordered by the owner himself or by a steward. The tenants bring their own tools and animals. The conditions under which this work is carried on vary widely. Where labour is scarce they are relatively favourable; in other parts they easily border on abuse. In the thinly populated yungas region, for instance, the tenant-labourer usually works on the estate for the first three days of the week and has the rest for himself; in other parts he works for the owner on alternate weeks; and in still others the rule is that the work is to be carried on without a break until it has been concluded, so that the tenant only has the less favourable days in which to work on his own land. Particularly in the mountain areas, this frequently results in considerable

Slavery

harm to production. Apart from purely agricultural work the tenant-labourers perform other individual services in turn; some of these may be considered as accessory to agriculture (tending of stock), while others are genuinely domestic or personal in character (cooking, cleaning, sweeping, keeping watch), etc. The latter services are known under the general title of pongueaje, derived from the Aymara word "puncu", door, because the job of night-doorkeeper is generally included. The employer, on the other hand, has no legal obligations or restrictions of any sort in connection with minimum wage rates, payment of specific personal services, observance of a specified working day, compulsory rest, provision for food, housing conditions, maternity protection, women's and children's work, compensation for industrial accidents, medical care, etc. In fact it may be summed up as a characteristic feudal system.'[1]

Another Latin-American country in which the aboriginal Indian people form a high proportion of the whole population, about one-half, is Guatemala. Here too the best land is owned by the immigrant Spanish settlers and most of the Indians have to live on the mountain slopes, where soil is poor. There are several systems of tenant-labour. Under one the Indian cultivates a piece of land on condition that he gives the landlord one-third or one-half of the crop, depending on whether the tenant provides his labour only, or his labour and the seed and tools. Under another system the Indian pays for his holding a rent of up to twenty manos of maize (a mano being about a pound) for each unit of twenty-five square yards. Under yet another the Indian undertakes to work on the landlord's estate during one week a month or three months a year for a wage of five to fifty centavos a day in return for the plot of land assigned to him for his own use. Cash tenancies are unusual and are met with only near the capital.

Several measures have recently been taken, however, which have greatly improved the living conditions of the Indians of Guatemala. The Labour Code now forbids landowners 'to induce or compel their workers to buy consumer goods from a particular establishment or person', and requires them 'to permit peasant workers to use the fruit and produce of the parcels of land granted to them and to allow them to use the conduits, wells and reservoirs on the estate to draw sufficient water for their own use'. A National Indian Institute has been set up to study problems affecting the welfare of the Indian population; and in 1948 the Government established two collective farms for Indians on fertile valley-land. In addition several

[1] ILO Report, CEIL/1/3, pp. 82-90.

Serfdom or Peonage

agricultural societies of the co-operative type have been incorporated.

It is along such practical economic lines that the most permanent solution of the problem must be sought; for as the League of Nations found in 1936, 'The root of the trouble lives in the system of land tenure'. There is ample legislation to protect the Indian in Latin-America, but the majority of laws are not enforced. They satisfy the good intentions of the legislator and can be paraded as evidence of benign government; but however genuine the spirit influencing them may be, it does not extend to those responsible for applying them. Atttempts to secure enforcement of the law are therefore only part of the answer. The real way forward lies in economic reform, in redistribution of the land and in the setting up of communal enterprises.

In this the experience of Mexico is of great value. In 1922 a system of co-operative agriculture was established, known as the Ejido system. Under it, in the thirteen years up to 1935, one million rural workers had been settled on ten million hectares of land. The Agrarian Code of Mexico provided that a group of not less than twenty persons has the right to petition the Government for the grant to them of a collective agricultural unit known as an 'Ejido'. Their petition is examined and usually land is found for them, at the rate of ten hectares of cultivable land per person and sixty hectares of pasture land. The ejidario must conform to certain standards of good husbandry and must pay the land tax, which is limited to a maximum of five per cent of the annual production of the ejido. When the ejidario dies the ejido passes to his widow.

The scale of the scheme was enormous, and it has proved successful. 'There is no doubt,' wrote the ILO in 1951, 'that conditions in Mexico[1] have considerably improved in the past ten years, thanks to the ejido system of agriculture.' One-quarter of the population of Mexico, i.e. five million people, are now living in ejidos; and of these no less than one-and-a-quarter million are American Indians.

Although Bolivia's past efforts to improve the lot of the Indian have not been very successful, a reform of land tenure has recently been begun in the country. A census taken in 1950 revealed that 4½ per cent of the population owned 70 per cent of the land, and the Bolivian Ambassador to the USA, in a speech on agrarian reform in New York in 1954, admitted the depressed condition of the land worker. He said, 'Remnants of feudalism cling to land ownership patterns in some Latin-American countries. Bolivia is among them. The workers are attached to the land as the peasants and serfs were

[1] Described by a named writer in 1940.

Slavery

in the Middle Ages. They do not own the land. They belong to it and in turn the land belongs to a comparatively few men. The workers are share-croppers, but they have not the freedom of movement or the share in the crops which the Southern share-croppers in the United States have. Many of the Bolivian workers on the land are actually serfs. They even render personal service to the land-owners. There is a regular rotation of men and women servants at some of the great haciendas as the farm-hands discharge their obligations to cook the meals, hew the wood and draw the water'.

By a decree of 1953 Bolivia aimed 'to impose such conditions on property ownership as the public interest may dictate, to raise the present level of production, to transform the feudal system of land tenure and use by a just redistribution of the land among those working on it, while respecting small and medium-sized holdings and to integrate the indigenous population in the national community by restoring to it its rightful economic and human status'. The Government acquired the unused lands of the large estates (latifundia), and paid the former owners with land bonds. Every Bolivian, without distinction of sex, over the age of eighteen was given the right to ask for a grant of land, provided that he cultivated it within two years; and all lands taken from the Indians since January 1, 1900, were restored to them.

By August 1954, according to the American magazine *Time*, 160,000 Indians of the Andean highlands had been granted ownership of land, in holdings varying from five to sixty acres. It was claimed that the reform would eventually abolish the colonato system, and thus free some two-and-a-half million Indians from peonage. It is to be hoped that this good beginning will indeed be pressed to a successful conclusion.

While agrarian reform is obviously a matter for the national governments concerned, other practical measures have recently been initiated by an international body, a joint mission of the UN Technical Assistance Board and the ILO. This Committee of Experts is at work in Bolivia, Peru, and Ecuador, at their invitation, trying to improve the condition of the Indians living on the 'altiplano', the high plateau 11,000-16,000 feet above sea level which runs for some 2,000 miles through these countries into Argentina. An account of their work has been given in a book published by the Carnegie Endowment for International Peace.[1] The debilitated state of the population, numbering about ten million, is described thus:

'These people are for the most part poor herdsmen or small farmers with only a few miners, who find part-time employment in

[1] *Indians of the Andes*, published May 1956.

Serfdom or Peonage

the declining mining industry. The Indians produce little for the outside world. Their subsistence economy affords a diet sometimes of only 700 to 1,000 calories a day (1,800 calories is usually considered the minimum necessary for good health), and existence is possible only because the chewing of the cocoa leaf enables them to become somewhat anaesthetized to hunger. There are some ten million of these isolated people, and their importance becomes even more apparent when one realizes that the proportion of the Indian population to the total population of each country ranges from 50 to 80 per cent of the whole. Their fuller participation in the economic, social and cultural life of the national community would increase greatly the economic and social welfare of their respective countries and of Latin-America as a whole. These people are not only a potential labour force. They are also human beings.'

The practical work of the Committee in 1954 and 1955 has been in the development of community centres to which the Indians are encouraged to migrate, and where they are trained in better methods of production. Four centres were established in Bolivia, where they are concentrating on the production of livestock, dairy produce, rice and wheat, commodities that have accounted for one-third of the value of Bolivian imports in recent years. One centre is at Cotoca, on the plains, at 900 hundred feet above sea level, and to this 113 Indian families had migrated from the altiplano up to the end of January 1956.

In Peru and Ecuador the Mission has been less successful so far. Three community centres have been established in Peru, but they have not developed so rapidly as those in Bolivia, partly because the Government has not fulfilled its promises to build roads and supply material. In Ecuador no community centre has yet been set up, because of difficulties in getting land for it; but assistance has been given in the hand-weaving industry.

The Indian population of the altiplano has been estimated at ten million by the ILO's Andean Mission, but how many of these are actually living in peonage is uncertain. Two members of a mission sent by the American Presbyterian Church in 1946 told the author that they estimated the number of peons in Bolivia, Peru and Ecuador at eight million.

This big problem of a conquered people long suppressed in a state of misery and apathy is now at last receiving some of the attention it needs. It is by any reckoning an unwholesome state of affairs for the growing republics of South America to have such large scale destitution behind their modern façades. A move towards a more complete integration of the indigenous population is long overdue

Slavery

and can only be an enrichment of the countries. The success of the community centres, especially in Bolivia, augurs well for the uplift of the Andean Indians, and it is to be hoped that closer co-operation will come between the Governments concerned and the Mission, and that more land and funds will be made available.

In the other former Spanish colonies, the Philippines, greater progress has been made in abolishing serfdom. But again, legislation alone was not always enough. The Philippine Government told the United Nations that, 'Such practices, which are remnants of the country's colonial past, are on the way to complete abolition. Practices arising from traditional forms of involuntary services rendered by tenants to their landlords have been reduced to a minimum by the passage of enlightened legislation'.[1]

While this is true enough, the limits to legal effectiveness were pointed out in a memorandum by Bruno Lasker. 'An attempt was made in 1912,' he wrote, 'to legislate the status of peonage out of existence in the Philippines; however, this law was neither complete nor final but rather seemed to recognize peonage by regulating it, and it was eventually repealed. On the other hand the Rice Share Treasury Act has done much to protect the farm worker. . . . The measures worked out by the Philippine Government for the resettlement of overcrowded farm populations may prove more effective in getting rid of the last remnants of serfdom than have legal prohibitions.'[2]

In South America and the Philippines peonage was the outcome of the attempt by the Spanish landowners to cling to their privileges. In the southern states of the USA, where peonage also survives still, in an attentuated form, something of the same sort occurred. When slavery was abolished by the Thirteenth Amendment in 1865 some of the ex-slave-owners sought to evade its provisions by keeping negroes in peonage. The Thirteenth Amendment clearly prohibited every form of servitude—slavery, serfdom and peonage.[3] But it was found necessary in 1867 to outlaw peonage specifically by passing the Peonage Abolition Act. Yet even this was not enough to suppress all forms of involuntary servitude. The Peonage Abolition Act covered compulsory service based on indebtedness, the characteristic of peonage; but it did not cover involuntary service not so based. In 1909 therefore consolidated enactments were passed in the fol-

---

[1] UN Doc. E/AC.33/10. Add. 67.
[2] UN Doc. E/AC.33/R11, pp 40-41.
[3] 'Neither slavery nor involuntary servitude, except as a punishment for crime whereof the party shall have been duly convicted, shall exist within the United States or any place subject to their jurisdiction.'

Serfdom or Peonage

lowing terms: 'Whoever knowingly and wilfully holds to involuntary service or sells into any condition of involuntary service any other person for any term shall be. . . .'

Nevertheless, as the US Government has informed the United Nations, two or three cases of involuntary servitude or peonage come to light every year and are prosecuted. The Department of Justice began such prosecutions early in this century, and they have clearly checked the practice. The law reports of the US contain many of these cases; the last was United States v Dial (Alabama, 1944), in which six persons were indicted. Two were convicted and imprisoned.

India, as we have seen, is struggling with the problem of rehabilitating its millions who are held fast in debt-bondage; it is therefore scarcely surprising to find that allied feudal practices also flourish there. In Bihar, in the words of the Indian report to the United Nations, 'serfdom exists in various forms. In other parts of the State, where the property is that of private landlords, the service holdings are hereditary and the occupants are liable to ejectment only on cessation of the required services. . . . Involuntary unpaid services exists in various forms. . . . In some districts of Madras landlords sometimes exact involuntary unpaid service from their tenants'.[1] And similar information was given about Orissa and West Bengal.

Madras, Bombay, and Bengal each has laws against labour for debt; but such labour continues in these states. A policy of allotting new cultivable lands to aboriginal groups, and of granting them loans and other facilities is being pursued by the state governments. But according to the ILO excessive indebtedness has sometimes reduced them to 'the status of a serf working their own fields on a bare maintenance for the profit of others'.[2]

These practices are, of course, part and parcel of the huge economic and social difficulties that India is facing. There is every hope that in the course of time they will be overcome by the spirit of social progress that is animating the whole country.

The other great region of the world where traces of serfdom still linger is Africa. Two instances are of the 'classic' type. In the British Protectorate of Bechuanaland, in the Bamangwato Reserve, a primitive tribe known as the Masarwa lives in a state of serfdom to the Bamangwato. The Masarwa are probably descendants of the aboriginal inhabitants, who were conquered by the Bamangwato and subjugated by them. They are not regarded as being entitled to any of the tribal lands, but they are allowed to use them for

[1] UN Doc. E/AC.33/10. Add. 70.
[2] Report CEIL/1/3, January 1951.

Slavery

pasturing their cattle and other animals in return for unpaid services as cattle minders to Bamangwato notables, to whom they are attached; and they are allowed to have some of the milk and meat of the cattle they mind. The Chief of the Bamangwato, moreover, claims the right to take a child from any Masarwa family to be attached to him for domestic service in his house. Any remuneration given to the Masarwa depends on the whim of his master and is irregular and meagre. But the bondage is firm. Custom does not permit the Masarwa to engage in any occupation or transfer his services from one master to another without the permission of his master at the time, nor can he move from the area of his master's authority without his permission.

The British Government has tried to end the practice. In 1936 a law was passed directing that the Masarwa should be paid in cash or kind for any services rendered by them, and it prohibited the removal of children from the custody of their parents. But the Bamangwato are a stubborn, strong-willed people. How successful the British administration has been in enforcing the law is not known.

A similar serf class, though with an added, gruesome obligation, exists in the Gold Coast. Captives in war used to be settled in villages on so-called 'stool' lands, i.e. on land belonging to the King or Paramount Chief, or the Queen Mother in the Akon states; and for the use of this land they had to pay tribute. Today their descendants still have to do so. The tribute takes the form of a prescribed part of the produce of the land and the obligation to furnish some of their children, from the age of seven upwards, for domestic service without payment, other than food and clothing, in the house of the Paramount Chief or the Queen Mother. But in addition to these typical services the serf class is drawn upon when victims are required for human sacrifice. On the death of someone of royal birth, his spirit has to be accompanied into the next world by that of another, to minister to his needs; so the choice naturally falls on the serfs.

In the Cameroons there is a far less serious and declining feudal practice. As the French Government informed the United Nations, 'in the north of the Cameroons a custom derived from serfdom exists, although it should be noted that the "serfs" are completely at liberty to change their overlord or, more accurately, landlord. During the last fifteen years, the "heathen" tenants of the Moslem landlords, making use of their favourable demographic position, have been taking possession of arable lands and refusing to pay the customary dues. The authorities encourage this full emancipation of the settled peasants, while taking the necessary measures to protect

Serfdom or Peonage

the pasture lands of the semi-nomadic Moslem landlords'.[1]

Recent information of serfdom in North Africa is not plentiful, though in 1955 two French anthropologists prepared a memorandum on Algeria, showing that serfdom exists in Algeria.

There is, finally, one other country in which current feudal practices have been brought to light. This is Abyssinia or Ethiopia, where besides slavery itself a most onerous system of land tenure keeps the cultivator in a state of subjection under the name of 'gabor'. As for slavery, Margery Perham is our authority. In describing the importance of the garbar she writes, 'The main support of the Ethiopian State and society was not the slave but the theoretically free cultivator, the "gabar".... It was not the land but the labour of the gabar on the land which provided the support for the provincial as well as the imperial administration. Hence the importance of the forms of tenure and tribute'.[2]

The word gabar means literally one who pays gibr, or tribute, and the gabar system is bound up with Ethiopian methods of land tenure, about which, unfortunately, too little is known. In payment for the land he cultivates the gabar renders tribute in the form of produce and/or services. But unlike the serfs of the Middle Ages the gabar is not tied to a particular piece of land for life; he can have one holding and seek another elsewhere. He is therefore neither a slave nor a serf. Yet he is undoubtedly subject to a servile status.

The manner in which the gabar, in spite of his theoretical freedom, becomes ground down has been described by another woman writer, Mrs C. Sandford. For many years she and her husband ran a farm in Ethiopia near the capital; her testimony is therefore authoritative and her devotion to the country manifest. According to her the gabar owed one-tenth of his produce to the Emperor, and a further fifth of it to the provincial governor or soldier to whom he was allotted. To the latter he also had to render one day's service out of every three, eight or ten days. Mrs Sandford remarks that this might have been reasonable had the gabars dared to use their right of appeal against the exactions imposed on them. 'But in fact the abuse proved stronger than the system. The masters exacted more than their due, and the system was as extortionate as those of old Roman days. Officer and soldier were equally rapacious.'[3]

This is borne out by Margery Perham. 'It will be easily imagined,' she writes, 'that Amhara soldiers in charge of conquered tribes, which were mostly pagan or negro, or both, and far from such supervision

[1] UN Doc. E/AC.33/10/42.
[2] *The Government of Ethiopia*, p. 278.
[3] *Ethiopia under Haile Selassie*, pp. 48-9.

Slavery

as existed near the centre, were not likely to treat these gabars with much forbearance. The principle that the tribute rested on the land rather than on the gabars was easily forgotten, and in these wide, depopulated regions it was more important to be allotted so many gabars than so much land . . . generally speaking, especially in the negro and Sidamo provinces, the position of the gabar became hardly distinguishable from slavery.'[1]

Indeed, according to a British visitor to the negro provinces in the middle 1930s, who was sympathetic towards Ethiopia, it was far worse;[2] and at the same time the slave trade itself was a constant drain on the subject people. Mrs Sandford, too, writes that the gabar status 'was responsible for much of the misery of the distant provinces, where appeal was impossible and resistance useless'. It was thus the extension of the gabar system to the conquered provinces that was mainly responsible for the peculiarly evil significance which the word acquired outside Ethiopia.

When Ethiopia abolished the legal status of slavery in 1942, it also abolished the legal status of gabar; but as with slavery it is uncertain how successful this has been in practice. The United Nations was informed in 1950 that, 'No compulsory and hereditary attachment to land ever existed in Ethiopia. If, however, a person attached himself to land voluntarily, such voluntary attachment was accompanied by obligations to render service to the landlord, but this was practised only in a certain part of Ethiopia, until repealed by an Imperial Proclamation on November 1, 1942'.[3]

Since then savage sentences, including death, have been imposed on convicted slave-dealers in Ethiopia; and these sentences have been given much publicity, to create the impression that the anti-slavery laws of the country are being vigorously enforced, and that slavery and other forms of servitude have been stamped out. Certainly in the main centres to which Europeans have access there is little sign of slavery; but we have the reports of British officials, mentioned earlier, to the effect that escaping slaves from Wallega province were seeking asylum in the Sudan up to 1955. If slavery itself continues to exist in the remoter parts of Ethiopia it is not unreasonable to assume that the gabar system does also.

The matter of the escaping slaves is supposed to be under investigation by the Ethiopian Government. It was brought to the attention of the Ethiopian delegate to the United Nations by the

---

[1] *The Government of Ethiopia*, p. 296.
[2] Mr G. T. Garratt, in an article entitled 'Abyssinia' in the *Journal of the Royal African Society*, Vol. 36, no. 142, pp. 36-49.
[3] UN Doc. E/AC.33/10. Add. 58.

author in April 1955, when he was promised that it would be taken up and the Anti-Slavery Society informed of the Government's findings. However, up to the present time no such information has been forthcoming from the Government of Ethiopia. Though the truth cannot be known until the present regulations are lifted and impartial observers are admitted into the country, one must conclude that slavery and the gabar system, which is near-serfdom, have not yet completely disappeared from Ethiopia, and any statements to that effect must reluctantly be discounted.

In South America, India, Africa and China, where the state of the land worker is relatively unknown, many millions are still living today in the semi-bound condition of serfdom. Improvement of their impoverished way of life may not be possible for many years to come. But the ending of their servile status, which is itself frequently a barrier to economic improvement, can and must be achieved throughout the world with the least possible delay. In this work the United Nations and the International Labour Office are playing an important part, not only in gathering information, and action, but also, as in South America, by sponsoring technical missions to give direct aid.

CHAPTER VIII

THE SALE OF WOMEN INTO MARRIAGE

ಣಿ

THE fact that all social life inevitably restricts the full and unqualified liberty of the individual, especially that of the weakest, makes it hard in some cases to draw a line between practices that are necessary, or of some social value, and those that are inherently evil. In this none has been more controversial than the custom of paying a bride-price in order to acquire a wife, which is widely practised in Africa and Asia.

It can easily be justified. The transfer of property on the occasion of marriage cements the bond between the families and makes for a stable institution. It may also have a symbolic value. But on the other hand it can all too frequently degenerate into a purely commercial transaction, in which a human being is the helpless victim, herself no more than a piece of property. If one adds to this the possible complications of child marriage, polygamy and concubinage, it can be seen that the position of women in primitive societies can be a subject fraught with difficulties.

So much so that the League of Nations could not make up its mind, let alone any progress in combating abuses. The Temporary Slavery Commission of 1925 wrote that, 'The Commission refrains from discussing questions of native marriage, because, on the one hand, the subject is so complex that it would be difficult to do so within reasonable limits; on the other hand, because the Commission is of the opinion that, generally speaking, both native customary law and Moslem law regarding marriage properly so-called do not, from a native standpoint, involve the purchase of a wife or any act of enslaving, and that cases which might approximate to slave-dealing are entirely opposed both to the Koranic law and to native customary law. The custom of concubinage under Moslem law and according to certain local practices is, on the contrary, much more likely to lead to slave-dealing, since the acquisition of a concubine is generally effected by means of payment of a sum of money, by whatever name —"present" or "dowry"—it may be called, which, in this case, is, in fact, a real purchase. But a general amelioration of the lot of

The Sale of Women into Marriage

women can only be looked for in the growth of civilization and education, together with a more widespread knowledge of the right of every slave of either sex to assert his or her freedom'.

Yet 'the acquisition of girls by purchase disguised as payments of dowry' was assumed by Lord Cecil of Chelwood and the Committee of the League of which he was the Rapporteur to be included in the League's definition of slavery; and Lord Lugard is on record as agreeing with this.[1]

By 1932 the League was ready to take a stronger line, though still cautious. After recapitulating the report of its predecessors, the Committee of Experts on Slavery wrote that, 'The present Committee is also of opinion that there is a great deal of misunderstanding in regard to the lobolo system, i.e. the sum paid to the girl's family by the fiancé. The most competent authorities regard this, not as a purchase price, but rather as a guarantee of proper treatment and an actual certificate of legal marriage. However, there is no doubt that this system has given rise to abuses, especially on the part of natives who no longer belong to any tribe and who carry on a regular trade in wives. When the handing over of a dowry is in fact a disguised purchase—that is, when it confers on the person handing over the dowry rights analogous to those of an owner of a chattel—this practice comes within the category of slave-dealing'.

But three years later it was in full retreat again. The Advisory Committee of Experts on Slavery of 1935 reported negatively on the subject, and never returned to it in the remaining years of its existence.

The custom of paying a bride-price, 'dowry', lobolo or boxadi is almost universal in tribal African societies south of the Sahara. Very few Africans, except those who have become de-tribalized or who live in towns, would consider themselves married unless cattle, goats etc., or a sum of money, or both, had been given to the bride's father or guardian by the suitor or his father. Among tribal Africans it is the only pledge of marriage, and even Christian Africans do not marry without it.

It has its origin in the earlier custom of arranging marriages by an exchange of women between tribes. At a later stage property was substituted in 'inter-group exchange'. One group would give property for a women from another group. Finally, in modern times, with the circulation of currency cash has taken the place of property. Bearing in mind that the woman becomes the property of her husband on marriage, that her consent to the transaction is not sought, and that she is often only a child, it can readily be imagined how

[1] In *Encyclopaedia Britannica*, 14th ed., article on Slavery.

Slavery

the payment of a cash sum can turn marriage into a mere sale.

One of the members of the Temporary Slavery Commission of the League of Nations, Mr H. A. Grimshaw of the ILO, has described the dangers. In a memorandum to the Commission he wrote, 'Girl children are frequently the victims of customs associated with marriage. In many instances where custom prescribes the payment of a dowry by the family of a prospective husband to the parents of the prospective wife, it is difficult to distinguish between this dowry payment and the actual purchase of the girl. Since the transaction may at times take place whilst the girl is of very tender age, she may lose all contact with her own family and her future will be entirely in the hands of her purchaser'.

Polygamy can make the commercial element even more prominent. Mr Grimshaw writes, 'There is also difficulty in distinguishing between marriage and sale in polygamous areas where divorce is easy and frequent. In illustration of this I may quote from the Report (to the Permanent Mandates Commission of the League) for 1923 on the British Cameroons: "Owing to the general tendency of the pagan polygamist to invest his money in women . . . they are often his only tangible assets, and when called upon to satisfy a debt, he is by force of circumstances compelled to realize. The method he adopts is to find another man willing to marry one of his wives and thus obtain a refund of any money he may have paid as so-called dowry. It may therefore be said that it is difficult for the administration to distinguish between marriage and a transfer for value received." '

There has been, however, a mitigating influence in Mohammedanism, both on marriage customs and on the general status of women. In Tanganyika, according to the Report to the Permanent Mandates Commission of the League on the country for 1922, the older pagan marriage customs are being replaced by Mohammedan marriage laws, 'a beneficial change, as child marriage is thereby discouraged and also the trade in young girls by near relatives, who previously received the dowry money'.

On the status of women under Koranic law Mr Grimshaw writes, referring to Tanganyika, 'The position of women among the Mohammedan population in Africa differs in some respects from that of their tribal sisters. The Mohammedan woman has a right to her own earnings and to a certain amount of personal property. Part of the dowry paid is spent on household furnishings, clothes and jewellery which is henceforth the property of the wife. If she is divorced she takes those things with her and a further part of the dowry is reserved to be paid to her if she is divorced. A Mohammedan

The Sale of Women into Marriage

woman is sometimes taught a trade, such as embroidery or carpet-making and she sometimes trades in the market. Moreover, widows are not automatically inherited. Wives and daughters receive a definite portion of the late husband's and father's estate, but less than a son, and if there is no son, part of the property goes to more remote relatives. Early betrothals are the rule though not always child marriage, and in any case consummation of the marriage does not take place until after puberty. Nevertheless, a father has the right to marry his daughter to whom he pleases without her consent. Marriage being a family affair, consent by the parties to the marriage is not required. The marriage is arranged between the parents. Moslem law allows polygamy to the extent of four wives plus concubines. The husband has the right to divorce his wife, but the wife has no corresponding right.

'Mohammedanism is not at its purest in Africa south of the Sahara; it has been affected by tribal custom, and it affects tribal custom. This inter-diffusion causes deterioration in both. It varies in different districts, but Mohammedanism is purer in the towns. Although the status of a Mohammedan wife is better than that of a tribal wife, she is still the inferior of her husband and there is no real attempt to interpret Koranic law in the sense most favourable to women.'

The status of a tribal wife on the other hand is usually little more than that of a chattel. The power of the head of the family often allows him to dispose of his women as he pleases; and while the system of doing so in exchange for a bride-price, euphemistically called a 'dowry' by some Europeans, can lead to an acceptable form of marriage it can equally lead to slavery. Mr Grimshaw remarks, 'Marriage in itself, though carried out in full accord with tribal custom and usage, may, as the Report for 1923 on French Togoland indicates, constitute a form of servitude. Where native custom provides that young girls should obey their parents in their choice of a husband, they are often promised in marriage at a very early age or even before birth. This often means that when the girl reaches marriageable age the husband is an old man'.

One must of course bear in mind the hard economic basis of marriage in primitive communities. R. H. Lowrie rightly points out that, 'Marriage until the most recent period has never been primarily directed towards the sentimental gratification of the spouses'. 'Savage matrimony,' he continues 'is preponderantly a means of cementing group alliances between families. In simpler conditions a wife is not normally a liability but an asset . . . since a girl in ruder societies represents economic value, her family surrenders her only for an equivalent.' He shows that the tribal African husband in such a union not only bought his wife but the right to any children she might have, even by a union with another man; and in case of barrenness he was entitled to restitution of the price paid. In conclusion he writes categorically, 'A West African woman is the property of her husband'.[1]

This is to look at it, and to some extent justify it, from a sociological point of view. As a contrast it is worth quoting an English feminist on the subject. Miss Nina Boyle, writing in the 1930's, summed up its personal implications thus: 'In many parts of Africa the native woman is so completely "property" that she is not only purchased and bartered but inherited. Unmarried girls whose fathers die are assessed among the divisible goods to be shared among the male heirs. They may be used to pay a debt or a compliment, to cement a bargain, to please a friend, to placate an enemy. No man may have a wife without paying her owner a price which in some cases has a maximum fixed by law.'[2] And she cites the Native Code of Natal, which lays down the maximum price which may be asked for a wife.

Defenders of the bride-price system usually advance three arguments in favour of it: that it makes for stability in marriage, since it must be paid back in the event of divorce; that it enhances the value of the girl; and that it acts as an incentive to young men to go out and work for sufficient to pay it. But each of these arguments is readily answered. Firstly, in spite of the bride-price divorces are of frequent occurrence. Secondly, it can hardly be considered desirable to encourage African girls to think of themselves as having a monetary value, as though they were animals. And thirdly, the incentive to work; its disadvantages outweigh any advantage, for as often as not it is simply an incentive to immorality.

Before the war the matter may indeed have been open to debate; but today it is less so. There is much evidence to show that the bride-price system has degenerated yet further, and that its social consequences are nothing but evil. In 1951 Madame Jane Vialle, a member of the United Nations *ad hoc* Committee on Slavery, and Senator for French Equatorial Africa, and herself daughter of an African mother, reported that, 'The dowry has lost its original symbolic meaning and has become a source of profit for the fathers, brothers or relatives of women. . . . The practice of competitive bidding for wives handicaps African social development in many ways. Rich men can obviously acquire several wives, thus condemning the less

---

[1] *Encyclopaedia of Social Sciences*, Vol. X, Marriage, pp. 147, 194.
[2] Pamphlet entitled *What is Slavery*, p. 6.

The Sale of Women into Marriage

well-to-do and often the youngest men to celibacy, and in many cases condemning women to prostitution'.[1]

Strong evidence on this decline comes from Sister Marie Andre du Sacre Coeur, LLD of the University of Paris and a member of the White Sisters' Mission, who spent seventeen years in Africa before the war. In 1939 she made the following factual description of African marriage customs: 'All black women marry, like their mothers and grandmothers, accustomed for centuries to submission to servitude. Marriage denotes almost always basically a certain transfer of property, of the kind which makes the woman pass from one family group to another, for the power of the head of the family is like that of the Roman *pater familias* and is by its nature a right of property.... A marriage regularly contracted gives to the husband a certain right of property in his wife and in the children she may have. A husband deserted may recover his wife in a court of law; if she is with a third party who wishes to marry her, the first husband has the right to exact repayment of what he paid for the woman.'[2]

But by 1949, whatever mitigating features this system may have possessed had been replaced by naked commercialism. In that year Sister Marie André visited French West Africa again for several months. On her return to France she wrote: 'Marriage has become a market which is discussed just as one discusses any other commercial business, and the daughter is given to him who offers the most. In 1948 the dowry reached in Yaounde (Cameroons) was 3,000 francs, besides four goats and the usual presents. In March 1949 it was 40,000 francs and thirty goats. In September 1949 it was 50,000 francs and 20 goats. This year it has reached 100,000 francs and more. One should add that the presents double the cash paid. A Chief found it simpler to put his daughter up to auction and she was acquired by a chauffeur for 100,000 francs, a motor truck and three cows. The dowry used to be symbolic, but it has come to have a fantastic monetary value.'[3]

The degradation of marriage in French West Africa was at its worst in the Cameroons, according to Sister Marie André. There fathers talk freely of selling their daughters. They even extort a supplementary dowry from the husband by claiming the right to take back the bride to sell at a higher price. As potential wealth,

---

[1] Memorandum on Slavery in African Territories, E/AC.33.R13, submitted to the Economic and Social Council of the United Nations.
[2] *La Femme Noire en Afrique Noire.*
[3] Pamphlet entitled *The Brazen Law of Marriage by Payment of Dowry in The French Cameroons*, p. 5.

Slavery

women often figure in lawsuits concerning inheritance. Sister Marie André quoted several cases from the records of a native court. In July 1949 a man claimed the goods of his deceased brother and was granted them. These included his two widows and a daughter. In another case a boy of fourteen demanded as his inheritance one widow, three children, three sewing machines and two saucepans. The widow was his own mother. He too was awarded them by the court. In yet another a boy of fifteen sued his mother because she would not marry the man to whom he had sold her. The customary law of the Cameroons clearly leaves no doubt that women are property.

The social consequences of such abuses of the bride-price system are prostitution, sterility and depopulation. Sister Marie André found one village of seventy households without a single child. In another sixty per cent of the men were unable to marry because rich men had bought up the women. The vital statistics for a group of villages in 1949 were 207 deaths and only 94 births; and out of a total of 1,013 women only eight were pregnant.

The advanced African sees the evil of the bride-price. The notables of two districts in the Cameroons voted for its abolition in January 1950. And as for the women, the more enlightened feel nothing but disgust, saying, 'We are not goats to be sold'. In Gabon too similar views exist among the women, according to M. Ballendier, a sociologist at the Institute of Scientific Research in French West Africa.

In other parts of Africa the present-day status of women is little better. In Nigeria the main problem is child marriage. A social welfare officer, Miss Alison Izzett, has said that in the course of her work in Nigeria she had come across child wives of from ten to fourteen years old, all married to men not of their own choosing. When they grow up they often leave their husbands and resort to prostitution, or form irregular unions. The whole stability of marriage is thus threatened. Miss Izzett also found that many young widows had run away from their villages in order to avoid a forced marriage with their deceased husband's heir. They had become prostitutes, simply because they could remain independent in no other way.

'We are fighting two things,' wrote Miss Izzett, 'Firstly that no marriage contract shall be made in respect of a girl under fourteen and that no consummation of a marriage shall take place before fourteen, and that it shall be illegal to have sexual intercourse with a girl under fourteen, whether married or not. At present intercourse with a girl under eleven is illegal only if she is not the man's wife.'[1]

[1] Article in *The Catholic Citizen*, January 1948.

The Sale of Women into Marriage

In South Africa payment of bride-price is customary among the Bantu, and it has an important bearing on the legitimacy of children. Prof. I. Shapira writes, 'Marriage among them is accomplished by the transfer of some form of material wealth, such as cattle, by the bridegroom, or his father acting on his behalf, to the bride's father or guardian. This transfer, customarily known as lobolo or boxadi, is generally held to be adequate legal proof of the marriage. All children born to a woman for whom lobolo or boxadi has been transferred, or promised, are considered to be the legal offspring of her husband, even though he may not be their physiological father. On the other hand children born to a woman for whom no lobolo or boxadi has been transferred or promised are regarded as illegitimate. They belong to their mother's family or clan and their physiological father has no claim on them unless he can make a special payment'.[1]

In East Africa, too, the status of married women is typically restricted, though in Tanganyika, as we have seen, Mohammedanism has raised it a little. For Kenya Dr Philip Mayer, sociologist to the Government, is our authority. He writes, 'The legal position of a woman for whom bride-price has been paid is definable in terms of duties and obligations rather than in terms of rights. She is indeed entitled to ask for a divorce, if persistently ill-treated or insulted, but she has little personal liberty, no right of property, no claim against her husband for the custody of her own children (even if they are not physically his), and no power to restrain him from cruelty towards her or from adultery'.[2]

The bride-price system is also practised in Swaziland, though here it seems to have retained some redeeming features. In reporting to the United Nations the British Government wrote, 'Under native custom "lobolo" is paid to the wife's family by the husband when he marries her. This is strictly not a purchase of the woman, but may perhaps be better described as a means of strengthening the bonds between the husband's and the wife's parents and of compensating for the loss of their daughter's services. There is provision under the "ngena" custom for the husband's eldest brother to take over his wives on his death for the purpose of raising seed for the deceased. There is, however, no compulsion on the widow to accept the position. She may choose another brother or refuse altogether to carry out the custom'.[3]

Attempts by colonial powers to modify native marriage customs

---

[1] Article in *Africa*, Vol. VI, No. 1, January 1933.
[2] *Gusii Bridewealth Law and Custom*, p. 63, Pub. 1950.
[3] UN Doc. E/AC.33/10/Add. 50.

Slavery

have naturally been discreet. Legislation has not aimed at abolition of the bride-price, but at such limitations of it as securing the consent of the girl and fixing a minimum age for marriage. In only one territory under British control, however, has anything of the kind been done. This is British Somaliland, where a law was passed in 1930 which 'allows any unmarried woman or widow to register her refusal to marry any specified person, and thus forms a safeguard for any unmarried woman who may have been betrothed by her father or guardian without her consent and also for a widow to obtain freedom to marry whom she may wish regardless of Somali custom'.[1]

France has gone rather further in making such legislation. The Mandel Decree, enacted in 1939 and named after its promoter, M. Georges Mandel, Minister for the French colonies at the time, prohibited marriage in French West Africa and French Equatorial Africa without the consent of both spouses, and required that the man should have attained the age of sixteen and the woman fourteen. This was reinforced in 1946 by another decree, which provided that a marriage contracted in violation of the Mandel Decree should be treated as enslavement. That these laws are only a mitigation and do not reach the real evil is clear from the evidence on current abuses in French West Africa.

Similar legislation to the French has been enacted in three other parts of Africa, in the Belgian Congo, in Southern Rhodesia, and in the Union of South Africa.

The most hopeful recent development, and one which could have far greater influence than any outside recommendations, or even legislation, has been the work of an all-African committee set up in 1954 by the Government of Eastern Nigeria. This committee, consisting of three African men and one African woman, was 'to investigate the social effects of bride-price and to make any recommendations it might think fit with a view to the removal of any anomaly or hardship'.

The Committee found that the bride-price at its present inflated value forced men and women to remain single longer than is normal and has resulted in many children being born out of wedlock, and in the spread of prostitution. 'Far less people marry,' said their report, 'and many have died celibates—what a tragedy! . . . Villages and towns teem with unmarried girls creating a large door for a regular visitor, the Devil. . . . The men burden themselves with heavy debts at exorbitant rates and pledge land and personal belongings and

---

[1] UN Doc. E/AC.33/10/Add. 50. The law is 'The Native Betrothal and Marriage Ordinance', Ch 67 of *Laws of Somaliland*, 1930.

The Sale of Women into Marriage

are even tempted to steal. Wives who are maltreated can no longer seek the protection of their family as the parents cannot refund the dowry; the element of choice is disappearing and the social status of women has deteriorated; for if a man pays much for a wife he expects much from her, and she is more like a serf than a partner.'

The value of daughters has ministered to the greed of parents, and these have cashed in on the desire of men for educated wives, so that where the 'dowry' is perhaps £50 for an illiterate girl the amount demanded for one with secondary or higher education may be as high as £150-£200. Pressure is brought to bear on girls to marry rich men, and there is an added temptation to child betrothal.

Yet in spite of widespread alarm at the excessive amounts asked as bride-price, which had led in many places in attempts to fix it, the Committee found that the idea of abolishing 'dowry' was received everywhere with horror. The reason is not hard to find. As one letter to the Committee aptly pointed out, 'Remember that when the slave trade was on the people who became rich by it were never pleased to see it abolished'.

In making its recommendations, therefore, the Committee did not include abolition of bride-price; though it expressed the hope that with the spread of education it would eventually disappear. Instead it concentrated on abolishing its worst features, particularly child marriage. It recommended that, 'No marriage shall be valid where either party is below the age of sixteen'. And that, 'The consent of parents or guardians shall be required if either party is below the age of twenty-one, but it should not be unreasonably withheld'.

The Committee strongly disapproved of the premium on education: 'The practice tends to create a social caste and should be regarded as against public policy.' It recommended that both the dowry and the incidental expenses of a marriage should be limited; that all marriages under native law and custom should be registered, with details of the dowry agreed and the amount paid, etc; and that an official marriage certificate should be issued.

On the subject of female circumcision, too, the Committee expressed its strong disapproval; but again it did not recommend its sudden abolition at present. It only recommended making it a punishable offence to carry out the operation on anyone over the age of one month.

Though these recommendations do not go as far as a non-African would wish they are a valuable step forward. For an all-African committee to recommend radical modification of ancient marriage customs provides a lead which other African territories may not be slow to follow. The Government of Nigeria, moreover, in a preface

Slavery

to the Report of the Committee, has stated that it undertakes to carry out its recommendations energetically by legislation.

The difficulties in the way of bringing about such a fundamental reform as the abolition of the bride-price system of Africa are immense. But it must be emphasized that in the eyes of the world the custom falls within the practices condemned as analogous to slavery. By paying a bride-price the husband acquires rights of ownership over his wife, which brings it within the definition of slavery in the Slavery Convention of 1926. Such other customs as the right of the husband to sell his wife to another man and the right of his heir to inherit his widow are also clearly rights of ownership. They have been included specifically in the definition of slavery in the Supplementary Convention of 1956.

The number of African women who have been married in accordance with these customs cannot be known; but it must be many million. The immediate need, to halt this degradation, is to secure that the consent of both parties shall be an essential to the validity of a marriage; and that there shall be a minimum age of consent. The age recommended by the Conference which approved the 1956 Convention was fourteen; but this was not inserted in the Convention. It is to be hoped that the Contracting States will enact laws without delay, where they do not already exist, to give effect to this expression of international opinion; and that it will not long be followed by the complete sweeping away of all that tends to turn a social institution into a commercial transaction.

CHAPTER IX

THE SHAM ADOPTION OF CHILDREN

∞

WE have seen in previous chapters how men have been exploited by their stronger conquerors, and how women in primitive societies or under harsh economic conditions tend to suffer the same fate. It remains to consider the lot of children under similar circumstances.

It is not easy for an impoverished and numerous family in an already over-populated country to regard the birth of a child as a blessing. As one more mouth to feed it brings with it the temptation of infanticide, or, where this is resisted, the later one of exploitation. As soon as the child is capable of performing any manual work he or she tends to be regarded as a supplementary source of income for the family. The child's potential labour acquires a market value. Under such conditions it is not uncommon for a parent to sell the right to the labour of one or more of his children to the head of another household in consideration of a money payment and an undertaking to maintain the child. While the transaction may retain some humanity, it is often little more than a sale into slavery.

Among the Chinese, in China, Hong Kong and Malaya, the custom was widespread and of long standing. It also exists in Japan, and it is known to exist in some form in Singapore, Brunei, Sarawak and Ceylon; while on the other side of the Pacific it is known in Peru and Bolivia. Since it has its origin in poverty legislation against it has often proved useless, and the only hope for its complete eradication is likely to be in improved economic conditions.

In China, Hong Kong and Japan girls are usually the victims, but it is not confined to girls. There the adoption of a young girl has traditionally been regarded, by those able to afford it, as a convenient means of securing a household servant, one young enough to be trained and at the same time unlikely to run away, however hard the work or however severely she may be treated. And it need hardly be pointed out that the girl may easily be required to serve as a concubine or prostitute. Besides the affluent, poor people may also adopt girls, from still poorer families. When the customary price for a bride from a better-placed family might be exorbitantly

Slavery

high, this is one way of securing a future wife for a son of the family. The adoption system is of immemorial age and has its roots deep in the social and economic condition of the country. In China it is known by various names; among them are 'pei-nu' or 'ya-t'ow'. The name under which it has become known to Europeans, however, is 'mui tsai', or 'little sister', which is what it is called in the British colony of Hong Kong.

Historically the custom may be said to date from the third century B.C. For some seven hundred years prior to this slavery had actually been abolished in China, by the Chow dynasty in one thousand B.C. But in the third century the Han dynasty restablished it, and at the same time parents were given the right to sell their children in cases of extreme poverty. The consequences, and the social background of the custom, have been described by Dr E. J. Eitel, who was at one time Inspector of Schools and Chinese Secretary to the Government of Hong Kong. 'The sale of persons, whether children or adults, for purposes of domestic servitude is the ruling custom all over China. . . . The large majority of all female domestics in China are young girls of more or less tender age who enter upon their domestic servitude when four or five years old. The reason for this immense demand for young female domestics lies in the system of polygamy which obtains all over China, and which has a religious basis. A son being required to continue the family sacrifices, any one whose first wife proves childless will consider it his religious duty to adopt a son, or to take a second, or third, or fourth wife until he has a son. To die without a son is considered a heinous sin against one's ancestors.'

To meet this demand, 'A family in urgent distress, and requiring immediately a certain sum of money, would take one of their female children to a wealthy family where the child becomes a member of the family and perhaps has to look after a baby. . . . The child may be sold out and out. In that case a deed is drawn up, called by a common legal fiction "a deed of gift". A sum of money is paid, and the child becomes the domestic servant of the family and is as entirely under the *patria potestas* of the head of the family as if she were a slave, with the exception that an all-powerful custom requires the master to find a husband for her when she is of age; and the moment that she is married she is as free as any married woman can be, and no touch of servitude clings to her descendants'.

So described the practice is not without its mitigations, and the Chinese view of it is naturally very different from our own. Dr Eitel goes on to say, 'Considering the deep hold this system has on the Chinese people, it is not to be wondered at that the Chinese can

The Sham Adoption of Children

scarcely comprehend how an English judge could come to designate this species of servitude as slavery. On the contrary, intelligent Chinese look upon this system as the necessary and indispensable complement of polygamy, and as an excellent counter-remedy for the deplorably widespread system of infanticide, and as the natural consequence of the chronic occurrence of famines, inundations and rebellions in an over-populated country. But the abuses to which this system of buying and selling female children is liable in the hands of unscrupulous parents and buyers, and the support it lends to public prostitution are facts too patent to require pointing out. To foreigners, of course, it seems unnatural that children should be sold into domestic servitude. But the Chinaman sees nothing unnatural in it, because almost every social arrangement in China, betrothal, marriage, concubinage, adoption, servitude, is professedly based on a money bargain'.[1]

The economic basis of the Mui Tsai system has been emphasized by Sir George Maxwell. In 1935 he contributed an illuminating memorandum on it to the Advisory Committee of Experts on Slavery of the League of Nations, of which he was vice-president. Drawing on his considerable experience of Mui Tsai in Malaya he wrote, 'In any discussion of the Mui Tsai system it is necessary to remember the social and economic aspect of the problem. The basic reason is that the parents, by reason of their poverty, are anxious to be relieved of the burden of feeding more children than they can support, and are tempted to dispose of girls to families which are able to maintain them, and which require their services for household work. From the point of view of both families, it is both a social and an economic affair. It is essentially an economic business from the point of view of the family which acquires the child, for her services are cheaper than those of a paid domestic servant. It is obvious, therefore, that it is easier to control the system at a time when the country is prosperous and when people are able to afford to pay the wages of ordinary domestic servants than at a time of economic depression'.

But Sir George Maxwell did not take such a complacent view of Mui Tsai as Dr Eitel, and he pointed out how the system had degenerated in modern times. 'Originally in the past,' he continued, 'there was undoubtedly a human side to the Mui Tsai system. In an earlier social organization, the "adoption" side of the transaction was more real, and the child in her new family lived not far from her parents. But with the growth of towns and cities, and the ever-increas-

[1] Appendix to the Report of the Commission on Mui Tsai in Hong Kong and Malaya, 1937, Colonial No 125.

Slavery

ing facilities of transport, the situation has changed. The children are now taken to places at great distances from their parents' homes. All the benefits of propinquity and surveillance of the parents and relatives disappear, and the opportunities for over-work and ill-treatment increase. This is made all the worse by the development on a very large scale of a system of regular "traffickers" in Mui Tsai. These people obtain children in one place and transport them to other places. Often they travel great distances by river, by road, or by railway. It may be regarded as an axiom that the further the child is taken from her parents, the greater the evils of the system and the more flagrant the abuses of it. In any consideration of a method of suppressing the system, it would be unwise, however, to pay too much attention to the instances of its abuse. Most unfortunately, terrible cases of unmerciful punishment, sometimes amounting to torture, have been proved, and cases of heartless ill-treatment are not uncommon. But it is the system (with the normal practices which prevail under it) — and not the abuses (which are an offence against the system) — which requires our attention.'

Sir George Maxwell also remarked that girls were not the only victims of "adoption". He wrote, 'The Mui Tsai system — as is apparent from its name — applies only to girls. There is reason, however, to believe that an analogous system under a different name is also in force (but perhaps only to a small extent) in respect of small boys. These boys perform menial services in the household and are sometimes employed in gangs to perform really heavy work, such as carrying firewood, earth or stones for their master, who hires out their services, and receives the payment for them. Very little information is available in regard to the employment of boys in such circumstances, and the matter requires investigation'.

So widespread was the custom in China that there were no less than four million transferred children in 1930, according to the estimate of a Chinese organization; and yet the legal status of slavery had been officially abolished in 1909. In 1927 another attempt was made to check the Mui Tsai system, but its only effect was to change the name to 'adopted daughters'. The girls were employed, remarked Sir George Maxwell, under the impression that the system was allowed by the Government provided that there was no gross cruelty. Cases of cruelty were certainly prosecuted, but a girl detained against her will would have had difficulty in getting access to a police officer and in persuading him to listen to her complaint against her employer. Few of the girls, moreover, were aware of their legal rights.

How things stand today under the Communist regime is impos-

The Sham Adoption of Children

sible to say. There is no recent information on the prevalence of the Mui Tsai system. According to travellers, however, it has greatly diminished since the abolition of landlordism by the Communists.

In the British colony of Hong Kong, so closely connected with the Chinese mainland, 'adoption' has naturally proved difficult to eradicate. Indeed, it was some time before any attempt was made. Slavery was abolished in British possessions in 1833, but the Mui Tsai system was allowed to continue in Hong Kong with the full knowledge of the Government and without interference until as late as 1922. And in spite of legislation it is only recently that it has been reduced to vanishing point.

The first step was taken in 1923 with the passing of the Female Domestic Servant Ordinance. This provided that no person might take any Mui Tsai into his employment, nor employ any female domestic servant under the age of ten years. A Mui Tsai was defined as 'every female domestic servant whose employer for the time being shall have made, directly or indirectly within or without the Colony, any payment to any person for the purpose of securing the services of such female as a domestic servant', or 'any female domestic servant acquired from another employer who had made payment for the purpose of securing her services'. Ill-treatment and gross cruelty to Mui Tsai was made punishable, and the Secretary for Chinese Affairs was empowered to remove any Mui Tsai from her employer and place her where he thought fit. The Mui Tsai was also given the right to apply for restitution to her parents.

The next measure secured the registration of Mui Tsai. Part 3 of the 1923 Ordinance provided for this, but it was not brought into force until 1929, when it was proclaimed effective. Besides requiring that all Mui Tsai should be registered with the Government, it provided for regular inspection of them by welfare officers and for wages to be paid to them, in accordance with a scale to be fixed by the Government.

The success of this registration is hard to gauge. In 1921 the census of Hong Kong revealed a total female population of 242,309. Out of this 8,653 were Mui Tsai, i.e. 3.5 per cent. By 1931 the female population had risen to 357,893. In this census the Mui Tsai were not enumerated separately, but on the above percentage basis the number was estimated to be about 12,000. Yet when registration became compulsory in 1929 only 4,368 were registered.

By May 31, 1936, the number of Mui Tsai on the register had fallen to 1,723. But in that year the minority report of a visiting Commission disclosed a possible loophole. The Commission, consisting of three members, was sent by the British Government 'to

Slavery

investigate the whole question of Mui Tsai in Hong Kong and Malaya and of any surviving practices in those territories of transferring women and children for valuable consideration, whether on marriage or adoption or in other circumstances'.

The minority report[1] was presented by the lady member, Miss E. Picton-Turberwell. In it she stated, 'Again and again witnesses told us people still buy Mui Tsai, but now call them "adopted daughters". There is undoubtedly a danger that the custom, which we were told repeatedly was of great antiquity, deeply rooted in the lives of the Chinese people, may continue under a different name. In China an order has been issued that Mui Tsai shall be called "Adopted Daughters" (Chinese Regulations for the Emancipation of Slaves and Mui Tsai, 1927). Canton is close to Hong Kong, and Chinese pour in every day from Canton. It is not unreasonable to fear that the name "adopted daughters" may in fact mean Mui Tsai'.

Miss Picton-Turberwell recommended a new ordinance of wider scope. She favoured 'abandoning the attempt to define and legislate separately for the Mui Tsai, and instead applying the machinery of protection, i.e. notification and, where necessary, inspection, to all transferred girls under twelve years of age'. She recommended that all persons who had in their houses any children, not being 'near relatives', who left their parents' custody before they were twelve, and who are still under the age of eighteen, should notify the Protector appointed under the law. 'Near relative', she said, should be defined as 'any relative less remote than a fourth cousin'

'Again and again,' she emphasized, 'witnesses in both Hong Kong and Malaya asserted that the status of a Mui Tsai existed under the cloak of "adopted daughter", or prospective daughter-in-law.' And she named witnesses who had testified to that effect.

One of the appendices to the Commission's report was a draft ordinance submitted by Sir George Maxwell, which was intended to repeal the ordinance of 1923 and substitute wider provisions. Miss Picton-Turberwell declared her approval of it. As before it prohibited the employment of female domestic servants under the age of ten years and made provision for the payment in wages at specified rates. But in addition it required the registration of all females under the age of twelve living in the house of anyone who was not a near relative, unless the householder could show that she had been genuinely adopted by him. It prohibited the delivery of a girl under twelve to a person not a near relative, as well as the acceptance of such a girl. And it gave the parents of a female domestic servant the right to apply for restoration of her to their custody.

[1] Colonial No 125, pp. 214-248.

The Sham Adoption of Children

Most of these ideas were incorporated in a comprehensive piece of legislation passed in Hong Kong in 1938, the Protection of Women and Girls Ordinance.[1] This covers three fields:[2]

(a) It prohibits, with drastic penalties, any form of sexual exploitation of any woman or girl, and any attempt to harbour or detain any woman or girl for the purpose of prostitution or emigration.

(b) It gives the Protector (the Secretary for Chinese Affairs) extremely wide powers of investigation, if necessary by forceful entry, into any suspected case of exploitation or illegal detention of women or girls, or of ill-treatment (including as a drudge) of girls under twenty-one.

(c) It makes all adopted daughters (unless the adoption has been the subject of an order by a competent court) automatically the statutory wards of the Protector, and makes it a criminal offence for the custodian of any such girl not to register her with the Protector.

In addition the Protector may declare as his ward any other unmarried girl under the age of twenty-one, if he has reason to believe that the girl's parent or guardian has agreed to transfer her for a valuable consideration, or to part with her permanently, or has not treated her properly. Finally, the Protector is empowered to make suitable home provision for all his wards, and to carry out inspections. The Ordinance thus extends full protection to clandestine Mui Tsai, as well as to girls who, though not employed as prostitutes, may reasonably be suspected of being trained or earmarked for that purpose.

With regard to numbers, in September 1950 the Women and Children's section of the Social Welfare Office had over 1,300 girl wards and over 500 voluntarily registered adopted boys on its books. And during the year 1949 nearly 5,000 visits were paid to the homes of registered children by officers of the department.

This machinery of protection seems to be succeeding. According to the latest information, a letter from the Colonial Office to the Anti-Slavery Society of April 1954, 'the system of Mui Tsai has almost ceased to exist in Hong Kong. The legal prohibition against the keeping of Mui Tsai is well known to the local population, and no cases of actual Mui Tsai have come to light for a number of years. On the other hand there are occasional instances of "adopted daughters", whose status approximates to that of a Mui Tsai, but in which the terms of the original adoption deed, and the treatment

[1] No. 5 of 1938; amended by No. 17 of 1946.
[2] As described in British report to United Nations, Doc. E/AC/33/10/Add. 50.

Slavery

accorded by the adoption parents, would not warrant a prosecution. In such cases the powers conferred by the Protection of Women and Juveniles Ordinance No. 1 of 1951 may be invoked, and the child registered as a ward of the Secretary for Chinese Affairs, and kept under regular supervision by women welfare workers of the Social Welfare Department. There are over 2,000 registered wards, including a number whose status at the time of discovery approximated to that of a Mui Tsai'.

In Malaya more than half the population is Chinese, and as on the mainland and in Hong Kong, the practice of transferring children to persons who are not near relatives is prevalent among them. Legislation to control it has been similar to that in Hong Kong. Mui Tsai were first registered in 1933, the number in that year being 3,006. One provision of the principle ordinance, however, the Children and Young Persons Ordinance of 1949, is not included in the Hong Kong ordinance. This prohibits the employment of a child under the age of eight years in any form of labour, and also the employment of a child under fourteen in any factory or workshop. According to the most recent information[1] there were, in 1950, 572 cases requiring the visits of officers of the Women and Children's Welfare Departments.

Traces of the Mui Tsai system also exist in other territories in the Far East under British control, in Singapore, Sarawak, and Brunei, where it follows the familiar pattern. In 1950 Britain reported to the United Nations that 'although in Sarawak and Brunei slavery as such does not exist, mention may be made of the following practices relating to the transference of children. Adoption of children is very common amongst the Chinese and the Malays, and in Sarawak amongst the Dayaks. Adoption by the Chinese falls into three main types:

'1. Adoption of orphaned children, usually by their relatives. Both male and female children are adopted in this manner.

'2. Purchase of young children, normally of girls only. If the parents have too large a family, or if the child is illegitimate, the parents often receive a small sum of money, which is regarded not so much as a sale price but as compensation for the expense of rearing the child plus "heart balm". If the adopted child is a girl, and there is a boy child of suitable age in the family, they may become provisionally engaged.

'3. Mui Tsai. As the Mui Tsai system is still firmly ingrained in Chinese custom, complaints are rare except in cases of ill-treatment, and offences are difficult to detect. In Sarawak a Protector

[1] British report to United Nations.

The Sham Adoption of Children

and a number of Assistant Protectors of women and girls have been appointed.'

The description of the second group of this useful classification indicates the difficulty of distinguishing between practices that are relatively harmless and those that are inherently undesirable.

Another country in which poverty and over-population have long led to the exploitation of young people is Japan, where girls especially are exploited for sexual purposes. As in China the custom of transferring children is traditionally accepted and still of frequent occurrence. An illuminating article on the subject appeared in the *Manchester Guardian*, for August 24, 1953. Written by its Tokyo correspondent, Mr Hessel Tiltman, it discloses an ugly trade.

'The traffic in minors,' he wrote, 'which originates in the poverty found in farming communities, has always existed in Japan. Before the war, the daughter who sold herself to ease her family's financial situation was regarded as exemplifying filial piety. The practice was abolished—on paper—by the occupation authorities, and today there is on the Japanese Statute Book a whole series of laws designed to stamp out the traffic and ensure the punishment of those participating in and profiting from it. Nevertheless, the Ministry of Labour published in 1953 a Report which states that between July 1951 and June 1952 there occurred nearly 1,500 known cases of young boys and girls being illegally sold by parents through authorized "employment agents" in return for cash payments that averaged between £10 and £15 for a year's work, but in some cases amounted to only the equivalent of 10s. The sinister purpose and real tragedy of this "trade" in young lives is shown by the fact that 89 per cent of all recorded cases concerned young girls. The overwhelming majority of them were discovered working as "waitresses" and barmaids in small and often dubious establishments (many according to the Tokyo police investigators being obliged to sell themselves to customers) and the largest single category as avowed prostitutes.'

All these young people were under eighteen, which is the age at which a minor attains his legal majority in Japan. 683 were found to be seventeen years old; 448 were sixteen; 285 were fifteen; and four were under ten.

Among the cases investigated was a girl of seventeen who was found working in a Tokyo restaurant as a maidservant in return for an 'advance payment' of £12. Two months after beginning her duties the proprietor of the restaurant bought her an attractive kimono, and forced her to 'entertain' customers. She thereupon fled back to her home. But her parents, who had received the advance payment, insisted on her returning to the restaurant. She was ex-

Slavery

pected to work for two years to pay back the debt of £12 which her family had contracted.

In another case a boy of eleven had been sold by his father as an odd-job boy to a farmer for ten years for £10, the understanding being that the boy would receive clothes, food and pocket-money during this period. It is illegal in Japan for a juvenile to work until he has reached the school-leaving age of fifteen years; but this transaction was arranged by an unlicensed 'employment agent', who received the equivalent of 5s. for his services. He was traced, however, and convicted, his sentence being four years' imprisonment.

The underlying causes of the business emerge all too clearly from a third case described by Mr Tiltman. This concerned a coalminer earning £17 a month who was the father of sixteen children. Because he could not maintain them he declared that he had had to sell one of his daughters.

The total number of children victimized in this way, according to an official of the Women and Children's Bureau of the Japanese Ministry of Labour, is considerably larger than the public figures indicate. There is no lack of legislation to combat it; the difficulty is economic. It was found that some of the children, when questioned, did not wish to return to their home, where their parents could not feed them. The parents, too, take the view that the children are happier in the 'jobs' assigned to them. For this reason officials of the Ministry of Labour believe that the traffic in young lives can really only be halted by an improvement in the social and economic conditions of Japan.

On December 27, 1956, the *Manchester Guardian* published another article by Hessell Tiltman, written in Tokyo, in which he said that figures compiled by the Ministry of Labour of Japan showed that in 1956 no less than 40,291 people in Japan had been sold and 'according to the police the total number of cases may well be higher. Some 80 per cent of known cases involve young girls aged from 17 to 25 "bought" by white slavers and destined for the licensed premises in the cities and for dubious "employment" at inns at hot springs and pleasure resorts. In spite of the newly enacted Anti-Prostitution Law, the authorities report that those engaged in the human traffic are paying from £10 to £70 each for young girls. . . . Basic reasons for the continuance of the traffic—in spite of the human rights guarantees in the Constitution, laws and the commendable effort of the authorities—are over-population, poverty and at times lingering feudalistic ideas in farming districts that when times are hard it is the duty of daughters to sacrifice themselves for their

The Sham Adoption of Children

parents'. He added that in North-East Honshu and Hokkaido farming families frequently have to exist on incomes as low as the equivalent of £3 a month. So the traffic in human beings is increasing.

The only remaining place in the East where children are known to be transferred in this kind of way is Ceylon. According to a report of the ILO for 1947,[1] 'In Ceylon there is a system resembling the Mui Tsai system, but somewhat different from it, which has been called, for want of a better term, "quasi-adoption"'. But there is no evidence on the harshness or humanity with which it operates.

The West is happily free from the practice, with the exception of South America, where children are sold into domestic servitude on a considerable scale, certainly in Peru and Bolivia. A high percentage of the young domestic servants in the provincial cities of Peru, and even in Lima, the capital, are American-Indian children who have either been given directly by their parents or else sold by unscrupulous traffickers, who have taken them from their native places.[2] As in other countries, legislation has had little effect. In 1936 and again in 1947, laws were made prohibiting parents from selling their children under the age of sixteen. But the practice continues. And in Bolivia, too, it goes on. The Bolivian Government has admitted as much in a statement to the United Nations; and a Bolivian sociologist has estimated the number living in this condition at 200,000.

The undeniable economic pressure which produces the custom of transferring children for the sake of their labour, the humanity with which it may sometimes be done, and the wide toleration of it, must not blind us to the fact that it is undoubtedly a form of slavery. In the words of Sir George Maxwell:

'1. The child is always of tender age. She is not able to consent, and her consent is not required.

'2. The girls are often terribly over-worked and sometimes are cruelly beaten and maltreated.

'3. Enforced and unpaid labour over a period of years from childhood to the adult age is not the "fair and humane treatment" which is required by Article 23 of the Covenant of the League of Nations.[3]

'4. Powers of ownership are inherent in the system (unless the system is modified and regulated by local legislation, and unless the legislation is actually enforced by the executive action of the Government), and the system is therefore slavery within the definition in Article 1 of the Slavery Convention of 1926.'

[1] Report 2 of the ILO for the Preparatory Asiatic Regional Conference of 1947.
[2] Bulletin of the Department of Native Affairs for 1950, pp. 67-78.
[3] Now Article 73 (a) of the Charter of the United Nations.

Slavery

And it has, of course, also been included in the 1956 Supplementary Convention of the United Nations.

The immediate need, as with other forms of slavery, is to secure the passing of necessary legislation wherever this is lacking, and, most important, the setting up of efficient machinery of protection. It is a melancholy fact that even this may prove insufficient until economic conditions are sufficiently improved to make the practice less necessary. But the very act of attempting to stamp it out draws attention to the economic problem and promotes a more humane, and productive, solution of it. It is certain that without vigorous measures, even if material standards of living go up, no custom that has struck deep roots in a society is likely to be broken.

PART II
THE FIGHT

CHAPTER X

SLAVE CHARITIES

೧೧

BY the seventeenth century freedom could be sufficiently taken for granted in Britain for her involvement in fresh enslavement to arouse concern. Of the two areas in which this was going on, in one, the West Indies, she was among the enslavers, but in the other, the Mediterranean, her citizens were among the victims. And sometime before the long fight against slavery began, before the moral indignation of the country was roused by the negro slave trade, her more easily awakened charitable impulses were called forth by the raids of the Barbary Corsairs. What might be called a compassionate phase intervened, in which awareness of slavery was limited and reactions to it, though practical, were relatively shallow.

The recognized way of rescuing those captured by the pirates of North Africa was by payment of ransom. In the course of the three or four years preceeding 1622 four hundred British ships were captured, with their cargoes, and their crews enslaved; and in the first quarter of that century two hundred and forty British slaves were ransomed for £1,200, at that time a large sum. This method of rescue presented no difficulty to the rich, but the poor were in an unenviable position. To help them many charitable testators in Britain left part of their estates on trust, to be invested and the income devoted to the redemption of Christian captives. By these means many were saved from the slave markets; but after 1830, when the French captured Algiers, there were no more slaves to redeem. The charities then became the subject of legal action to determine how their funds should be applied. Several of them are still in existence today, with greatly increased incomes.

In English law, when the particular purpose of a trust comes to an end after the testator's death, the Court may direct that the income of the trust fund shall be applied to another object as close to the intentions of the testator as can be found. This is called in Norman French an *object cy-près* to the intentions of the testator, and the doctrine is known as the Cy-près Doctrine. Its application, however, in the face of conflicting interest, has not always been

Slavery

favourable to anti-slavery purposes.

One of the two main charities whose funds have continued to be applied to objects connected with slavery is the Charity of Rebecca Hussey, who left money on trust 'for the redemption of slaves'. By 1865 this fund had amounted to £22,000. Since the need to apply it for the original purpose had ceased by then a fresh scheme was devised. On June 26, 1865, the Court authorized the trustees to 'apply a moiety of the income of the fund in Lagos (Nigeria), and the remaining moiety in St Helena'. Local trustees were to be appointed in each colony. Those in Lagos were to use their share of the income to redeem 'from slavery such slaves as shall escape from the tribes surrounding Lagos to the latter place, and as the local trustees shall, after inquiry into the circumstances of each case, consider to be deserving objects of charity, or in the establishment or maintenance, at one or more places in Lagos, of schools for the general and industrial education of Africans and providing buildings for the purpose or by giving aid to such schools as are or may be there'. The trustees of St Helena, on the other hand, were to use their share solely for educational purposes, for the establishment and maintenance of schools for Africans.

The scheme for the Lagos half of the charity was later amended. On May 4, 1906, it was directed that the income should be applied to, 1. The redemption of slaves on the coasts or other parts of the continent of Africa; and 2. The relief and assistance of liberated African slaves in need of assistance, either by way of making contributions to any institution established for the rendering of such assistance, or otherwise. But if the trustees were unable to apply the income usefully in these ways they were authorized to make grants to 'such established institutions in Africa as are devoted to the education (technical or otherwise) of native African races'.

A second charity which is still helping to undo the work of the slavers is the Lady Mico Charity, whose funds are used for educational purposes in the West Indies. Lady Jane Mico was the wife of an alderman of the City of London. By her will of July 1, 1670, she bequeathed the sum of £1,000 on trust, the income from which was to be used 'to redeem poor captives in what manner my executors should think most convenient'. The Charity was not actually established until 1680, and it was not until June 1686 that the trustees were directed by the Court to invest the trust fund in land. However, they invested so successfully, by buying a freehold wharf and premises in Castle Bayard above London Bridge, that by 1827 the fund amounted to £115,510, then invested in Consols.

None of the income was in fact applied for the redemption of

Slave Charities

slaves, except for £1,500, which was paid to Sir Charles Wagner in March 1737, for this purpose. By 1827 a fresh scheme for the Charity was being devised, and in November of that year the Court was asked to approve it. In 1834 four trustees were appointed, Mr Gibson, Dr Lushington, Mr (later Sir) T. Fowell Buxton, and Mr Barber, and the scheme they submitted was for applying the income towards the education of apprentices in the British Colonies recently emancipated from slavery. Approving it the Court stated that it believed that 'the testatrix by her will contemplated the redemption of poor slaves in the Barbary States but such intention could not now be carried into effect, and the proposed scheme was as near to the intention of the testatrix as circumstances would admit and that the same was a proper scheme and he (the Judge) approved thereof'.[1]

The trustees were authorized to spend part of the capital on school buildings. A teachers' training college was established in Jamaica, and another in Antigua. In addition schools were opened in Trinidad, Demerera, Bahamas, St Lucia, Mauritius and the Seychelles Islands. Of all these, however, only the Lady Mico Training College in Jamaica is still in existence today. But this is running successfully. In it students receive free tuition, board and medical attention. After remaining there for three years they are bound to teach in elementary schools for a further six years. The annual expenditure on it in 1931 amounted to £5,294, and according to the Jamaica Handbook for that year, 'The school run in connection with the Mico Training College is high on the list of first-class elementary schools in Jamaica'. Since 1834 the trustees have usually included a member of the Buxton family; the present one is Mr D. A. J. Buxton.

Three other existing slave charities are worth mentioning, though none of them is devoted to anything connected with slavery today. One, Betton's Charity, was the subject of legal proceedings in which the Lady Mico Charity sought unsuccessfully to claim a portion of its funds. It was created on the death of Thomas Betton, of the Parish of St Leonards, Shoreditch, London. By his will dated February 15, 1723, Thomas Betton bequeathed 'the rest and residue of my estate wheresoever and whatsoever to the Worshipful Company or Corporation of Ironmongers of the City of London and to their successors upon trust etc. That they do pay one full half part of the said interest and profit of my whole estate yearly and every year forever unto the redemption of British slaves in Turkey or Barbary'. The other half of the income was again divided in two. One part, that is to say one-fourth of the whole income, he bequeathed to

[1] A.-G. v Gibson.

Slavery

charity schools in the City of London and suburbs, where education was according to the Church of England, with the stipulation that not more than £200 per annum should go to any one school. The remaining fourth, after the payment of ten pounds to the Chaplain of the Company, was to be applied to the relief of 'necessitated decayed Freemen of the company, their widows and children, not exceeding ten pounds a year to any family'.

Thomas Betton died in 1724, and for the next hundred years sums of money were paid out of the slave fund income for the redemption of British captives in Turkey or Barbary. But after the last payment was made in 1825 the fund accumulated, and its future had to be determined. The other half of the income from the estate, that from the London and suburbs fund and the decayed freemen fund, presented no difficulties, and it has always been applied according to the will.

The prolonged legal deliberations concerning the slave fund began in 1829, when the Attorney General filed an information asking the Court to approve a scheme for applying its income. The Court of first instance held, in 1833, that it had no jurisdiction to direct application of the money to objects inconsistent with the intentions of the testator. On appeal, however, the Lord Chancellor, Lord Brougham, cited the Doctrine of Cy-près and directed that the income of the slave fund be given to the objects of the other trusts created by the testator because 'when a testator gives one charitable fund to three several classes of objects unless he excludes by most express provisions the application of one portion to the purpose to which the others are destined, it is clear that the Court may thus execute his intention in the event of the impossibility of applying that portion to its original destination'.

To establish this impossibility the Master advertised, inviting any organization with a charitable purpose connected with the Testator's intentions to put forward its claim. Among those who answered were the trustees of the Lady Mico Charity. They claimed that their activities, the education of British emancipated negroes, was an object cy-près to the intentions of the testator, and that the Betton's slave fund should be applied to it. The Court, however, held that Betton's bequest was made in more limited terms than Lady Mico's. Whereas Lady Mico's trust was 'to redeem poor captives in what manner my executors should think most convenient', with no restriction on the kind of captive, Betton had limited his benefaction specifically to British captives in Turkey or Barbary. The Court therefore dismissed the claim of the Lady Mico trustees;[1]

[1] A.-G. v Ironmongers' Company (1840) 2 Bearan 313 (1841) Cr. and Ph. 208.

Slave Charities

a judgment which was upheld by the House of Lords in 1841.

The last time Betton's charity came before the Court was in 1908, when an important point was established. On June 25, 1907, the Charity Commission had made an order under the Charitable Trusts Acts 1853-94 disposing of the income of the slave fund. The trustees appealed against it to the Court of Chancery, because they feared that under the order the entire income of the fund would be devoted to educational trusts, permanently and in all events. But Mr Justice Swinfen Eady gave a reassuring ruling. He held that the order merely determined the controlling body for the time being and did not in any way restrict, alter or affect the objects of the charity or prevent the income from being applied by a future scheme to non-educational purposes, 'if circumstances should arise making that course expedient'.[1] And there the matter rests today.

The same diversion into purely educational outlets occurred with Lord Craven's Charity for Poor Scholars and Christian Captives.

This trust was created on the death of John, Lord Craven, whose will, dated May 28, 1647, directed that a part of his estate was to be invested and the income therefrom was to be used to assist 'four poor scholars, whereof two were to be in the University of Oxford and two in the University of Cambridge', and the residue was to be used 'for the redemption of English Christian captives and prisoners in Algiers, or in any other places under the domination of the Turk'.

This was duly done, until the French conquest of Algiers in 1830 put an end to the Barbary slave-raiding. In 1834 the Court of Chancery was asked to approve fresh uses for the slave part of the Charity, as it had been found that there were now no more Christian captives to redeem. The scheme the Court approved increased the number and income of the scholarships created under the first part of the Charity. A 'moderate portion' of the fund, however, was set apart 'in case captives should be made'.

In 1895, when its terms were slightly modified, the Charity amounted to £56,491 12s. 3d., invested in new Consols. The Court then approved that there should be two fellowships and six scholarships at the University of Oxford and six scholarships and one studentship at the University of Cambridge. Since then Lord Craven's Charity has been undisturbed.

The largest of the slave charities, and certainly the one which is most open to criticism, is the Charity of Henry Smith (Kensington Estate). The story of the Anti-Slavery Society's hitherto unsuccessful efforts to secure even a modest portion of the income, which

[1] In re Betton's Charity, 1908. 1 Ch. 205.

Slavery

amounts to no less than £150,000 a year, makes strange reading.

The Charity came into existence in 1628, on the death of Henry Smith, an Alderman of the City of London. By his will, dated April 24, 1627, he left £2,000 on trust to be invested in land. Of the income half was to be divided among his 'poor kindred' and half was to be applied 'for the use of poor captives being slaves under the Turkish pirates'. The trustees invested wisely. They bought eighty-four acres of land in the Parishes of Chelsea and Kensington, which were then outside London. Now that they are well inside it these lands, let on building leases, yield a large income. In 1954 it was £139,523.

Slaves were ransomed in accordance with the will until 1723. Why none was ransomed after that date, when Barbary slave-raiding did not cease until 1830, is not clear. At all events, in 1849, as no income was being spent on 'poor captives', an application was made to the Court to approve other uses of the money, related to the intentions of the testator. Then in 1875 when the Charity again came before the Court, it was directed that in the absence of claims on behalf of 'poor captives' the entire income of the Charity should be applied for the benefit of the testator's 'poor kindred' and subject thereto to general charitable purposes.[1]

On the next occasion when the matter came before the Court, in 1889,[2] all reference to 'poor captives' had disappeared. Under the fresh scheme of distribution for the income approved by the Court, after provisions had been made for the 'poor kindred' the trustees were authorized to grant money out of the remaining unapplied income to hospitals in London and to charities for organizing holidays in the country for the children of the poor in London. Neither in 1875 nor in 1889 was any evidence adduced that slavery still existed and that the testator's intention to benefit slaves could be carried out, if not in the original way, in some other way *cy-près* thereto. It was apparently assumed that no *cy-près* object of benefaction existed.

The charity was administered under the 1889 scheme for the next fifty-seven years, until the hospitals were nationalized under the National Health Service Act of 1946. The trustees then took the view that grants to hospitals would be in relief of taxation, so they discontinued them. A new scheme was devised and on July 27, 1951, the trustees took out a summons to bring the matter before the Court for its approval. This time the Anti-Slavery Society heard of the legal proceedings, and determined to take part in them if possible.

[1] A.-G. v Duke of Northumberland (1877. 7 Ch.D. 745).
[2] A.-G. v Duke of Northumberland.

Slave Charities

The Attorney-General, Sir Lionel Heald, was asked to receive a deputation led by the late Viscount Simon, and he promised to appeal to the Court to join the Society as 'relator' in the proceedings, and to hear their counsel.

The Society's efforts met with some success; for when the summons came before the Court on July 1, 1952, the scheme of 1889 was amended, Mr Richard Wilberforce, QC, was heard on behalf of the Society, and an anti-slavery organization was once again included among the legitimate objects of the fund. The trustees were authorized to give a maximum of £5,000 annually to the Clergy Fund, which was also created by the Testator's will, to augment salaries of clergymen of the Church of England, and to make grants to hospitals, convalescent homes, charities for giving children holidays in the country, charities for the relief of aged persons, medical research, charities for the relief of widows and children of clergymen, and of deceased and disabled servicemen, charities for the promotion of moral welfare or social services, and finally, to 'organizations or bodies engaged in restoring slaves or serfs to freedom, or the relief and rehabilitation of freed slaves or serfs, or for preventing the seizure of human beings for slavery or serfdom'.

But this was only the beginning of the story. When the Anti-Slavery Society, as the most prominent organization engaged in combating slavery, applied to the trustees in 1953 for a grant under the new scheme, which had been approved by the Court, they met with a rebuff. In a letter dated May 13, 1953, they were informed that 'the trustees in their discretion did not consider that they should make a donation towards the purpose for which one was asked'. And in each of the next three years a similar answer was received when the application was renewed. In 1954 the trustees wrote that they 'saw no reason to change the decision which they made at this time last year'. In 1955, that the trustees 'consider the purpose of your Society calls for international action and should be sponsored by the United Nations Organization'. And in 1956, the trustees were 'still of the same opinion as previously expressed'.

The trustees' attitude towards anti-slavery work emerged when the Society's solicitor discussed the matter with the Treasurer of the Charity in March 1954. He learnt that 'the trustees have never considered the relief of slaves was, as such, contemplated by the Testator. Their view is that the trust was for the rehabilitation of seamen who were captured on the Barbary Coast and that the trustees were surprised when the Court included organizations for the restoration of slaves to freedom as one of the objects of the scheme, and even though the Court included a Society of this kind

Slavery

as an object of the Charity, the trustees have complete discretion and they are not convinced that the relief of slavery should be treated as an object for the Testator's benefaction'.

Could any opinion be more perverse? Far from limiting his benefaction to seamen the Testator expressly stated that it should include 'poor captives being slaves under the Turkish pirates'. Furthermore, since lands under the domination of the Turks were the only ones then known by Englishmen to be inhabited by slaves, the limitation to the Barbary Coast was by implication only. The generality of the Testator's intentions was recognized by the Court of Chancery in the 1952 hearing, when, after being excluded from the scheme of distribution of the income of the Charity for sixty-three years, benefaction to slaves was reinstated as a fitting object. The trustees did not at that time oppose the Anti-Slavery Society's application for slavery to be included in the scheme; nor did they appeal against the judgment of the Court. Yet since then they have persistently challenged the correctness of its decision and refused to abide by it.

Finally, to point their perverseness even more sharply, it was proved to the satisfaction of the Court not only that slavery exists in the world today, but that it exists in the Hejaz, which was a Turkish colony until 1919, and therefore a country in which the Testator intended to benefit slaves. Yet the men who control the income from his trust fund, now amounting to some £150,000 a year, refuse to allow one penny to be spent on carrying out his wishes.

Today Englishmen are happily no longer in need of rescue from slavery. But there are many others who are including British subjects. Although it is many years since the thought of it aroused the charitable impulses of these free and liberal-minded people, the doctrine of *cy-près* recognizes the continuity of general intentions in spite of changed conditions. It is unfortunate, therefore, that both Betton's Charity and the Charity of Henry Smith should be wholly lost to the cause of ameliorating the lot of any remaining slaves. As we have seen, there is still much to be done and a continuing need for funds with which to do it. The testators would surely be the first to rejoice that their legacies should have a wider application and no longer be required merely to pay a pirate's ransom.

CHAPTER XI

THE ANTI-SLAVERY MOVEMENT:
SLAVE TRADING

ಬಿ

WHEREVER slavery has become established its convenience for the enslaver and supposed economic necessity have never failed to blind men's eyes to its evil basis, and only isolated voices have been raised against it across the centuries. 'Zeus takes away half a man's virtue,' wrote Homer, 'when the day of slavery comes upon him.' Plato however only condemned the right of a Greek to hold another Greek as a slave. For the most part, in spite of the mitigating influence of Christianity, the old systematic slavery became modified through economic changes, and it was not until the seventeenth century, when the true nature of the West Indian trade in negroes began to become known in Britain, that condemnation of it on moral grounds began in earnest. From then on, however, a noble body of men and women, free from the blinkers of self-interest, increasingly forced the problem on the attention of the world, stirred its conscience, and eventually secured its abolition in all but a few countries.

One of the first voices to be heard was that of Robert Baxter, the famous nonconformist. In his *Christian Directory* of 1673 he still accepted slavery itself, if strictly regulated, but denounced the slave-hunters as 'the common enemies of mankind'. A few years later, in 1680, came a pamphlet by Morgan Goodwyn, an Anglican clergyman from Oxford who had gone out to Barbados. This exposed the planters' brutal treatment of their slaves and described the slave trade as 'a cruelty capable of no palliation'. And at about the same time a novel appeared entitled *Oronoko, or the Royal Slave*, in which the savagery of the slaver-trader and the slave-owner was contrasted with the nobility of a slave. Written by Mrs Aphra Benn, who had lived in Surinam (Dutch Guiana), and afterwards dramatized by Southerne, it was the first work in English literature since *Othello* with a black man for its hero.

During the next hundred years the slave system was constantly attacked, by preachers, philosophers, poets and pamphleteers. 'Slavery is so vile and miserable an estate of man,' wrote Locke,

Slavery

'and so directly opposite to the generous temper and courage of our nation, that it is hardly to be conceived that an "Englishman" much less a "Gentleman" should plead for it.' These were the opening words of the first *Treatise on Civil Government*, published in 1689. Defoe, in his *Reformation of Manners*, directly assailed the slave trade; and the miseries of enslavement are alluded to in the poetry of Thomson, Pope, Savage and Shenstone. From the pulpit in 1760 came a declaration by Bishop Warburton that 'the infamous traffic for slaves directly infringes both divine and human law'; and he spoke of 'the vast multitudes yearly stolen from the opposite continent, and sacrificed by the colonists to their idol, the god of gain'. And among others Adam Smith, John Wesley, the Abbé Raynal, Thomas Payne and James Ramsay, all continued to attack slavery.

These remained, however, expressions of individual opinion; and they were words, not deeds. The first deeds came, as one might expect, from a body of people who have provided a moral lead in more than one field, the Society of Friends, or Quakers. Their founder, George Fox, as early as 1671 had urged the Friends in Barbados to mitigate the evils of slavery by treating their slaves well and by setting them free 'after certain years of servitude'. Then in 1688 the German Quakers in Pennsylvania pointed out that morally there was no difference between stealing and enslaving men. Gradually, by exhortation, censure and warning most of the Quakers in England and the colonies who owned slaves or were connected with the slave trade were induced to give them up or end their dealings. By 1774 the Quakers had sufficiently consolidated opinion within their ranks for the annual convocation of Friends to vote for the expulsion of any Friend engaged in the slave trade; and two years later all American Friends were required to free their slaves.

Having thus secured the abolition of slavery amongst themselves, the Quakers widened the scope of their activities. In 1783 they organized the first anti-slavery society, with the aim of influencing public opinion through the dissemination of information about negro slavery. Its executive committee consisted of Tom Dillwyn, George Harrison, Samuel Hoare, Thomas Knowles, John Lloyd and Joseph Woods. A year after its formation the society brought out a pamphlet, *The Case of our Fellow Creatures, the Oppressed Africans*, and sent a copy to each Member of Parliament. This society was the first organized attempt to attack the institution of slavery, and with the exception of the inhabitants of Bridgewater, who prepared a petition and sent it to Parliament, the Quaker Society was the only active group until it was absorbed in Thomas Clarkson's larger Society.

The Anti-Slavery Movement

The Quakers were indeed the first group to fight slavery, and continued to supply a steady moral force to the movement, but the first militant individual abolitionist was Granville Sharp, who by his determination and skill secured the historical legal decision which finally made slavery in Britain impossible.

Granville was one of fourteen children, several of whom rose to positions of distinction. His brother William was appointed to be one of the King's surgeons, and another brother, James, was a prominent merchant in the City of London. Granville showed his remarkable ability early in life. The intellectual audacity he displayed in his teens showed that no task was too difficult for him. When he learnt that his second employer had a claim to the barony of Willoughby de Parham he embarked on a detailed study of the case, and mastered it so thoroughly and was able to expound it with such force that his argument carried the worthy Mr Willoughby straight into the House of Lords.

His connection with slavery began one day in 1765 when he was leaving his brother's surgery in Mincing Lane. Among the poor patients waiting at the door for free treatment he noticed a negro, whose appearance was so 'extremely distressful' that Granville turned back and drew his brother's attention to him. His name was Jonathan Strong, and he was the slave of a Mr David Lisle, an irascible lawyer from Barbados, by whom he had been so savagely flogged that he could hardly walk. Lisle had abandoned him as almost dead, but William Sharp managed to get him admitted to St Bartholomew's Hospital, and here he recovered. On his discharge Granville found him a job as errand boy to a chemist in Fenchurch Street.

So far the episode had not planted in Granville's mind any idea of questioning the ancient institution of slavery. He regarded his assistance to Strong as a matter of private charity and forgot it. Two years later, however, Lisle saw Strong in the street, in good health and not dead, as he had thought. Since his property had thus recovered its value Lisle traced Strong to the chemist's shop where he worked, and promptly sold him to a Jamaican planter, James Kerr, who kidnapped his purchase and entrusted him to a jailer for safekeeping until he could ship him to Jamaica. But Strong succeeded in getting a message to Granville Sharp, who at once came to the rescue. He went to the prison, heard Strong's story and warned the jailer not to surrender the negro without a warrant. He then applied to the Lord Mayor to summon before him anyone who claimed Strong. When Kerr duly appeared and claimed him as his slave, the Lord Mayor held that no person slave or free could be

Slavery

imprisoned unless an offence was alleged, and he was therefore compelled to release him.

Outside the court Kerr tried to regain possession of his 'property' by holding on to him. But Sharp threatened to charge Kerr with assault, so he released Strong, who made good his escape. Kerr then decided to postpone dealing with his slave until he had punished this busybody who had interfered so gratuitously with his long-established rights as a slave-owner. He brought an action against Sharp.

At this point Sharp's determination and independence of judgment, and no doubt his experience with the Willoughby barony, came into full play. Some forty years earlier, in 1729, the Law Officers had given an opinion that a master's rights of property in his slave were unaffected by the residence of the slave in England, and that the master could 'legally compel him to return again to the plantations'. The Attorney General at the time, Yorke, had since become Lord Mansfield, the Lord Chief Justice, and he was destined in another two years to reverse this opinion. Sharp's own lawyers advised him not to fight the case Kerr was bringing, but he told them that 'he could not believe that the law of England was really so injurious to natural right as so many great lawyers for political reasons had been pleased to assert', and that he was not intimidated by the official opinion. He also told them that he would conduct his own defence.

As before, he worked away at the law books, and built his case on the contrary opinion expressed in 1729 by Chief Justice Holt that 'as soon as a negro comes into England he becomes free'. He composed a memorandum in which he supported this view with an exposition of the principles of villeinage and common law, and sent copies of it to eminent lawyers. This had such an unsettling effect that Kerr's lawyers advised him to withdraw his case, which he did —and paid the costs.

But Sharp was not satisfied, for the law remained uncertain. He wanted a judgment. Two years later he had his opportunity, and in spite of legal reluctance the decisive judgment was finally given. A slave named James Somerset, who had been brought to England from Virginia by his owner, Charles Stewart, ran away. On recapture he was put aboard a ship bound for Jamaica, whereupon Granville Sharp took legal proceedings to obtain his release. By this time Lord Mansfield, who was to hear the case, had become convinced that the opinion he had given as a law officer was wrong. But he tried hard to avoid having to admit it. He twice adjourned the case; he invited Stewart to end it by setting Somerset free; and

The Anti-Slavery Movement

he urged both sides to settle it out of court. But it was no use: the case went on. And on June 22, 1772, Lord Mansfield delivered his famous judgment. In the course of it he said, 'The power claimed never was in use here nor acknowledged by law. The state of slavery is so odious that nothing can be suffered to support it but positive law. Whatever inconveniences, therefore, may follow from the decision, I cannot say this case is allowed or approved by the law of England; and therefore the black must be discharged'.

The 'inconveniences' included some 15,000 other slaves in Britain at the time of the decision. All were now recognized as free, whether or not they chose to remain with their old masters. Thus, by one man's work, in the face of accepted opinion, slavery was abolished in the British Isles. Nor was this all. The Somerset case sounded the death knell of slavery throughout the British Empire; the anti-slavery movement now gained momentum.

Following on his success Granville Sharp wrote to the bishops, and from most of them obtained a promise of support for a campaign against the slave trade. Two more valuable recruits also came on the scene. One was James Ramsay, a clergyman who had served for nineteen years in St Kitts and was now a vicar in Kent. He joined the fray with a series of outspoken pamphlets denouncing West Indian slavery as he had seen it. The other was Thomas Clarkson, who was to do as much as any man to secure the triumph of the cause. Without his untiring zeal and industry, his personal researches and propaganda all over the country, and the prestige and authority he attained, the attack on the slave system in British countries could not have achieved its aim as quickly or as fully as it did.

Unlike Sharp and Ramsay, with their direct experiences, Clarkson's connection with slavery began as an intellectual one, with a prize-winning Latin essay at Cambridge University. Written in 1785, it was on the subject appointed by the Vice-Chancellor, 'Is it right to make men slaves against their will?' Clarkson has recorded that he drew most of the material for it from Anthony Benezet's *Historical Account of Guinea*. But what was begun for academic honour, and in some detachment, soon gripped his whole being. After winning the prize he left Cambridge on horseback, bound for London. As he rode along the horrors of the slave trade he had been reading about kept coming into his mind. When he got into Hertfordshire he dismounted, sat by the roadside and thought. The implications of his essay suddenly became clear and compelling: if what he had written was true, the time had come for somebody to see the matter through to its conclusion. From that moment the abolition of slavery became the supreme object of his life. The scene of his decision,

Slavery

Wades Mill, is marked today by a monument to his memory.

Under Clarkson's purposefulness and skilful management the various strands of the anti-slavery movement now began to come together. He prepared an expanded English version of his essay, which was published in 1786 by James Phillips, a Quaker. Through him Clarkson met Tom Dillwyn, a member of the Quaker Committee for the abolition of the slave trade, and began his life-long association with the Quakers. Shortly afterwards, he met Granville Sharp and James Ramsay, and decided not only that he could collaborate with them, but that he would abandon the clerical career he had begun and devote the whole of his energies to the abolitionist cause. It was a decision that meant much self-sacrifice; for unlike some of his colleagues Clarkson was not a rich man.

Together this group formed, on May 22, 1787, a new Society for the Abolition of the Slave Trade. Its standing committee of twelve absorbed the old Quaker committee, except for Knowles, and included Clarkson and Phillip Sansom, with Granville Sharp as chairman. Its declared object was to 'procure and publish such information as may tend to the abolition of the slave trade', and for this limited purpose it was sufficiently well equipped with men and money. The slave trade and not slavery itself was the target; for although every member of the committee was an exponent of the whole system of slavery, they saw that they must proceed with caution. The abolition of slavery was by no means forgotten, but it was held in abeyance until the primary object of abolishing the trade was achieved.

Even this was formidable enough. It required legislation; and to persuade Parliament to contemplate an Abolition Act in the face of apathy and vested interests must have seemed a desperate task in 1787. To accomplish it a dedicated parliamentarian was needed, a man who was popular, influential and persuasive, yet not a leader of either party, so that he could draw votes from each. The need produced the man in William Wilberforce.

Born at Hull in 1759 Wilberforce came of an old and well-to-do Yorkshire family. From unstrenuous days at Cambridge he went on to London, as MP for Hull, to enjoy the leisured life his independent fortune made possible. There his personal magnetism and spontaneous interest in everybody made him hosts of friends. Chief among them was an old one. William Pitt, with whom he had much in common. They were of the same age, they had been at Cambridge together and they were elected to Parliament in the same year, 1780. They now became the closest friends, sharing Wilberforce's house at Wimbledon; and when Pitt became Prime Minister in 1783 there

The Anti-Slavery Movement

was no one on whom he could more certainly rely for support in speech and vote than the gifted young Yorkshireman.

Thus far nothing had prompted Wilberforce to probe far below the surface of life. His adoption of more serious views, when it came, nearly ended his political career. In 1785, under the influence of Isaac Milner, who had been an usher at his school and was now a don at Cambridge, Wilberforce was suddenly gripped by the religious emotion which Wesley had set flowing. His conversion was completed when he met a man named John Newton and listened to the remorseful and lurid account he gave of his earlier life as captain of a slave ship, before his own conversion had led him to the Church. A changed man, Wilberforce decided to resign from Parliament; and he would have done so, but for the slave trade. He had heard of it first from James Ramsay and then from Newton; now he read Clarkson's essay, met the author and asked for more information. He soon became convinced that the slave trade ought to be stopped, and in his present frame of mind it was not much longer before he accepted the task of fighting it in Parliament as his own share in the crusade. The moment of his final decision came one summer's day in 1787, as he has recorded in his diary. He was sitting with William Pitt under an old oak tree in Holwood Park, Kent, overlooking the Vale of Keston, when Pitt remarked. 'Why don't you, Wilberforce, give notice of a motion on the slave trade?' From then on Wilberforce began to tread the long road which was to lead to the abolition of the British slave system and the consolidation of the British humanitarian tradition.

At about this time Wilberforce went to live at Clapham, which was then a quiet country village a few miles from Westminster. Though Clarkson became his close and constant collaborator, he was not one of the group of intimate friends on whom Wilberforce chiefly depended for the intellectual and spiritual sympathy and help he needed. These he found among some of his neighbours, with whom he became very friendly and formed a coterie which came to be known as the Clapham Sect. They included the first abolitionist, Granville Sharp, Henry Thornton, MP, Charles Grant, John Shore (afterwards Lord Teignmouth), James Stephen, Zachary Macaulay, Thomas Babington and William Smith, MP. While religion was the strongest link between these gifted men, added to this was their humanitarian activities; and the man they felt to be their leader was undoubtedly Wilberforce.

The attack on the slave trade could now be opened. Wilberforce's parliamentary talents, Clarkson's industry, and the propaganda of the Abolitionist Committee together made it possible. Wilberforce

Slavery

did not become a member of the Committee, for it was felt that he would be more influential in Parliament if he was not the direct representative of such a group. Needless to say, however, he constantly sought information and advice from it, and his diaries show that he could not have pursued his course without the central organization. It supplied him with the irrefutable evidence he needed to present his case effectively, and at the same time converted public opinion to the abolitionist point of view.

As soon as the Society was formed Clarkson wrote his *Summary View of the Slave Trade*, a more concise account of it than his essay, and then set out on a tour of the ports frequented by slave ships, especially Bristol and Liverpool, with the object of collecting firsthand evidence on board the ships. In the four months he was away he gathered a mass of information, and on his return to London at the insistence of the Committee in November 1787, he spent the next few months writing his *Impolicy of the Slave Trade*. At about this time, too, he met William Pitt, a meeting arranged by Wilberforce, whose health had become impaired and who therefore thought it advisable that the introduction be made. Clarkson has recorded that Pitt and he conversed for a considerable time.

Pitt was an ardent supporter of the anti-slavery movement. In February 1788 he requested the Trade Committee of the Privy Council 'to take into consideration the present state of the African trade'. The Abolition Committee, with Clarkson's tireless energy behind it, did all it could to ensure that the true facts came to light by bringing in witnesses. Among them was Dr Spaarman, who had been sent to Africa on a tour of investigation by the humanitarian King of Sweden. The Privy Council's examination of the question was protracted, however, and long before it had prepared its report, Parliament had passed its first measure concerning the slave trade.

Though it was only a palliative, an attempt to reduce the sufferings of the slaves in transit, it was a beginning. Sir William Dolben, Member for Oxford University, had visited a slave ship in the Thames, and been so horrified by the tight packing of its human cargo that he at once gave notice of a Bill to limit the number to be carried in proportion to the size of the ship. This challenge to the slave trade was accepted by its promoters, who denied the slaves' sufferings, and declared that any attempt to regulate the trade would ruin it. But their arguments made little impression on the House. The Bill was passed by an overwhelming majority. On reaching the Lords it was threatened with destruction; but when Pitt let it be known that he would resign if it was defeated the Lords also passed

The Anti-Slavery Movement

it, with a majority of two.

In 1789 the battle in the Commons was joined in earnest. In April the Report of the Privy Council committee was published, and though it stated no opinion but simply presented all the evidence on both sides of the question, its effect was damning. Then on May 12 Wilberforce moved a resolution, in a fine speech summarizing the case against the slave trade. It held the attention of the House for over three hours and no less a master of oratory than Burke declared it to be comparable with the eloquence of the Greek orators. But the House was not yet ready to make up its mind. Conscience was in conflict with native caution, and a decision was postponed until the next session, when it could hear all the evidence at its own bar.

Meanwhile, across the Channel similar moves were afoot, amid the greater events that were pending. In 1788 Lafayette and a group of French liberals had corresponded with the Abolition Society in London and had set up a similar organization in France, named Les Amis des Noirs. The French society, however, contained far more influential men than the English. Its president was Condorcet, and its members included the Abbé Gregoire, Brissot, Clairere, Lafayette, Necker, the Abbé Sieyes and Mirabeau. With the fall of the Bastille on July 14, 1789, the visible sign of a new era of universal brotherhood, conditions in France seemed specially auspicious for the success of abolition, and many of the revolutionaries were actively interested in it. To give this movement all possible support, and with the idea of trying to influence the French Chamber of Deputies to take action, Wilberforce had decided to visit Paris in the summer of 1789, on the adjournment of Parliament. But the threatening revolution made it unwise for one officially connected with the British Government to make such a trip. Wilberforce therefore turned to Clarkson, who knew more about the slave trade than any other abolitionist; and within a week he left for France.

On arrival Clarkson was received by the King, who accepted from him a copy of his essay, *The Impolicy of the Slave Trade*. Clarkson anticipated an early victory for the abolitionist cause; for he did not perceive, any more than his French friends, how fast affairs were moving towards anarchy in France. The anti-abolitionists, moreover, were well organized. As in England, the profits from the whole system of slavery had enriched a considerable number of people, who were able to exert tremendous influence. Three hundred men were said to have banded themselves together with the express purpose of assassinating opponents of the slave trade. Clarkson, along with several of Les Amis des Noirs, received a letter threatening his life

Slavery

if he did not desist from his anti-slavery activities. In spite of this, however, he remained in Paris for six months and continued to take part in the campaign.

But, as in England, the moment had not yet come for success; the French Chamber of Deputies could not be brought to the point. Mirabeau, one of the strongest figures in French politics, canvassed every member of the Chamber and found that 300 were unequivocally in favour of immediate abolition of the slave trade. Of the remaining 900, 500 promised to vote for it if England agreed to take similar action. But, of course, no such guarantee could be given, so Mirabeau had to abandon his plan for legislative action; and Clarkson, thwarted in his efforts, returned to England.

It was another four years before France took any decisive step, and then its effect was uncertain and of only short duration. On his return to England early in 1790 Clarkson continued to interest himself in French activities. For several months he wrote regularly to Brissot, the founder of Les Amis des Noirs, and to the Abbé Gregoire. Then, on May 14, 1791, the Abbé succeeded in bringing the matter before the National Assembly, and claimed for coloured people all the rights of citizenship. A bitter discussion followed, in which Robespierre exclaimed, 'Let the colonies perish if they must cost you your honour and justice'. As a result citizenship was granted to mulattoes; though slavery was far from being abolished in all the French colonies. The National Convention did not vote such a measure until February 5, 1794; and it is doubtful how far it was carried out. In any case the law was repealed by Napoleon in 1802, and this first attempt to end slavery in French territories, which seemed to have everything in its favour, came to nothing. The cause had to wait until 1823, for a fresh champion, Victor Schoelcher, who, after years of relentless effort, finally achieved success in 1848.

Back in England, too, the first impetus, about to be put to the test, was to prove insufficient. In January 1790 Wilberforce succeeded in getting a motion through the House of Commons for the appointment of a Select Committee to hear evidence on the slave trade, and for the rest of the session evidence was presented. When printed it filled three large volumes. Clarkson prepared an abridgement, however, and circulated 5,000 copies of it. At last, in April 1791, the case having been fully prepared, Wilberforce was able to propose a motion for the abolition of the slave trade. But it was defeated; and for the next thirteen years the struggle made scarcely any progress. Wilberforce, supported by the Clapham Sect, continued his efforts in Parliament; but he was unable to get any legislation passed, even for gradual abolition. In spite of all that had been done to demon-

The Anti-Slavery Movement

strate the evils of the slave trade, Parliament remained indifferent. As for Clarkson, the other great pillar of the movement, ill-health forced him in 1794 to discontinue his long journeys in pursuit of evidence and until 1804 he had to lead a quiet life. During these ten years of his retirement the work of the Abolition Committee came to a standstill; indeed from April 12, 1791, until May 23, 1804, no meetings were held. The anti-slavery movement was in the doldrums.

The way forward opened unexpectedly in 1804, when the Abolition Committee met once again, strengthened by new members. Among them were Henry Brougham, Zachary Macaulay and James Stephen. In the House, too, Wilberforce renewed the attack. He introduced another Bill for the abolition of the slave trade and managed to steer it successfully through its three readings. Unfortunately it was introduced into the House of Lords too near the end of the session, so that a division had to be postponed until the following year. But victory appeared to be in sight, and although Pitt, early in 1805, asked Wilberforce to delay the reintroduction of his Bill, he declined. Devoted as he was to his friend, he refused to make 'his holy cause subservient to the interests of a party'. In the event, however, he was again disappointed. The Bill was rejected by the Lords, by a majority of seven. The vested interests were still too strong.

Pitt for political reasons had tried to restrain Wilberforce temporarily, but he never ceased to be a supporter of the anti-slavery movement, and before his death in 1806 he was able to render it one further service. To legislate for settled colonies an Act of Parliament was, and still is, necessary, but for conquered or annexed colonies the Crown's prerogative is sufficient. Pitt utilized this distinction and contrived to prevent the introduction of new slaves into annexed colonies by an Order-in-Council in 1805.

The following year at last saw the turning point in the long campaign. In the early months another measure was passed which whittled down the slave trade a little further, an Act that prohibited British ships from taking slaves to foreign colonies. Then in June Fox, who had succeeded Pitt as Prime Minister, won the support of the majority of his Cabinet for abolition. He introduced a resolution in support of it, and this was carried by 114 votes to 15, a clear indication that victory was now certain. Although Parliament was dissolved in the autumn, a general election maintained the same government in office, and it was decided that the Abolition Bill should be the first and principal measure of the new session. It was to be started, moreover, in the House of Lords.

Slavery

And there, on January 2, 1807, Lord Grenville introduced the successful Bill. Its first clause, as finally enacted, provided that from and after January 1, 1808, all manner of 'dealing and trading in slaves' in Africa, or their transport from Africa to any other place, should be prohibited and unlawful, and any British subject found guilty of doing so would be fined £100 for every slave so purchased, sold or transported. The second clause declared that any British ship engaged in the slave trade should be forfeited; and other clauses provided for the penalization of insurance contracts made on behalf of the slave trade, for the payment of bounties to naval officers and men for the recovery of slaves from ships violating the Act, and for putting such rescued slaves at the service of the Crown.

The Bill had a far from smooth passage, however. On its second reading, on February 5, it was bitterly attacked by H.R.H. the Duke of Clarence and three other peers, Lords Hawkesbury, Eldon and St Vincent, who walked out of the House in protest. On the other hand it was supported by the Duke of Gloucester, the Bishop of Durham and seven other members of the House, and it was eventually carried by 136 votes to 36.

In the House of Commons the outcome was certain, and Wilberforce, whose indomitable perseverance had made it possible, now at long last received his reward. At the climax of the debate on March 16 the House rose to its feet and cheered him to the echo. When the vote was taken the Bill received a majority of 283 to 16; and with the Royal Assent, given on March 25, 1807, the first objective of the anti-slavery movement had been achieved.

The slave-traders had been defeated in Parliament, but so profitable was their business that fines alone were not enough to suppress it. When the Act came into force on January 1, 1808, British ships of war promptly saw that it was carried out, and the majority of British slavers were quickly driven from the seas. But the possible gains were so great that a contraband trade continued, with ships fitted out in continental ports. Though many of these were captured, one successful voyage in three was enough to show a handsome profit. To deal with the smugglers an amending Act was passed in 1811 making slave-trading a felony, punishable by transportation, and this was effective. Another, even more drastic Act was passed in 1824, making slave-trading piracy and a capital crime. But its purpose was mainly as an example to other nations. It was found to be unnecessary and was repealed in 1837.

From the time when such determined and clear-sighted men as Granville Sharp, Clarkson, Wilberforce and their little band of propagandists began to open their countrymen's eyes to its brutalities;

The Anti-Slavery Movement

when such public figures as John Wesley, Adam Smith, Bishop Porteus and Jeremy Bentham came out publicly against it; and when such statesmen as Pitt, Fox and Burke espoused the cause of Abolition, the British slave trade was doomed. The remarkable fact is that the vested interests proved so powerful, and the trade was regarded as so permanent, however regrettable, a part of European civilization, that it took twenty years to bring about the necessary revolution in thought.

In France, as we have seen, even a revolution in society was insufficient to bring about the permanent abolition of slavery. Readmitted to legality by Napoleon the French slave trade continued to flourish until the end of the Napoleonic wars in 1814. And then in the peace terms given to France in May 1814, when Louis XVIII was restored to the throne, France was permitted to continue the slave trade for a further five years. Not surprisingly this infuriated the people of England. Every effort was made to induce the British Government to demand at the Congress of Vienna, about to be held, the immediate abolition of the slave trade, not only of France, but also of Spain and Portugal. Public protest in England rose to fever pitch. Clarkson, naturally in the thick of it, succeeded in winning a distinguished supporter, the Emperor Alexander of Russia, who was on a visit to London. With the help of his close Quaker friend, William Allen, Clarkson secured an interview with him and presented him with a copy of his *Abridgement of the Evidence given to the Select Committee of Parliament in 1789-91*. Crossing the Channel on his way back to the continent the Emperor became violently sea-sick; but when a nobleman offered his sympathy he replied, 'It is that book—the *Abridgement*—that has made me more sick than the sea'.

The Congress of Vienna was held early in 1815. In a determined effort to bring the whole subject of abolition to its attention Clarkson prepared a new analysis of the slave trade, which was soon printed, and addressed it to the various European delegates. He also approached the Duke of Wellington and influenced him to propose to Talleyrand that the Congress powers should agree to abolish the slave trade. But Talleyrand declined. The principal British delegate was Lord Castlereagh, who had originally been an opponent of abolition. But he had become converted to the cause and at the Congress fought tenaciously for the proposed agreement. France, however, insisted on retaining her right to continue the slave trade under the armistice of the previous year, and she was supported by Spain and Portugal. The continental powers regarded abolition as a strange British obsession, and the most that the Congress could be persuaded

Slavery

to do was to declare that the slave trade was 'the desolation of Africa, the degradation of Europe, and the affliction of humanity'.

Surprisingly enough it was Napoleon who took the next step towards abolition in France. Shortly after the Congress of Vienna, when he made his escape from Elba and his sensational return to power, he issued a decree to abolish the slave trade. But Waterloo and more distant exile soon followed, and after his defeat the rulers of Europe again gathered in Paris. Clarkson once more was among them. He renewed his contact with the Emperor Alexander of Russia by means of a letter from the Duke of Gloucester, which he presented. The Emperor promised Clarkson that he would never desert the cause and authorized him to write to him whenever he might be of use; but he believed that serious international complications were involved in the abolition of the slave trade.

The next twenty-five years, although they saw the legal abolition of the trade by most if not all of the nations engaged in it, were to prove him right. On his restoration to the French throne Louis XVIII reinforced Napoleon's decree with another to the same effect; but it was not until 1831 that France took effective steps to stamp out the traffic. Spain and Portugal signed a treaty to abolish the slave trade in 1815; but they had to be induced to do so by grants of the British taxpayers' money, disguised as an 'indemnity' for captured slave ships, and as late as 1842 Portugal found it necessary to declare the slave trade to be piracy. In America, meanwhile, President Jefferson, almost at the same time as George III assented to the British Abolition Act, approved a Congressional measure prohibiting the importation of slaves into the United States as from January 1, 1808, and penalizing all participation in such trade. In South America, too, between 1810 and 1812 the traffic was legally abolished by the newly-created republics of Venezuela, Chile and Argentina. Brazil gained her independence in 1825, and in 1831 she passed an Act providing for the punishment of slave-traders and for the confiscation of their ships; but the trade did not actually stop until 1853.

All these decrees were in fact so much waste paper. Only Britain took the necessary steps to ensure that her laws were obeyed; and in the absence of any international machinery of control British diplomacy now began the struggle to extract by treaty from all nations reciprocal rights of stoppage and search of ships reasonably suspected of conveying slaves, and to secure the condemnation of any such ships by a court of law. The struggle proved long, and might perhaps have ended unsuccessfully had not emancipation finally removed the cause of the slave trade in the West.

At about the same time as these treaties were being negotiated

The Anti-Slavery Movement

exploration in Africa began to make Western nations increasingly aware of the other, Eastern branch of the slave trade, from East Africa to Arabia and the countries of the Middle East, where slavery was regarded as a natural institution. In this region also an attempt was made by the British to curb the trade by means of treaties with the rulers of some of the states concerned. And here too the struggle was long, and often unavailing. It culminated eventually in the 'Magna Carta of the African slave', the Brussels Act of 1890. But long before this the first phase of the work of the anti-slavery movement had been done. A fresh climate of opinion had been created, and the field of action had become international.

CHAPTER XII

THE ANTI-SLAVERY MOVEMENT: SLAVERY ITSELF

THE abolition of the slave trade in British possessions was a great achievement, but it had always been regarded by its promoters as the means to a greater end, the abolition of slavery itself. As Wilberforce said in 1823, 'The emancipation of the slaves was the ultimate object of all those who took the lead as advocates for the abolition of the slave trade'. But any hopes he entertained, along with such leading public figures as Pitt, Fox, Grenville and Grey, that with the end of the trade slavery would automatically diminish and finally disappear were to prove vain. Another long fight had to be waged, this time against the colonial legislatures and planters, before slavery could be brought to an end.

At first, however, amelioration was the aim. It was believed in England that the planters, deprived of fresh supplies of slaves from Africa, would be forced to treat those they already had with greater consideration, to prolong their lives and hence their service, and to promote their natural increase. The British Government therefore began by proposing to the colonial legislatures measures designed to improve the condition of the slaves, to eliminate overwork and cruel punishments and to encourage marriage. Gradually, it was hoped, as things improved, a smooth transition from slavery to freedom could be effected.

If the planters had been amenable to reason the hope would not have been unfounded; but instead the vast majority of them were hostile to the whole idea of emancipation. They argued that the negroes were not ready to take their place as free citizens, and that a long period of preparation for citizenship must ensue. They instanced the disturbed history of Haiti since the slaves had risen there and with much bloodshed thrown off French rule. All the various uprisings and atrocities by slaves in the West Indies were given as evidence of the negro's unreadiness, and urged in the defence of the continuance of slavery. Above all, there was the economic argument. The abolition of slavery, it was predicted, would plunge

The Anti-Slavery Movement

England's richest colonial possession into ruin.

The British Government, for its part, hesitated to interfere too much in the affairs of the colonies, which had, after all, their own legislatures. Whether these could be overruled to the extent of forcing emancipation on them was open to doubt. The colonial legislatures, moreover, were thoroughly roused. They could see the writing on the wall, but their animosity to anything emanating from the home Government led them to resist or evade every suggestion for ameliorating the condition of the slave. The West Indian planters fought against emancipation much more vigorously than they did against abolition of the slave trade. Perhaps they attributed the success of the abolitionists less to the justice of their cause than to their own failure to resist more strenuously; in which case they were determined not to let it happen again. They hated the humanitarian leaders, and hated them so deeply that they lost sight of the fact that they had behind them the great body of British public opinion. It was this in the end which forced emancipation on the Imperial Parliament.

'If,' as Sir Reginald Coupland has pointed out,[1] 'they had recognized that they were now dealing not with the whims of a few pious fanatics—as they chose to regard the abolitionists—but with the sober good nature of the British people, if they had pocketed their pride and coolly consulted their own interests, if they had set themselves genuinely to improve the lot of their slaves, the end of slavery might have been long postponed. But they did none of these things. They stiffened their necks. They denied the right of anybody in England, of Parliament itself, to interfere in their domestic affairs. They would do what they liked with their own property. To accept suggestions, however gentle, of "amelioration" would be a confession of guilt, and an admission that those detestable busy-bodies knew better how slaves should be treated than they did themselves. The planters' policy was one of flat defiance; and in adopting it they lost their chance of successfully appealing to the inherent caution and fair-mindedness of British public opinion, and on playing on its love of compromise and dislike of violent courses. If they had been wiser, the abolition of slavery would have been none the less sure in the end, but, as the abolitionists themselves expected, it would have been slow. The planters' conduct made it sure and swift.'

The abolitionists began their first campaign, for emancipation through amelioration, with two steps in 1815. First, an address to the Crown was voted by both houses of Parliament asking that the

[1] In his book *The British Anti-Slavery Movement*, p. 13.

Slavery

colonial legislatures be urged to promote the physical, moral and religious improvement of the slaves. 'This means,' said Canning, in a speech intended for the planters' ears, 'you are safe for the present from the interference of the British Parliament, in the belief that left to yourselves you will do what is required of you.'

But they did not. One or two of the colonial legislatures inserted some minor improvements in their slave codes, but nobody in those colonies believed they were meant to be observed.

The abolitionists' second measure was a Bill introduced by Wilberforce for the compulsory registration of all slaves, in order to prevent the illicit importation of new ones—a simple and effective device that had been conceived by James Stephen. It had been applied to Trinidad in 1812, and later to St Lucia, which together with Demerara and Berbice (afterwards united as British Guiana) were Crown Colonies without elected legislative assemblies, and therefore subject to legislation by Order-in-Council. Wilberforce's Bill was fiercely opposed by the planter interests. They denied that there had been any smuggling, and denounced the measure as a wanton violation of their liberties. However, Lord Castlereagh persuaded the Commons, in accordance with the Government's policy, to allow the colonial legislatures to enact the necessary legislation themselves.

This time they did, though only Tobago and Grenada adopted the efficient Trinidad system. The other colonies omitted to make the sale of unregistered slaves illegal—an essential provision—and some of them, notably Jamaica, made little effort to complete or enforce legislation. To frustrate this the Imperial Parliament enacted in 1819 that duplicates of the registers should be lodged in London, and that the sale or mortgage in England of any slave not entered in the register should be invalid.

The abolitionists' activities had violent repercussions in the colonies. The slanderous abuse that was heaped on them had the effect of exciting the slaves. A rumour spread among them that their masters were withholding freedom from them when it had already been granted. In Barbados they rose and did considerable damage on sixty estates. Though they were easily suppressed by troops, several hundred slaves were killed; but no white man. Some of the prisoners were subsequently tried and executed. For the planters, of course, this was further ammunition. They held the abolitionists guilty of having inspired the rising, and pointed out what happened when those incorrigible meddlers in England played with fire.

By 1818 the planters' resistance to reform had led Wilberforce to lose faith in amelioration and decided him to press for outright

The Anti-Slavery Movement

emancipation. Could it now be denied, he said, that the slaves' only hope of betterment lay in Parliament? But at about the same time his health began to fail, and he realized he would have to retire. He did not have to look far, however, for a worthy successor. Among the younger members of Parliament, one of its most effective speakers and a man as devoted as himself to humanitarian causes, was Thomas Fowell Buxton. In 1821 therefore, after consulting James Stephen, Wilberforce wrote to him and asked him to undertake the task of leading the movement in the House of Commons.

Physically the two men could not have been more different. Wilberforce was small and frail, while Buxton was unusually tall and massive. One thing they had in common was that Buxton, like Wilberforce, had lost his father when only a few years old. But a serious view of life was instilled in him at an earlier age than Wilberforce, for his mother, who moulded his character, was a Quakeress. This earnestness of purpose was further strengthened by his intimacy with the Gurney family, who were also Quakers; by his marriage to Hannah Gurney and his friendship with his wife's sister, Elizabeth Fry, and his brother-in-law, Samuel Hoare.

Buxton had entered Parliament in 1818, and had at once thrown himself into the battle for the reform of prisons and the penal code. It was his success in this field that influenced Wilberforce, who had met him through the Gurneys, to invite him to undertake the Parliamentary leadership of the anti-slavery movement. Buxton had been attracted to the movement before, but feeling that it was safe in Wilberforce's hands, he had directed his energies elsewhere. When the call came to accept the mantle from the man he regarded as the best and greatest in public life, he hesitated and pleaded his ignorance of the subject. He promised to study it and give his answer later. For more than a year he applied himself to the matter until by the autumn of 1822 he had made up his mind. He accepted Wilberforce's invitation, and became the chosen parliamentary leader of the abolitionists. They could now begin to plan their second campaign, for outright emancipation.

In 1823 a fresh society was formed, the British and Foreign Anti-Slavery Society. Like the committee of 1785, for the abolition of the slave trade, it had a nucleus of Quakers; but it was bigger, and, unlike the earlier committee, it included many other men prominent in public life. Although Granville Sharp had died ten years before, Wilberforce naturally became a member, and Clarkson at sixty-three was still vigorous. But active control of the organization was in the hands of younger men, and they were unwilling to co-operate with the veterans. The years of delay in bringing about emancipa-

Slavery

tion had made them restless, and they now rose up in such numbers, and with such determined insistence, that the Government had to give attention to them.

The campaign opened with the presentation of a petition from the Quakers in the House of Commons on March 19, 1823. Then on May 15th, Buxton moved that 'the state of slavery is repugnant to the principles of the British constitution and of the Christian religion, and that it ought to be gradually abolished throughout the British colonies with as much expedition as may be found consistent with a due regard to the well-being of the parties concerned.' It could no longer be claimed that slavery was a necessary evil and that it could not be abolished without bringing ruin on the colonies. All that the planters' supporters could ask was that there should be progressive amelioration sliding gradually into freedom, the very course the British Government had offered them a few years before, and which they had so definitely refused.

The Government's mind was now made up, however. Its spokesman, Canning, Foreign Secretary and Leader of the House, denounced the evils of slavery as vigorously as Buxton and declared that the Government intended to abolish it. 'Effectual and decisive measures of amelioration,' he said, 'would be framed, and by determined and persevering, but at the same time judicious and temperate, enforcement of them, abolition would be gradually achieved.' Although Buxton would have preferred something more drastic he withdrew his motion when he saw that the House was with Canning. He also realized that it would not be fair for Parliament to impose emancipation on the planters without giving them one more chance to introduce it themselves. It was necessary, moreover, that the great majority of members of Parliament should become convinced of the wisdom of imposing it. But this process was to take a further ten years.

When the British Government informed the colonial legislatures what reforms it considered necessary, including the prohibition of the use of the whip for driving gangs at work and for punishing female slaves, the reaction was immediate. The planters exceeded all their previous efforts at denouncing interference from England, Jamaica being particularly vehement. One member of its legislature moved a request for the dismissal of the Secretary of State for the Colonies, and another for the secession of Jamaica from the British Empire. Finally, an address was passed declaring that the existing slave code did all that was practically possible to make the slaves 'as happy and comfortable in every respect as the labouring class in any part of the world'. Within a few weeks, however, these 'happy

The Anti-Slavery Movement

and comfortable' slaves were thought by the Government of Jamaica to be plotting an insurrection. Whereupon eleven of them were convicted and hanged on absurdly insufficient evidence.

In Barbados and Demerara, too, the planters' passion ran high, though it vented itself not on the slaves but on the missionaries In Barbados, William Shrewsbury was accused of defaming the planters in his reports to England. His chapel was pulled down and he was forced to leave the colony. In Demerara violent talk among the planters excited the suspicions of the slaves, and the old rumour circulated among them that freedom had been granted to them by the King but was being withheld. Some 13,000 slaves rebelled and locked up the white men on their estates and killed two overseers who resisted them. But there was no looting and no burning of property, and the troops put down the rebellion easily, with the loss of a few hundred lives among the slaves. The restraint of the slaves was due to the influence of John Smith, a missionary of the London Missionary Society; but this did not prevent Smith from being tried for having incited the rebellion—and condemned to death. The decision to execute was referred by the Government to the Colonial Office; but before an answer had been received, Smith died in prison of consumption. Forty-seven of the slaves were convicted and hanged, and others were flogged and imprisoned.

Once again the colonies had refused to do for themselves what was necessary, and had only responded with violence.

Yet the British Government was still not ready to force the issue; though it took definite action in the four Crown colonies. For them, in March 1824, a detailed code of regulations for the treatment of slaves was enacted by Order-in-Council. This provided for a protector of slaves to act for them in legal proceedings and make their evidence admissable in a court of law. It prohibited the use of the whip for driving gangs at work and for the punishment of female slaves, and forbade the breaking up of families by sale. It also facilitated the marriage of slaves and manumission.

As far as the other colonies were concerned, however, they were simply requested to legislate on similar lines; and their reaction was again negative. The legislature of Jamaica rejected the Bill making slave evidence admissible and declared that the time was 'unfavourable for the adoption of any measures interfering with long-established institutions'. The Barbados Assembly did pass a new slave law, but it was so inadequate that it was vetoed by the Colonial Office. Only Tobago, St Vincent and St Kitts enacted laws ameliorating the condition of the slave, and their slave populations were small.

Public opinion in England, meanwhile, had been growing stronger.

Slavery

The treatment accorded to Shrewsbury and Smith, and the insufficiency of the evidence on which slaves were convicted and hanged in Jamaica, had been ventilated in Parliament and in the Press, and it all helped the abolitionists' cause. In the spring of 1826 a petition signed by 72,000 people was presented to Parliament. But no decision was in sight. One more effort was made to get the colonial legislatures to introduce reforms; but once more the suggestion was contemptuously rejected.

The Anti-Slavery Society had been as active as its predecessor in disseminating facts and moulding public opinion, and in 1830 it held a large convention in London. Clarkson fittingly opened the proceedings by moving that Wilberforce be invited to take the chair. 'I may say that this chair,' he said, 'is his natural and proper right in this assembly. He is entitled to it as the great leader in our cause.' Wilberforce in accepting the invitation recalled their long labours together. 'I have been called to take this chair by no person more dear to me than my valued friend and fellow-labourer, for I wish to be known by no other name in this great cause. . . . I cannot but look back to those happy days when we began our labour together, or rather when we worked together (for he began before me), and we made the first step towards that great object, the completion of which is the purpose of our assembly today.'

But before the meeting was over the divergence of opinion between the old guard and the new became apparent. On the platform with Brougham and other political leaders was Buxton. When he moved the usual resolution calling for emancipation 'at the earliest period', the younger and larger part of the audience, ignoring protests against hasty action from the 'elder statesmen', demanded immediate emancipation, and their proposal was carried in a burst of cheering.

The Anti-Slavery Society now launched an intensive campaign, which was kept up throughout 1831 and 1832. For the first time—and it was a startling novelty—women took part. Monster petitions were signed and presented to Parliament. Leading newspapers, hitherto hostile or neutral, began to give their support, and all over the country a battle of posters began, in which the opposing organizations, for and against slavery, vied with each other in obliterating each other's posters with their own. In Parliament, too, the cause was gaining votes, until by the spring of 1832 Buxton felt ready to test his position. He courageously insisted on dividing the House, and though he was beaten by a majority of 136 to 92, the vote for his motion was so substantial that at last the Government agreed to yield and introduce an emancipation Bill.

The Anti-Slavery Movement

The climax to the struggle came in 1833. On April 18th another huge anti-slavery convention was held, in Exeter Hall. From it a delegation was elected to go to the Prime Minister and inform him that the country would no longer brook delay. A month later, on May 14th, the Government published its Bill.

All indirect methods of bringing slavery to an end by amelioration were now finally discarded. The Bill put an end to the long wrangle by providing for the abolition of the legal status of slavery within a year. To minimize the economic dislocation as far as possible all slaves over six years of age were to serve as unpaid apprentices for three-quarters of the working day, while for the remainder they were free to work for wages or not, as they chose. In return the owners were to be compensated for their loss by a loan of £15 million. Buxton and his supporters, however, were opposed to the whole apprenticeship system, and in deference to their wishes the Bill was modified. The period of apprenticeship was reduced, to six years for praedial or field labour, and to four years for non-praedial labour, and the loan of £15 million was made a free gift of £20 million.

The passage of the Bill, which was introduced on July 5th and became law on August 29th, was not without an element of drama. While it was being debated and brought to a successful conclusion, Wilberforce lay dying. The great veteran of the cause died on July 29, 1833. A few days before he had remarked, 'That I have lived to witness a day on which England is willing to give twenty millions sterling for the abolition of slavery'. And at about the same time another veteran, Zachary Macaulay, also died. He was described by Gladstone as 'the unseen ally of Mr Wilberforce and the pillar of his strength'. But these two devoted men had the satisfaction of living to see the victory of their cause.

A year later came the historic moment when emancipation became a fact, at midnight on July 31, 1834. The opponents of emancipation had predicted trouble, that if the slaves were freed they would give themselves up to drunkenness, disorder, insubordination and idleness. But though the occasion was celebrated with great rejoicings, the ex-slaves behaved with commendable decency and order, and obediently accepted the new apprenticeship.

The apprenticeship system did not last long, however, for nobody liked it. In 1836 Joseph Sturge, the founder of the Anti-Slavery Society, visited the West Indies and on his return reported against it. Then in 1838 both Brougham and Buxton declared in favour of bringing it to an end. Had it been necessary a second Act of Parliament would have been passed abolishing the system; but the planters

Slavery

themselves had no liking for it, and by August 1, 1838, all the negroes were completely free.

The effects of slavery in the British colonies, and the subsequent emancipation of the negroes, have been long and enduring. In colonies in which all the land was already under cultivation such as Barbados and Antigua, the freed negroes continued to work on the estates, for wages, as they had done as slaves, and the fall in the production of sugar was consequently slight. But in colonies in which there was much unused land, such as Jamaica, the apprentices preferred to buy or rent plots to cultivate themselves, and thus avoid working on the estates. In such colonies the estates, lacking labour to maintain their state of cultivation, sought to fill the void by bringing in contract labour from overseas. This was resisted by abolitionists like Clarkson, who regarded it as an attempt to revive the slave trade, but they were unsuccessful and the labour flowed in.

At first it came from Madeira; but India was soon found to be a more effective source of supply, and the importation of indentured Indian workers continued for many years, until it was brought to an end after the First World War. Under their contracts the immigrants were entitled to repatriation, but in fact the vast majority of them settled in the West Indies, with the result that their descendants today account for more than half the population of British Guiana and over a third of that of Trinidad. Jamaica imported rather fewer Indians, and there they form only about five per cent of her population.

A further source of contract labour was China, and though such immigration was neither so considerable nor so prolonged as the Indian, it had the effect of adding yet another race to those already assembled in the West Indies, making a total of four major types, European, African, Indian, and Chinese.

For the most part the freed men and women in the West Indies converted themselves with remarkable rapidity into a stable. contented and not unprosperous peasantry. They acquired land wherever they could and lived on the produce of their smallholdings. Marriage became more common and the population began to rise. Their standard of living also rose, and was reflected in their clothing, housing and furniture. In many places they paid for their children's education and subscribed for the building of churches and schoolhouses. The planters admitted the improvement, and when a Parliamentary Committee heard evidence in 1842, most of them spoke highly of all the negroes' qualities except one, their unwillingness to work for wages. According to one of them, the negroes had

The Anti-Slavery Movement

made 'a more rapid advance in the scale of humanity than probably any set of persons ever did in a similar period'. The bitterness which slavery had engendered between the two races, white and black, disappeared and race relations began to improve.

Although this rapid advance of the ex-slaves could scarcely be sustained, there can be no doubt as to the general benefit of emancipation. As Sir Reginald Coupland has written, 'If in some degree this dawn of a new age was a false dawn, if the negroes failed to maintain the heights they reached in the first inspiring years of freedom, nevertheless the general condition of their life and their prospects of future progress remained immeasurably better than in the deadening days of slavery'.

The effects of emancipation were felt, less happily, in two other British colonies, in Mauritius and Cape Colony. The proximity of Mauritius to India enabled its planters to get a regular and adequate supply of Indian contract labour more easily than the West Indian planters. In Mauritius, therefore, Indian labour almost came to supplant African on the estates. Of the 60,000 to 70,000 negro slaves released by emancipation the non-praedials continued to work as artisans for wages, as do their descendants; but the praedials failed to accept the benefits of freedom as successfully as their West Indian brethren. The majority of them even failed to earn a living. but drifted into vagrancy, thieving and destitution.

In Cape Colony emancipation precipitated events, and crystallized attitudes of mind, whose effects are still being felt today. There were at the time some 39,000 slaves in the colony, and the loss of this labour was a heavy blow to their owners. In addition the compensation assessed as payable to them was reduced by half. The British settlers, however unwillingly, at least accepted emancipation, but most of the farmers of Dutch origin found it intolerable. Their Calvanistic religion led them to adhere rigidly to the principle that 'there shall be no equality between white and black in church or state'. In 1835, therefore, thousands of them, seeking to escape British rule, set out on a Great Trek across the Orange river. On the other side of it they established the republics of the Transvaal and the Orange Free State, which lasted until they were defeated in the Boer War at the beginning of the century. But today, unfortunately, the Dutch still adhere to their principle, and harmony in South Africa seems as far from being achieved as ever.

With the abolition of British slavery it might be imagined that its chief architect, Thomas Clarkson, would allow himself well-earned rest. But slavery continued to be tolerated in many of the more progressive nations, in Spain, Brazil and the United States of

Slavery

America. To these countries British abolitionists, Clarkson not least among them, turned their energies. Clarkson took the greatest interest in the fierce struggle for abolition that was going on in the United States, and corresponded regularly with the leaders of the American anti-slavery movement, with Lewis Tappe, William Lloyd Garrison and John Greenleaf Whittier. He took an active part in it with a pamphlet entitled 'A Letter to the Clergy of the Various Denominations and to the Slave-holding Planters in the Southern Parts of the United States of America'.

But his health was failing, and in 1840 he made his last public appearance, at a convention in London organized by the Anti-Slavery Society and attended by 2,000 delegates from all over the world. Clarkson began by presiding, but his poor health prevented him from doing so throughout. In the course of his address he said, 'I was formerly under Providence the originator and am now unhappily the only surviving member of the Committee which was first instituted in this country in the year 1787 for the abolition of the slave trade'. In his tribute to Wilberforce he remarked that 'there never was a man dead or living to whom our cause was more indebted'.

The remaining years of his life Clarkson spent in retirement at Playford Hall, Suffolk, though he continued his benevolent exertions to the end. He died on September 26, 1846. Granville Sharp was the father of the anti-slavery movement and Wilberforce was its public spearhead, but no man laboured more strenuously for it than Thomas Clarkson. He it was who accumulated the vast body of evidence which first stirred the public conscience and then convinced public opinion of the evil of slavery and the need to bring it to an end.

The end of slavery in the French colonies required the devotion of another inspired individual, Victor Schoelcher. We have seen how under the stimulus of the Abbé Gregoire, Brissot, Mirabeau and others of Les Amis des Noirs slavery was abolished, legally though not effectively, in the French colonies in 1794, only to be reintroduced by Napoleon in 1802. The story of slavery in Haiti, France's most important colonial possession, with its negro rebellion of 1791, the uncertain hand of the French home Government, and Napoleon's equally disastrous handling of the island's affairs, was redeemed only by the emergence of Toussaint l'Ouverture, perhaps the greatest negro leader yet to arise. The French slave trade was eventually suppressed in 1831; but slavery was still tolerated until 1848.

The second French anti-slavery movement acquired its future leader in 1823, when Victor Schoelcher, aged twenty-five, read a

The Anti-Slavery Movement

passage from Homer: 'To live in slavery is not to live; it is dying in slow agony.' It was Schoelcher's call. He joined the Committee of Les Amis des Noir, and set out on a tour of the New World which lasted eighteen months. In Cuba, Mexico, Florida and Louisiana he saw the reality of slavery, and on his return to France he resolutely took up the struggle, which was long, unceasing, without compromise, and seemingly without avail.

The French abolitionists' chance did not come until 1848, when revolution broke out in France. Schoelcher was abroad, but he returned at once to France and went to Arago, the Minister for the Navy and the Colonies. An account of their meeting has been left by Arago himself. 'In an interview which we had together today, the 3rd March, 1948, Mr Schoelcher proved to me that it was absolutely necessary to return to the idea of immediate Emancipation. He demonstrated to me that the letter to the Governors of the colonies would not satisfy the slaves, that the vague promise it contained would seem to them a deception and that they would definitely try to take by force what should have been granted them willingly. The arguments of Mr Schoelcher brought complete conviction to my mind, and I resolved to present to my colleagues a decree of immediate Emancipation. I proposed at the same time to appoint Mr Schoelcher as Under-Secretary of State to help me in the great work of emancipation and to set up a Commission of which I would appoint this eminent philanthropist the Chairman, a Commission which would be charged with drawing up all the rules which the free State would make indispensable.'

The French Decree of Formal Emancipation was made on April 27, 1848.

Not long after his main purpose had been achieved Victor Schoelcher had to go into exile, in Belgium and England, for more than eighteen years, from 1851 to 1870. On his return to France, however, he became a senator for life, and put his customary fervour into his work. He died in 1893. In a recent tribute to him, made during an address to the Anti-Slavery Society on July 19, 1956, M. Emmanuel La Gravière remarked, 'If the name of Victor Schoelcher awakens too small an echo in the memories of the people of his mother country, the people overseas recognize his name and know what it signifies; I have seen the eyes of Africans and of West Indians fill with tears when pronouncing it'.

By far the most violent struggle over the issue of slavery was, of course, that in the United States of America, which came near to being disunited because of it. The cleavage that developed between north and south had deep historical roots, not least the puritan

Slavery

tradition of the north. The German Quakers of Pennsylvania, as we have seen, were among the first people to denounce slavery, and in the north anti-slavery sentiment was vigorous. American Quakers kept pace with their English brothers. In the south, however, although there was some anti-slavery feeling, the planters who depended on slaves for their labour, and who had behind them a more proprietary colonial tradition, did not share this view. When the American colonies united to oppose English impositions, the Revolutionary Congress of 1775 declared that, 'No slaves shall be imported into any of the thirteen United Colonies'. By 1778 five States, Rhode Island, Connecticut, Pennsylvania, Delaware and Virginia, had acted on this by passing laws prohibiting the importation of slaves. But the elements of the embryo nation were a long way from yielding much of their sovereignty to any Continental Congress. In 1783 it was still legal for citizens of New England or the Middle States to take part in importing slaves into the plantation States of the South; and there slavery remained as firmly established as in the West Indies.

Another attempt to prohibit the slave trade was made in 1787, when the Convention was held which drafted the federal constitution of the United States. But instead of immediate prohibition being written into the constitution, the chief slave States, South Carolina and Georgia, succeeded in getting it postponed for twenty years. It was enacted that 'the migration or importation of such persons as any of the States now existing think proper to admit shall not be prohibited by Congress prior to the year 1808'.

In the meantime the abolition movement in the north, led by the Quakers, had steadily been gaining strength. One of its most active members was Anthony Benezet (1718-84), the man whose book first inspired Clarkson. He was an exiled Huguenot who had joined the Society of Friends and taken charge of a school in Philadelphia. He published several pamphlets denouncing slavery, and corresponded with Granville Sharp, John Wesley, and the Abbé Raynal. Another valuable pen for the cause was that of Thomas Paine, whose tract on 'African Slavery in America' came out in 1775. Shortly after its publication the first anti-slavery society was founded in Philadelphia.

By March 1807 Congress was able to pass an Act abolishing the slave trade, which became effective on the earliest date permitted by the constitution, January 1, 1808. This, it will be remembered, was the date on which the British abolition Act also came into force. By then all the northern and central States had outlawed the slave trade and several had abolished slavery, too. Even Georgia and South

The Anti-Slavery Movement

Carolina had prohibited the importation of slaves for a while fearing that disaffected slaves from the West Indies might come in and incite a repetition of the slave revolt in Haiti of 1791. But when South Carolina reopened her doors in 1803, nearly 40,000 slaves were landed at Charleston in the course of the next four years.

Further Acts were passed by Congress against the slave trade, in 1818, increasing the penalty for it to imprisonment, and in 1830, declaring it to be piracy and a capital offence. The Act of 1818 also empowered the President to employ the American navy to seize American slavers on the coast of Africa and elsewhere. But neither of these Acts was rigorously enforced; no American was executed under the 1830 Act until 1862. The flow of slaves continued. In 1819 it was estimated that between 13,000 and 15,000 new slaves were entering the United States annually, and even as late as 1860 sixty to seventy cargoes of slaves were stated to have been landed that year.

Until about 1830 the American abolitionist movement, like the British, aimed at gradual abolition. But in 1831 William Lloyd Garrison began to publish his *Liberator*, courageously started without a dollar of capital and under the most inauspicious circumstances. From then on immediate abolition became the cry of the North. Since the foundation of the Union, however, the North had been in a minority in Congress. Of the thirteen original confederating States nine were slave States and only four had abolished slavery in their State constitutions, and had liberated their slaves. Thus the North could not force emancipation on the South. When new territories became ready for admission to the Union as member States, disagreement inevitably arose about whether they should be allowed to be slave-owning or not. At first it was an accepted convention that new States should be admitted in pairs, one slave-owning and the other not; and by 1819 four had been admitted in each category. But the purchase of the vast territory of Louisiana from the French in 1803 raised the problem in acute form.

Under the terms of the treaty of acquisition Louisiana was slave-owning, and was admitted as such in 1812, thus making five new slave-owning States and four non-slave-owning. But when Missouri came to be carved out of it as a separate slave-owning State opposition was vigorous. The dispute was only settled after long delay by the admission of Maine as a balancing State and by what is known as the Missouri Compromise, the drawing of the Mason-Dixon line along latitude 36.30, above which slavery was to be prohibited in the rest of the Louisiana Purchase.

The divergence of North and South was now already clear and

Slavery

though the question of slavery seemed settled for the time the stage was set for the final struggle. Texas was admitted as partially slave-owning in 1845. Then in 1854 the Missouri Compromise was set aside in favour of a more dubious principle of 'squatter sovereignty', under which Kansas and Nebraska were allowed to decide for themselves whether they would be slave-owing or not, in spite of the fact that they were both north of the Mason-Dixon line. This inept decision caused great bitterness, which was further increased by the judgment of the Supreme Court in the Dred-Scott case.

Scott was a slave who had been taken to Nebraska. There he claimed his freedom and the rights of an American citizen. But the Supreme Court, by seven to two, held that no slave or descendant of a slave could be a citizen of the United States. Furthermore, it questioned the validity of the Missouri Compromise. One of the constitutional functions of Congress, it held, was the protection of property, and slaves were recognized as property by the constitution. Most people in the North, of course, took the opposite view, that slaves, in the word of the constitution, were 'persons held to service or labour', and that a major function of Congress was also the protection of liberty.

The last of the incidents that exacerbated feeling was the raid of John Brown. He had been active in Kansas on the side of the anti-slavery movement in the fierce quarrels between the slave and anti-slave factions. In 1859, with a large body of abolitionists and negroes he invaded the nearest slave State and seized one of the United States' arsenals at Harpers Ferry. A United States force proceeded against him and in due course he was tried and hanged Some defend John Brown on the ground that he struck a blow for abolition. Others say that he was mad and that a lunatic asylum should have been his fate rather than the gallows. Whatever the truth, his raid helped to make compromise impossible.

By now the balance of power in the Union had shifted to the North, with its superiority in industry and numbers; and there the work of the abolitionists had successfully roused public opinion. In this one of the most influential works was *Uncle Tom's Cabin* by Mrs Harriet Beecher Stowe. Published in 1852, it exposed the harsh application of the Fugitive Slave Law.

The issue came to a head with the election of 1860. The Republican candidate was Abraham Lincoln. He had a horror of slavery and had plenty to say on the question, but he was not an abolitionist as far as the older Southern States were concerned. His plan was to move slowly towards amelioration of the condition of the slaves, and so to gradual liberation. He was not well known, however, in

The Anti-Slavery Movement

much of the United States, and was scarcely a public character at all. To the Southern mind he appeared from his general remarks on slavery as an arch-leader of abolition. So when he began to talk of the necessity of making State policy subordinate to Federal policy, the Southerners interpreted him to mean that if he were elected President he would force emancipation on them.

His chief opponent was the Democrat Douglas, whose party had already been split by the issue of slavery before the election. Douglas argued that since slavery was lawful throughout the United States under its constitution, each State had the right to continue it or to abolish it without interference from the Federal Government. This, then, was the election issue: whether Federal policy should overrule State policy in the internal affairs of the State, or whether the Federal Government was bound by the powers given to it by each State when the federation was formed. Furthermore, those who championed the State against the Federal power maintained that they had the right to secede if they disagreed and wished to.

When Lincoln was duly elected after the vote was taken on November 6, 1860, the Southern States felt it was time to leave a Union so antipathetic to their own ideas. The legislature of South Carolina had remained in session over the election. It now considered the right of secession, enthusiastically approved it, and on December 20th passed the necessary ordinance. By the following February six other States had taken similar action, and together they set about forming a new confederation. By the spring four more States had joined them, not because they particularly wished to secede, but out of sympathy with the principle of State sovereignty and the right of secession. The final total thus rose to eleven States. The break was complete. Could it or would it ever be healed? And how?

Except among a minority there was no immediate demand for war. Nor was the Republic equipped for it; it was in fact highly disorganized and uncertain. War broke out in the end, not by any deliberate declaration, but through the precipitate action of South Carolina, who resisted the Federal Government's attempt to provision its garrison at Fort Sumter. Feeling on each side soared at once, and it was four years before the country knew peace again, a million men poorer and financially nearly ruined. But with the victory of the North the United States emerged as a single political entity—and a country without slavery.

The Emancipation Proclamation which initiated the ending of it was made by Lincoln on September 2, 1862. It was made, however, less with the object of abolishing slavery than from a desire to

Slavery

preserve the Union. In it Lincoln threatened that unless the revolted States returned to their allegiance by January 1, 1863, their slaves would be declared free. No State returned, so the proclamation was issued. It was, of course, illegal; for the President had no such power. Lincoln is said to have done it to enlist support for his cause. At all events, he later had it validated by a resolution of the two Houses of Congress, which was passed on January 31, 1865. Since then it has been known as the Thirteenth Amendment, and it did indeed abolish the legal status of slavery in the United States. Not three months later the South surrendered, on April 9th, and within a few days Lincoln himself had been assassinated.

Emancipation in most other countries fortunately pursued a less violent course. The example of Great Britain was eventually followed by the other European nations. The Dutch emancipated their slaves in 1863. Portugal passed a law in 1858 which brought slavery to an end twenty years later. All the South American republics, with the exception of Brazil, wrote emancipation into their constitutions as they acquired them between 1810 and 1830, or else passed the necessary Act shortly afterwards. Cuba and Brazil were the last to lose their slave systems. It was not until 1870 that Spain enacted for Cuba a law providing for the gradual extinction of slavery; and the following year Brazil passed a similar measure.

So the sorry tale of slavery is nearly ended. But not quite.

CHAPTER XIII

THE ANTI-SLAVERY SOCIETY

HISTORIANS have pointed out that the attitude of the English people towards slavery changed completely between 1775 and 1800. Before 1775 few people had anything to say against it; through ignorance and apathy the majority of English people tacitly approved of it. But after 1800 the exact reverse was the case. The majority of people were convinced of its evil, and only a few, albeit powerful, individuals tried to defend it. How far was this change due to the growing humanitarianism of the day, and how far to the strenuous activities of the abolitionists?

The answer is probably a bit of both. In the first phase, which ended with the first attempt to secure legislation in the House of Commons, the abolitionists were undoubtedly fighting to make an impression on public opinion; in the second, when their ideas were understood in the wider context of humanitarianism, their function was more to canalise opinion and keep it informed. The purpose of this chapter is to give a fuller account of the organization which served this purpose so faithfully, and which went on to extend its vigilance to every quarter of the world; which it still does today.

There were actually three main societies, but as they succeeded each other, carrying over many of the same committee, they may be regarded as a single developing organization. The first, the anti-slavery society organized by the Society of Friends, lasted from its foundation in 1783 until it was absorbed by Clarkson's Society for the Abolition of the Slave Trade, which was founded on May 22, 1787. The difference between the two was mainly in the broader base and stronger purpose of the second. Right from its inception it was intended as an instrument to achieve a desired end. Besides the work of disseminating information in order to mould opinion, which was the Quakers' original aim, it was concerned with the more painstaking task of gathering the necessary body of irrefutable facts, with which its Parliamentary leader, Wilberforce, could present his case.

Clarkson's own contribution to this was strenuous. After his first

Slavery

tour of the slave ports, he made another in August 1788, to get additional evidence to lay before the Privy Council trade committee. On this tour he recorded that although he talked with forty-seven persons who had useful information, only nine would give him any. It was a busy time for the Society: Clarkson mentions that 'between May 1787 and July 1788 the Society held fifty-one meetings and printed and distributed no less than 51,430 pamphlets and books, besides 26,526 reports, accounts of debates in Parliament and other small papers'. Much of the writing and preparation of this material naturally fell on Clarkson's shoulders.

The work reached its peak in 1790, when a Select Committee of the House of Commons was appointed to hear evidence on the slave trade. A lot of this was marshalled and presented through the efforts of the Society, and at the conclusion of its proceedings Clarkson prepared his famous *Abridgement*. At about this time, too the Society acquired its seal. This was designed by Josiah Wedgwood, the famous potter and philanthropist, and represented a negro slave bound with chains and kneeling in a suppliant position. The inscription read, 'Am I not a man and a brother?'

After April 1791, when Wilberforce made his first, and unsuccessful, attempt to get an abolition motion through the House, and when Clarkson's health gave way under his labours, the work of the Society in England came to a temporary end. But although it had failed to achieve its purpose in Parliament, it had done its work outside. And its members were far from idle during this lull, one of their activities being the promotion of the Sierra Leone Company.

As early as 1787 Granville Sharp had been troubled about the poverty of the liberated negroes in England. With the help of some others he now organized a settlement for them in Sierra Leone. To manage it the Sierra Leone Company was incorporated in 1791 and an area of land on the coast was bought from an African chief. There Freetown was established, with the idea of making it a trading centre for African products. The British Government assisted with the transportation of the English negroes and the following year another influx was organized, of ex-slaves from Canada, who had fled there from the north American colonies. Their passage to Africa was accomplished in fifteen ships under the supervision of Clarkson's naval brother, Lieutenant John Clarkson. During the long voyage, with all the hazards and trials of the sea at the time, only sixty-five died, and the convoy arrived in Sierra Leone in March 1792 with 1,131 negroes. Lieut. Clarkson was then appointed Governor of the little colony of Freetown by the directors of the Sierra Leone Company. Although this company was not actually

The Anti-Slavery Society

organized by the Abolition Society as such, so many of its members were active in it that it was virtually an offshoot of the main society. Granville Sharp was its president and Wilberforce a director; and a later Governor of Freetown was Zachary Macaulay, another active abolitionist.

When the Society again took up its campaign at home in 1804, it was only three years before its object was achieved. The hard battering at an indifferent public or House of Commons was no longer necessary, and a sustained, skilful political effort won the day.

With the abolition of the slave trade in British possessions the Society could turn to its abolition elsewhere, and, at last, the greater object of abolishing slavery altogether. It began by trying to get Europe to outlaw the slave trade as piracy, and by working for the amelioration of slavery in the British colonies. But with the resignation of Wilberforce and the assumption of the parliamentary leadership by Buxton in 1822, the Society underwent a reorganization and adopted a new name to indicate its changed purpose. The new society, the British and Foreign Anti-Slavery Society, founded in 1823, had, in addition to its core of Quakers, the support of a large number of public men. Its first President was H.R.H. the Duke of Gloucester, who had spoken in the House of Lords in support of the Bill abolishing the slave trade, and among its Vice-Presidents were five members of the House of Lords and fourteen of the Commons. On its Committee were many members of the old guard, Clarkson and Wilberforce, of course, Thomas Babington, John Stephen and William Smith, and now Buxton and Henry (afterwards Lord) Brougham. Its first secretary was J. H. Tredgold.

As soon as the Society was formed, Clarkson, now sixty-three, went on a long tour through England to make it known and encourage the establishment of branches in provincial centres. As a result an ever increasing number of petitions began to flow towards Westminster. In 1823, 225 were delivered, and in the following year nearly 600. There was, at the same time, a continuous output of literature; the most important pamphlet being the 'manifesto' with which the campaign for amelioration was superseded by the campaign for emancipation by Parliament.

An even more effective instrument of propaganda, which the Society was now strong enough in personnel and funds to forge, was the *Anti-Slavery Reporter*. It first appeared in 1823, and is still being published today. From 1825 its editor was Macaulay, and in his hands it proved to be a regular arsenal of up-to-date facts which could be relied upon, because they had been collected, or at least

Slavery

reviewed, by an editor who was known to be as scrupulous as he was indefatigable. It was freely admitted that 'whatever Macaulay says may be taken for gospel and quoted'.

From 1823 onwards, therefore, public opinion was subjected year by year to a continuous barrage, until its pressure convinced Parliament of the need for drastic legislation. The Society's great meeting of 1830 began the final push. The intensive campaign of 1831-2, run mainly by George Stephen and three Quakers, Emmanuel and Joseph Cooper and Joseph Sturge, sent speakers to lecture all over the country. Within a year the number of affiliated societies rose from 200 to 1,300. In all this activity women played an important part, two being responsible for one of the largest petitions, signed by 187,000 people. The climax to the campaign came with the Exeter Hall meeting on April 18, 1833, and the publication within a month of the Government's Bill. When this became law on August 19th of that year the decision wrung from the Lord Chief Justice by Granville Sharp sixty-six years before, that 'whoever sets foot on English soil is free', was finally extended to all parts of the world where British rule prevailed.

The Society was now free to attack slavery in foreign countries. In 1840 it gathered to its Convention in London delegates from all over the world. This great occasion has been given permanent record in a painting by Benjamin Haydon which hangs in the National Portrait Gallery in London. It contains no less than 138 portraits, ranging from careful studies of the delegates on the platform to indistinct outlines of members of the audience.

The attention of the anti-slavery movement was focused primarily on East Africa and Arabia, and it was anxiously watching the treaty-making efforts of the British Government to stop it. As these were proving of doubtful success, the Society held another large meeting in London, in 1872, to maintain the pressure of public opinion. It was held, by permission of the Lord Mayor, in the Mansion House, and its outcome was the Government's decision to send Sir Bartle Frere to the Sultan of Zanzibar to negotiate a more decisive treaty. But in the event this too proved unsuccessful.

Africa, meanwhile, was rapidly being taken over by the European powers, with two paradoxical results from the point of view of slavery. On the one hand it enabled the European powers to put an end to the slave trade from East Africa, but on the other it gave rise to a fresh and scandalous form of exploitation in the Belgian Congo. In both these developments the Anti-Slavery Society played an important part. Thanks mainly to the efforts of Mr Sydney (later Earl) Buxton, a member of its Committee, it helped to bring about

The Anti-Slavery Society

the Brussels Conference of 1890, which led to the Brussels Act of 1890, and it helped to fight the evil state of affairs in the Belgian Congo.

The Congress of Berlin of 1885 had confirmed the partition of Africa and created the Kingdom of the Congo, of which Leopold II of the Belgians was recognized as the king. With the declared object of uplifting the backward inhabitants of Africa, Leopold founded the International African Association and sent Stanley on a tour of the Congo. Stanley returned with a batch of treaties with African chiefs inviting the International African Association to come in and usher in civilization. So far the intentions of the European powers towards the Africans were nothing but benevolent. But the Act of the Berlin Congress which gave Leopold complete administrative control over this large area of Africa also allowed him to create and arm an African force for the avowed purpose of putting down the Arab slave trade and to disarm the people of the Congo. By this means a tool of oppression was forged, and the Africans were left defenceless.

For a few years all went well, but in 1890 trouble began The principle was established that the Africans had no right to the land outside their own gardens and villages, nor to its products. The produce of the land was declared to be the property of the Government. This conception was carried so far that Africans who collected it for sale to white men were denounced as poachers and the white men who bought it as receivers of stolen goods. 'The native is entitled to nothing,' said one Prime Minister of Belgium, and the phrase became a system. Force was substituted for administration and the main object became the pillage of the natural wealth of the Congo to enrich Belgian interests. Villages were ordered to produce a fixed amount of rubber every week, and if they failed to do so soldiers were sent to capture their women, children and old men to be held as hostages until the required rubber was produced. But the treatment did not stop there. The women were raped and villages were looted and set on fire. Every form of brutality was practised. Soldiers brought back human hands to be checked against cartridges expended. Women and children were crucified and villages were hung with the intestines and sexual organs of slaughtered males. The population of the Congo during this period of terror is said to have been reduced by twelve million.

The remoteness of the Congo meant that it was some time before news of this ghastly story reached Europe. It was not until 1897 that a Swedish missionary, the Rev. E. N. Sydblom, addressed a letter to the Anti-Slavery Society describing its horrors. But as a result the

Slavery

Congo Reform Association was founded by a member of the Society, Mr E. D. Morel, who worked for it for nine and a half years. The Society worked in close connection with the Association, and a later secretary of the Society, Mr (afterwards Sir) John Harris who had been a missionary in the Congo and an eye-witness of some of the horrors, with his wife, Mrs (now Lady) Alice S. Harris, was active in publicising them. Opinion was roused, Parliament debated the matter, and King Leopold was compelled to invite an international commission, composed of three judges, a Belgian, an Italian and a Swiss, to go out in 1904-5 to investigate it.

When the Commission reported to the King it was some time before he would allow its findings to be published. But it leaked out that in ten years the King and his associates had made three million pounds profit. Public opinion was incensed. The King continued to defy it; but the Powers signatory to the Berlin Act of 1885, led by Britain and the United States, forced him to surrender his personal control of the Congo. It was vested instead, in 1908, in the Belgian people and Parliament. Since then reforms have been instituted, and another hideous chapter in African exploitation, all the more hideous for its supposedly humanitarian beginnings, was ended. The Belgian administration of the Congo is now economically one of the most progressive in Africa.

In 1905 there were two developments in the Society's affairs; women were admitted to membership of the committee, and it moved its premises. The old offices which it had long occupied were at 55 New Broad Street in the City of London. From there it moved to Denison House, 296 Vauxhall Bridge Road, London, where it remains today. The old offices were subsequently demolished. At this time the Society had H.M. King Edward VII as its Patron, and as President, Sir Thomas Fowell Buxton, GCMG, the son of the famous emancipator. Its Secretary was Mr Travers Buxton, who took over the office in 1898 and held it until he was succeeded by Mr John Harris in 1910. Mr Buxton thereafter became a Vice-Chairman of the Committee and did long and faithful service for the Society, which did not cease with his death; for he left it a legacy of £1,200.

In 1909 the Society underwent another change of name. It absorbed by amalgamation the Aborigines Protection Society, and became known as the Anti-Slavery and Aborigines Protection Society. The Aborigines Protection Society had been founded in 1837 mainly through the efforts of the emancipator, the first Sir Thomas Fowell Buxton, and Thomas Hodgkin, 'to assist in protecting the defenceless and promoting the advancement of uncivilized

The Anti-Slavery Society

(i.e. backward) tribes'. But for long the work of the two organizations had overlapped, and when the Secretary of the Aborigines Protection Society, Mr H. R. Fox Bourne, died in 1909, it was felt that amalgamation would make for economy of effort and money. Mr Travers Buxton remained as Secretary of the joint organization, but in 1910 Mr J. H. Harris and his wife, Mrs Alice S. Harris, became the Organizing Secretaries.

The next big scandal to require the immediate energies of the Society came in 1909. In that year Mr E. Hardenburg, a civil engineer, arrived in London with a manuscript containing an account of his experiences at Putomayo in Peru. There, he maintained, the Peruvian Amazon Rubber Company, a company registered in England, was enslaving American Indians to gather rubber for them from the forests. Although he offered his manuscripts to several London publishers, all refused to touch it for fear of possible libel actions. The editor of *Truth*, however, was bolder. He published extracts from Hardenburg's story, and these showed that it was once again the desire to obtain the greatest production in the shortest time at the least possible expense that had led to the virtual enslavement of the Indians. The Company operated a system under which they advanced European goods to the Indians, who then became the Company's debtors, forced to pay off the debt in rubber. As the debts were transferable they became saleable assets, and with the sale went the right to the body of an Indian. In other words it was a form of debt-bondage. To enforce it the Company maintained a corps of armed men, and in 1910 owned Winchester rifles to the value of £1,700.

These allegations drew no comment from the London Office of the Company, but public interest increased and would not let the matter rest. Two enquiries were therefore set on foot, one by the company and the other by the British Government. The Government of Peru, strangely enough, was unmoved, and even ignored a resolution by the Peruvian Senate calling for an inquiry. The evidence gathered by the British, submitted to a Select Committee of the House of Commons, disclosed monstrous labour conditions, which were later described by the Court as 'indistinguishable from slavery'. It was a system of outrage and robbery; the Indians had everything taken from them and finally their bodies were hunted in the forests.

The winding up of the Company, and hence the end of their pernicious activities, was finally brought about by the Anti-Slavery Society. The Chairman of the Select Committee of the House of Commons was Mr Charles Roberts, MP, who was also Chairman of

Slavery

the Committee of the Anti-Slavery Society. Armed with a Speaker's Warrant he entered the office of the Peruvian Amazon Rubber Company, seized their books and carried them off to Westminster. This provided the necessary evidence to justify winding up the Company. In March 1913 a small group of the Company's shareholders gave the Society the necessary power to do so. An application was made to the Court, which was granted, and the Company was liquidated.

The formation of the League of Nations began another chapter in the activities of the Anti-Slavery Society, quite as strenuous as many previous ones. It first became concerned in the League's affairs when the chapter of the Covenant of the League dealing with backward territories was being drafted. The Principal Allied Powers invited the President of the Society, Sir Victor Fowell Buxton, and its Secretary, Sir John Harris, to assist them. Unfortunately, Sir Victor Fowell Buxton died from injuries received in a motor-car accident before he could go to Versailles. But a member of the Committee, Lord Henry Cavendish Bentinck, was appointed to go in his place. The outcome of the deliberations in which he and Sir John Harris took part was the establishment of the Mandates system.

On the general subject of slavery, however, the League was to prove lethargic. Once founded it was continually lobbied by the Anti-Slavery Society to get it to make a Slavery Convention. But this was not done until 1926; the final Convention being based largely on information supplied by the Society. Next, the Society pressed for machinery to enforce it. From its experience of the Brussels Act of 1890, the Society knew that the most effective method was to set up a Slavery Bureau and a system of patrols. But the League could not be persuaded even to examine the proposal until six years after its Convention had been made.

The Society's campaign continued to be an uphill one. The League had convened a Temporary Slavery Commission in 1922; but it remained temporary. By 1931 it needed all the insistence of the British delegate to the League's Assembly, Mr Charles Roden Buxton, MP, a Vice-Chairman of the Anti-Slavery Society, to persuade the League to reconvene its Commission; and the Society had to raise the necessary funds for it. However, the Society was asked to give its views on what modifications, if any, were needed in the League's machinery for the abolition of slavery. They recommended the establishment of a Standing Committee of Experts on Slavery to advise the League; and this was duly formed. The most tangible result of the Society's efforts during this period was probably the abolition of slavery in Nepal and the Sierra Leone Protectorate in 1924, due largely to the efforts of Sir John (later Lord) and Lady Simon.

The Anti-Slavery Society

In the remaining years up to the outbreak of the Second World War the Society continued its work, with the League and independently. It was concerned particularly with Ethiopia, the last remaining Christian country to tolerate slavery. In 1933 it sent a deputation there consisting of Lord Noel-Buxton and Lord Polwarth. They were received by the Emperor Haile Selassie II, who promised that he would abolish slavery within fifteen years. And so he did, legally, when he regained his throne in 1942.

The year 1933 was also the centenary of the abolition of slavery in the British colonies. The Society naturally celebrated in suitable style, and to mark the event Sir John Harris wrote *A Century of Emancipation*.

The coming of war necessarily put an end to anti-slavery work, though the Society never ceased to function. 1940 saw the death of Sir John Harris, suddenly from a heart attack. He had been Secretary for thirty years, and no one who held that office did more for the Society than he. His death was deeply regretted, and as a tribute to his memory a fund was opened, to which about £2,800 was subscribed. The Sir John Harris Fund, as it was named, was to finance research and any special aims of the Society.

One of Sir John's principal assistants was another distinguished member of the Society, Lady Kathleen Simon, the wife of Sir John (later Viscount) Simon, and the author of a classic book on slavery. She was led to join the Society by the memory of her early life in Tennessee, in which she lived with her first husband, Mr. Manning, where the racial discrimination that remained as the aftermath of slavery had made a deep impression on her. She was an attractive speaker and for many years drew large audiences, from which she seldom failed to recruit one or two new members for the Society. She also collected money for the Society. Before she died in 1955 she handed over £4,350, all of which she had collected herself. Besides her own valuable services to the anti-slavery movement she kindled the interest of her husband and drew him into it, until Lord Simon became almost as ardent a supporter of the cause as she herself. He rendered the Society many valuable services, and the death of them both within fifteen months of each other was a great loss. Lady Simon was a President of the Society and Lord Simon a Vice-President.

My own term of office with the Society began in 1941, when I succeeded Sir John Harris as Secretary. As I am West Indian by birth, a retired colonial official, and as the war prevented any anti-slavery work, the early years of my service were devoted to efforts to improve condition in the British colonies.

Slavery

One of the first matters to need the Society's attention in this period was the diversion of funds from West Africa into the coffers of the United Kingdom. At the outbreak of war the British Government had assumed by law the sole right to buy all West African cocoa. In the first and second years of the war there was a loss on its purchases and sales of this valuable commodity, but thereafter there was a substantial profit each year. The Anti-Slavery Society heard of this, and heard, furthermore, that these profits were being put into the general revenue of the United Kingdom. Representations were made to the Government pointing out that West African producers of cocoa had been deprived of the right to sell in the best market, and if there was a profit it should be returned to West Africa. As a result of our pressure the Government agreed to this. They promised that the net profits on the sale of cocoa would be returned to the territories concerned, and eventually about six million pounds was returned in this way. It was used to finance the Gold Coast and Nigeria Cocoa Marketing Schemes, the capital funds of which now amount to nearly a hundred million pounds.

Shortly afterwards the Society was able to help in another part of Africa. The Paramount Chief of Swaziland, Sobhurwa II, informed the Society that thousands of his people were landless, and were wandering about in a destitute condition. The Society arranged a deputation to the Minister responsible, Mr C. R. (now Lord) Attlee, which put forward a suggestion that land should be bought with a grant from the Colonial Development and Welfare Fund and the Swazis settled on it. The suggestion was taken up, and the scheme has proved on of the greatest successes in land resettlement in the Commonwealth, 27,000 landless Swazis being provided for in this way.

The end of the war brought further changes in the Society's personnel, though family connections with it remained remarkably strong. In 1946 Mr Charles Roberts retired from the Chairmanship of the Committee and was succeeded by Mr Henry Tapscott. Mr Tapscott had been Treasurer for several years, and under his wise care the Society's investments had increased considerably in value. Before Mr Tapscott took it over the office of Treasurer had been held by two successive members of the Brooks family, into which Mr Tapscott had married. He had succeeded his father-in-law, Mr Alfred Brooks, who in his turn had succeeded his father, Mr Edward Wright Brooks. Now another member of the family, Mr Basil Brooks, Mr Tapscott's brother-in-law, took over. Unfortunately, a few years afterwards Mr Basil Brooks was killed in an aeroplane disaster. But the family tradition remained unbroken. He was succeeded by his

The Anti-Slavery Society

elder son, Mr Edward Brooks, thus making four generations of the family to serve in the office of Treasurer. Several other families connected with the Society's early days are still represented on the Committee. There are still Wilberforces and Buxtons, and there is still a Samuel Hoare (Lord Templewood). Until recently there was a Tredgold, and there is still a Thomas Hodgkin. And the generosity of the Society's members, in service and money, remains as strong as ever. In 1950 Miss Beatrice Allen, daughter of the late Mr Charles Allen, a former Secretary of the Society, left it half of her fortune, amounting to about £4,000.

With the foundation of the United Nations Organization, the Society turned again to pursuing international objectives. As with the League of Nations, the first step, amidst the end-of-war confusions, was to try to interest it in the subject of slavery at all. In 1946 the Committee of the Society sent its Secretary to New York, to the headquarters of the United Nations. But he met with little response. Two years later, he made more headway, when he attended the General Assembly of the United Nations in Paris in 1948. He won the support of the Belgian delegate, Professor F. de House, and the French delegate, Professor René Cassin, and they introduced a resolution requesting the Economic and Social Council of the United Nations to study slavery. This was carried, and the Council appointed an *ad hoc* Committee of Experts on Slavery.

A matter the Society was particularly anxious to have settled was the amendment of the 1926 Convention on Slavery, which experience had shown to be deficient. It was now possible to achieve this through the *ad hoc* Committee, of which I was a member. It sat in 1950 and 1951, and one of the results of its deliberations was the making of the Supplementary Convention on Slavery of 1956.

To-day the strength and prestige of the Society is as high as ever. In 1950 it applied for, and was granted, consultative status to the Economic and Social Council of the United Nations. Supporting the Society's application, Britain informed the United Nations that it regarded the Society as the only effective voluntary organization working for the abolition of slavery and that it had helped H.M. Government form its policy on slavery over a long period of time. Each year since then, whenever slavery has been on its agenda, the Society has sent a representative to the spring session of the Economic and Social Council.

The present Secretary of the Society is Commander Thomas Fox Pitt, also a retired colonial official, who took over from me in 1955, on my retirement and appointment as Director. He bears two names famous in anti-slavery endeavour.

Slavery

In the course of its history the Society has attracted the services of many distinguished men and women, and much more might be written about them. That they have not worked in vain is certain; but the cause still needs serving. Although the Society's pioneering days are long since past, and its activities today are inevitably less stirring, they are none the less necessary, and will continue to be until that time, still an unpredictable way off in the future, when all men are free, and known to be free, everywhere in the world.

CHAPTER XIV

INTERNATIONAL ACTION
BEFORE THE LEAGUE OF NATIONS

୧୨

PRIOR to the Congress of Vienna, held in 1815, there was no collective international agreement or action to abolish the slave trade, still less slavery itself. Until then Britain had led the way in making treaties to control it; and she continued to do so. Beginning with her treaty with Tripoli of 1622, designed to protect British subjects from enslavement by the Barbary pirates, the British Foreign Office has been engaged constantly in anti-slavery treaty making. During the hundred years following the abolition of the slave trade in British possessions, nearly six hundred treaties and international instruments were concluded by successive British governments. Eighty of them were with Portugal alone.[1] That they were directed mainly against the slave trade reflects the astonishing fact that it was many years before any international statesman grasped that slave-trading could not be suppressed until slave-owning was also abolished.

With the Congress of Vienna slavery and the slave trade were forced upon international consciousness for the first time, though very reluctantly. Shortly before in August 1814, the Duke of Wellington had proposed to Talleyrand that an agreement should be suggested at the Congress in which the contracting parties granted each other reciprocal rights of search of merchant vessels suspected of carrying slaves north of the Equator. But Talleyrand utterly refused to consider it, on the grounds that it would be an infringement of sovereignty. This was, indeed, the general feeling of the continental statesmen, who regarded the abolition of slavery as a strange British obsession rather than a subject about which practical statesmen could be expected to concern themselves seriously. The principal British delegate, Lord Castlereagh, had been won to the cause by Wilberforce, and the Czar Alexander of Russia, who had been won by Clarkson, was full of idealism and support. It had been

[1] For a full account of Britain's efforts the reader must be referred to *The Cambridge History of British Foreign Policy* (Vol. II, Ch. VI). *A Century of Emancipation*, p. 217.

Slavery

hoped that a fully-fledged charter of abolition might have been obtained from the Congress, outlawing slave-trading as piracy; but the majority of the powers were only willing to denounce it, without being prepared to agree to any sanctions against it.

The Declaration which emerged from the Congress represented in fact little more than a pious hope, though even this was progress. The principle of abolition was accepted. The Declaration, signed by eight powers, Austria, France, Great Britain, Portugal, Prussia, Russia and Sweden, stated that 'the commerce known by the name of the slave trade (Traite des Negres d'Afrique) has been considered by just and enlightened men in all ages as repugnant to the principles of humanity and universal morality, and at length the public voice in all civilized countries calls aloud for its prompt suppression ... and several European governments have virtually come to the resolution of putting a stop to it'. But it could not 'prejudge the period that each particular Power may consider as most advisable for the definitive abolition of the slave trade'.[1]

The Declaration was renewed in 1822 by a similar Declaration signed at Verona on November 28, by Austria, France, Great Britain, Prussia and Russia.

By 1870, by one means or another, the main hopes of the abolitionists at the Congress of Vienna were realized and slavery in the West, and hence the need for a slave trade, had come to an end. But between 1830 and 1870 a large number of treaties concerned with this branch of the trade were concluded. Though none of them was particularly effective, the most important were the Treaty of London of 1841 and the Treaty of Washington of 1862.

The Treaty of London was an effort to stamp out the remnants of the trade as carried on by European powers. It provided that any vessel flying the flag of the contracting parties engaged in conveying slaves on the high seas, should lose the protection of that flag. Furthermore, it authorized warships of any of the signatory powers to arrest such ships and search them. If they were found to be conveying slaves, they were to be handed over to the appropriate tribunal of the country to which the arrested ship belonged. This treaty was signed by Austria, Great Britain, Prussia, Russia, and by France, though France never ratified the treaty.

The Treaty of Washington, between Great Britain and the United States of America, executed in the midst of the Civil War after Lincoln's Emancipation Proclamation, was of a similar nature, and was directed against the importation of slaves by the Southern

[1] The full text of this Declaration may be found in Hertslet's *Map of Europe by Treaty*, Vol. II, No. 7, p. 60.

International Action before the League of Nations

States. The two countries granted each other a reciprocal right of search of ships suspected of conveying slaves on the high seas; and it provided for adjudication by a mixed court composed of an equal number of judges of each nation, appointed by their respective governments.

Various powers entered into a number of other treaties giving similar reciprocal rights of search.[1] But most of them, of course, have since been either formally abrogated or recognized as obsolete.

The slave trade to the East, however, was a tougher problem, not yet solved today. At first treaties were attempted in this area also, but with little success, and it was not until some form of international control was instituted that the trade was all but wiped out; only to revive when the control was removed. The need for effective patrolling unfortunately remains.

The first treaty concerned the slave-exporting towns on the East African coast, which had been established long before by colonists from Oman. It was found that the Sultan of Oman had an ill-defined right of sovereignty over them, and in 1822, he was persuaded to sign a treaty in which he agreed to prohibit 'all external traffic in slaves', and in particular the sale of slaves to Christians. But the treaty was not easy to enforce. The slaves were conveyed in small dhows, which could hide in creeks by day, and slip out at night, to continue on their way in the darkness. Attention was therefore transferred to Zanibar, which was known to be an entrepot for a large number of slaves en route from East Africa to the Middle East.

A treaty was successfully negotiated with the Sultan of Zanzibar in 1845, by which he agreed to prohibit the export of slaves from all his African dominions. But again, it was only a treaty. Fleets of little dhows from South Arabia continued to bear down on Zanzibar with the southward monsoon in December, and in spite of all the British cruisers could do, they collected their cargoes of slaves and slipped off for home with the northward monsoon in April.

Further treaties were negotiated later by Sir John Kirk, who was appointed British Consul in Zanzibar in 1866. He had gone out to Africa with Livingstone, whose exploration and writings did so much to expose the extent and cruelty of the traffic in slaves. Dr Kirk, as he was then, was a scientist of distinction and a man of singular charm. Besides his dominating personality, he had a fluent command of Arabic and a sound knowledge of Mohammedan law, all of which soon enabled him to acquire great influence with the

[1] Their titles may be found in the *British and Foreign State Papers*, Vol. II, 6, pp. 91, 118, 161 and 196; and in the *League of Nations Treaty Series*, 1-39, p. 816.

Slavery

Sultan of Zanzibar, Syed Barghash. At that time the Sultan was a wealthy, powerful, and independent potentate exercising a claim to rule as far as the Great Lakes of Africa. Sir John Kirk managed to get him to sign two treaties with Great Britain, in 1873 and 1876, the first forbidding the export of slaves from his territories, and the second prohibiting their transport to the coast.

Even these treaties, however, were only partially successful, and the Arab slave trade with Zanzibar did not really come to an end until Zanzibar became a British Protectorate in 1897. But today the slave trade is finally exorcized, for a cathedral stands where the slave market used to be.

Similar treaties were made with the Sheikhs of the Persian Gulf between 1838 and 1847, with the Shah of Persia in 1851, and with the Somali chieftains in 1855 and 1856. But they proved to be of little avail, and the ultimate lesson of the long fight with the Arab slave trade in East Africa was that it could not be completely suppressed by treaties. This could only be achieved either by the cessation of the demand for slaves at the import end, or by stopping it at its main source of supply in Africa. As regards the first alternative the demand for slaves still continued in Arabia. As regards the second, when the European powers engaged in their sweeping annexations of territory in Africa in the eighties, the position was completely transformed.

The 'scramble for Africa' was conducted at such high speed that by the end of the nineteenth century, only Morocco, Tripoli, Egypt, the Sudan, Abyssinia and Liberia had not been subjected to European occupation. All the slave-owning African kingdoms, whether Moslem, as in French West Africa and Nigeria, or pagan, like Benin, Ashanti and Matabele, fell before the arms of the new rulers of Africa. The European powers could not stop the demand for slaves in Asia, but they could now stop the export of slaves from Africa. King Leopold II of the Belgians had organized his International African Association for exploring and civilizing Africa in 1876, and had sent H. M. Stanley to open up the Congo area in 1879. To settle the newly arisen problems of central Africa an important conference was held in Berlin in 1885, the Berlin Congo Conference. The resulting convention, the General Act of Berlin of 1885, signed by seventeen states, was the second important step in collective international action against slavery.

The area to which this convention applied was the whole geographical region of the Congo. This included the basin of the Congo and defined areas watered by the Loge, Zambesi, Ogowe, the Nile and the Niger, and Lake Tanganyika. The declared aims of the Con-

International Action before the League of Nations

vention, all of which became matters of international concern, were freedom of trade in the area, protection of native rights and interests, future occupations on the coast of Africa, navigation of the rivers, the encouragement of missionary endeavour, and the suppression of slavery.

The particular articles concerned with slavery were Articles 6 and 9. Article 6 was general in tone, and read: 'All Powers exercising rights of sovereignty or influence in the said territories engage themselves to watch over the conservation of the indigenous populations and the amelioration of their moral and material conditions of existence and to strive for the suppression of slavery and especially of the Negro slave trade.'

Article 9 was more specific and made definite demands on the signatory powers. It read: 'Seeing that trading in slaves is forbidden in conformity with the principles of international law, as recognized by the signatory Powers, and seeing also that the operations which, by sea or land, furnish slaves to the trade ought likewise to be regarded as forbidden, the Powers which do or shall exercise sovereign rights or influence in the territories forming the conventional basin of the Congo declare that these territories may not serve as a market or way of transit for the trade in slaves of any race whatever. Each of these Powers binds itself to employ all means at its disposal for putting an end to this trade and for punishing those who engage in it.'

This Convention, the General Act of the Berlin (Congo) Conference of 1885, to give it its full title, is still in force.

The next two conferences on African affairs were held in rapid succession, in 1889 and 1890. That of 1889 was held in Belgium and resulted in her being assigned the Congo Free State, as it was named, and a declaration 'to help in suppressing slavery and the slave trade within the area covered by the General Act of the Conference'. That of 1890 was the far more important Brussels Conference convened by King Leopold. Its object, once again, was 'to put an end to the crimes and devastations engendered by traffic in African slaves'. But this time, the third international drive, a really comprehensive convention was produced.

The Brussels Conference of 1890, though formally convened by Leopold, came about largely through the perseverance of the Anti-Slavery Society; and in particular, the efforts of a member of its Committee, Mr Sidney Buxton, in the House of Commons. In March 1899, Mr Buxton proposed a motion suggesting such a conference, and during the debate the results that might be hoped from it were clearly formulated. Speakers were concerned that slave-trading

Slavery

should be outlawed, and declared similar to piracy, that all nations should allow the mutual right of search of ships suspected to be carrying slaves, that the status of slavery should no longer be recognized by international law, and that the import of arms into Central Africa should be restricted. Most of these points were incorporated in the Brussels Convention.

The Conference was attended by the representatives of seventeen nations. In addition to the whole of Europe, the United States of America, Turkey, Persia, and Zanzibar all signed the resulting convention of 1890, and ratified it in 1892. The dominant influence in the framing of the Convention, which has been called the Magna Carta of the African slave trade, was widely known to be that of Sir John Kirk, the British plenipotentiary.

The detailed provisions of this magnificent weapon against the slave trade were contained in 100 articles, divided into seven chapters. The first chapter dealt with the actual capture of slaves. It laid down the practical measures that were to be taken by the signatory powers who exercised authority in the countries where such capture might take place. The first Article recognized that the most effective means of counteracting the slave trade in the interior of Africa lay in the progressive organization of administrative and other civil and military services in the territory; in the improvement of communications and means of transportation, the restriction of firearms, and in the establishment in the interior of occupied military stations to prevent the capture of slaves and to intercept caravans, as well as to organize mobile expeditions.

In other articles of the first chapter the contracting parties confirmed their former declarations and agreed to do all they could to repress the slave trade. The legal measures they were required to take included laws to bring within their penal provisions relating to grave offences against the person 'the organizers and abettors of slave-hunting, those mutilating male adults and children, and all persons taking part in the capture of slaves by violence'. Laws were also to be enacted to bring within penal provisions relating to offences against individual liberty 'carriers and transporters of, and dealers in slaves'. Provisions for the welfare and repatriation of liberated or fugitive slaves were also accepted, and finally a group of articles contained provisions regarding the prohibition of the import of firearms into territories in Africa affected by the slave trade.

Chapters II and III dealt specifically with the transport of slaves. Chapter II, concerned with their transport on land, provided for the maintenance of a watch on caravan routes, and for the inspection of caravans. Chapter III, concerned with their transport by sea, defined

International Action before the League of Nations

a Maritime Zone and provided for mutual rights of search of vessels less than five hundred tons in weight. It also laid down regulations concerning the use of the flag and the supervision to be exercised by cruisers. The cruisers of any of the signatories were authorized to examine suspected vessels and, if there was sufficient evidence, to arrest them and surrender them for trial by courts of the state whose flag they were flying.

Chapter IV was concerned with the destination of the slaves. A pledge was given by contracting powers whose institutions still recognized the existence of domestic slavery that they would not only prohibit the trade in slaves but also the importation into, transit through, or departure from their territory of African slaves. Special assurances were given by the Ottoman Empire, Persia, and Zanzibar; and the diplomatic and consular agents and naval officers of all signatories pledged themselves to assist the local authorities in repressing the slave trade where it still existed.

Having thus bound its signatories to take specific measures, the convention, for the first and only time either then or since, went on to the equally important matter of seeing that they were carried out. Chapter V provided for the establishment of an International Maritime Office at Zanzibar, and for an International Bureau at Brussels. The object of the Zanzibar Office, at which each of the signatory powers might be represented by a delegate, was to centralize all documents and information to do with the slave trade in the Maritime Zone. The information the powers were obliged to submit was defined in five groups, and included instructions given to commanders of men-of-war navigating the seas of the Maritime Zone, summaries of reports to governments concerning the grounds of seizure and the results of searches, lists of territorial or consular authorities and special delegates, copies of judgments and condemnations of vessels, and all information that might lead to the discovery of persons engaged in the slave trade in the Maritime Zone.

The International Bureau at Brussels, which was attached to the Belgian Foreign Office, was intended to deal with the legal and statistical sides of the trade, and to circulate information. The signatories undertook to communicate to each other the text of their laws and administrative regulations connected with the General Act; and all statistical information concerning the slave trade, slaves detained and liberated, and the traffic in firearms, ammunition and alcoholic liquors. The Zanzibar Office was to report annually to the Bureau at Brussels, which was to arrange for the collection and publication of documents and information.

The sixth chapter of the General Act went on from control to

Slavery

contemplate the establishment and institutions for the liberation of slaves and for their protection. Finally, the seventh dealt with legalistic provisions, rectifications, and administrative questions. Article XCVI provided that the 'present General Act repeals all contrary stipulations of conventions previously concluded between the signatory powers'.

It was indeed the most detailed international code against the slave trade ever devised, and during the following twenty-four years, from 1890 until the outbreak of the First World War, it led to great and successful activity in suppressing it. The Shah of Persia and the Sultan of Zanzibar co-operated actively with the other contracting states, and they all played their part so effectively that when the Temporary Slavery Commission of the League of Nations met in 1925, it could say with truth that the slave trade between Africa and Arabia had almost ceased. Alas! it has revived.

But what one international gathering created was undone, or virtually undone, by another. The outbreak of the First World War suspended activities under the Brussels Act of 1890, and at the end of it, in 1919, a fresh convention, the Convention of St. Germain-en-Laye, was made. This was signed and ratified by the Principal Allied Powers, the United States of America, Belgium, the British Empire, France, Italy, Japan, and Portugal.

In sentiment the Convention was admirable. It was based on Article 6 of the General Act of Berlin of 1885, and even strengthened its language. Article II (1) of the Convention of St Germain-en-Laye read:

'The Signatory Powers exercising sovereign rights or authority in African territories will continue to watch over the preservation of the native populations and to supervise the improvement of the conditions of their moral and material well-being. They will, in particular, endeavour to secure the complete suppression of slavery in all its forms and of the slave trade by land and sea.'

But unfortunately it made no provisions or suggestions about how this was to be achieved. Furthermore, Article XIII of the Convention was interpreted as abrogating the valuable provisions on slavery in the Berlin and Brussels Acts, at least as far as the signatories to the St Germain-en-Laye Convention were concerned. For nearly forty years this was the general international view, and it was greatly regretted by abolitionists. Recently, however, there has been a hopeful development; the British Foreign Office now appears to believe that the Brussels Act was not abrogated.

In a statement to the House of Commons made on November 1, 1956, the Parliamentary Under-Secretary of State for Foreign

International Action before the League of Nations

Affairs said that, 'The United Kingdom . . . is party to the Brussels Act of 1890. The Brussels Act specifically recognized reciprocal rights of visit, search and detention of vessels suspected of engaging in the slave trade within certain defined maritime areas. The United Kingdom is also a party to the Convention of St Germain-en-Laye of 1919, which, though it purported to abrogate the Brussels Act as between the parties to that Convention, imposed an obligation to "secure the complete suppression of the slave trade by land and sea", and this tacitly reaffirmed, or left untouched, the general provisions of Chapter III of the Brussels Act regarding the slave trade on the high seas. In pursuance of the obligations of the United Kingdom under the above-mentioned instruments British naval vessels have regularly patrolled the high seas in the Persian Gulf and the Red Sea'.

This is good news indeed. We have seen in Chapter IV that a slave trade into Arabia is still flourishing. Many believe that it will not be abolished until the Brussels Act, with its excellent machinery of control, or something very like it, is revived. As long ago as 1933 Lord Lugard, one of the greatest authorities on slavery, deplored its alleged abrogation. It was unfortunate that it should have been set aside so lightly after the First World War; for the provisions which were substituted for it were far too brief and inadequate, and lacked the specific agencies of the Brussels Act. The Brussels Conference of 1890 at which it was formulated undoubtedly represented a high-water mark of international concern over questions of slavery. Through it the full vigour of the anti-slavery movement was able to make its effect felt in the less tense international conditions of the time.

CHAPTER XV

THE LEAGUE OF NATIONS
AND AFTER

THE problem of slavery after the First World War was no longer one of sentiment, on which the widespread agreement almost amounted to indifference, but of how to secure the practical action that was still needed. The Convention of St Germain-en-Laye was useless in this respect, and so was the League of Nations at first. Its Covenant contains no express reference or undertakings in regard to slavery, except in connection with the mandate system. For other countries action on slavery depended entirely on the interpretation any nation might place on the rather general wording of Article 23 of the Covenant. This provided that: 'Subject to and in accordance with the provisions of international conventions existing or hereafter to be agreed upon, the Members of the League of Nations (a) will endeavour to secure and maintain fair and humane conditions of labour for men, women and children both in their own territories and in all countries to which their commercial and industrial relations extend, and for that purpose will establish and maintain the necessary international organizations; (b) undertake to secure just treatment for the native inhabitants of territories under their control; (c) will entrust the League with general supervision over the execution of agreements with regard to the traffic in women and children.'

Over the territories under mandate, however, the League of Nations did exercise general powers of supervision and inquiry into progress made in abolishing slavery. In many of these countries slavery had formerly been a well established institution, and since the idea of the mandate system was to promote the welfare and advancement of the peoples concerned, the abolition of slavery and the slave trade were clearly desirable ends. The Covenant of the League stipulated that any general existing or future international conventions on the slave trade were to apply in all classes of mandate. Besides this, in both B and C class mandates express provisions were inserted not only for the suppression of the slave trade but also for the

The League of Nations and After

prohibition of forced labour, except for essential public work and in return for adequate remuneration. For class B mandates, moreover, there were also undertakings to provide for the eventual emancipation of all slaves and for as speedy an elimination of domestic and other slavery as social conditions would allow. Since the mandatory powers were obliged to render the Council of the League of Nations, through the permanent Mandates Commission, annual reports about their territories on, among other matters, measures taken for the abolition of slavery and the slave trade, some measures of progress was assured.

The wider question of slavery in the whole world was first accepted by the League in 1922, and given international shape in its Slavery Convention of 1926. In 1922 the League established its Temporary Slavery Commission, which was instructed to examine the situation and make suggestions for dealing with any problems that might be found to exist. Many of the Commission's proposals naturally required joint action, and its principal recommendation, contained in its second report, was that an international Convention should be made to give effect to them. The Council of the League forwarded the report to the Assembly, to receive its consideration on September 2, 1925.

The British Government meanwhile had prepared a draft Convention, and this was submitted to the Sixth Assembly of the League in 1925. The proposal to adopt a Convention was approved by the Assembly on September 26th that year, on the recommendation of the Sixth Committee, and the draft was then submitted to member governments for their approval. Governments were also asked to appoint plenipotentiaries to meet at the opening of the next session of the Assembly in 1926, to examine the draft.

Finally, having been re-examined and amended by the Sixth Committee, the Convention was approved by the Assembly in a resolution of September 25, 1926, and signed on that date in Geneva by the representatives of thirty-six states. Twenty-seven of these subsequently ratified the Convention at various dates; but since then it has been ratified by a total of forty-six states: Afghanistan, Australia, Austria, Belgium, Bulgaria, British Empire (the self-governing British Dominions adhered separately), Canada, China, Cuba, Czechoslovakia, Denmark, Ecuador, Egypt, Estonia, Finland, France, Germany, Greece, Haiti, Hungary, India, Iraq, Irish Republic, Israel, Italy, Latvia, Lebanon, Liberia, Mexico, Monaco, Netherlands, New Zealand, Nicaragua, Norway, Poland, Portugal, Roumania, South Africa, Spain, Sweden, Switzerland, Syria, Turkey, the United States of America and Yugoslavia. Eight other nations signed or

Slavery

acceded to the Convention, but have not yet ratified it: Albania, Colombia, Dominican Republic, Ethiopia, Iran (with reservation), Lithuania, Panama, Uruguay.

The Convention is still open to accession by a further nineteen states: Saudi-Arabia, Argentine Republic, Bolivia, Brazil, Chile, Costa Rica, Guatemala, Honduras, Iceland, Japan, Liechenstein, Luxembourg, Paraguay, Peru, El Salvador, San Marino, Thailand, Union of Soviet Socialist Republics, and Venezuela.

The Slavery Convention of 1926 was not a long one—it contained twelve Articles—and it did not achieve all that might have been achieved; but it was the best that could be managed in the circumstances. The first Article defined slavery and the slave trade, which had never been considered necessary before. Slavery was defined as, 'the status or condition of a person over whom any or all the powers attaching to the right of ownership are exercised'; and the slave trade as, 'all acts involved in the capture, acquisition or disposal of a person with intent to reduce him to slavery; all acts involved in the acquisition of a slave with the view to selling or exchanging him; all acts of disposal by sale or exchange of a slave acquired with a view to being sold or exchanged, and, in general every act of trade or transport in slaves'.

The definition of slavery proved sadly inadequate. According to the Rapporteur of the Sixth Committee, Viscount Cecil, the definitions were primarily the result of the work of the League's legal experts, and they were based 'on the minimum provisions of existing colonial legislation and on the previous international conventions on the subject'. The Committee stated that the definition of slavery was intended to apply 'not only to domestic slavery, but also to those conditions mentioned in the Temporary Commission . . . i.e. debt slavery, the enslavement of persons distinguished as the adoption of children, and the acquisition of girls by purchase disguised as payment of dowry'. But in spite of this it has been widely interpreted as embracing chattel slavery only, and countries have evaded their responsibilities under it.

Article 2 (b) of the Convention imposed on the contracting parties the obligation 'to bring about progressively and as soon as possible the complete abolition of slavery in all its forms'. Commenting on this the Report of the Sixth Committee explained that 'the abolition of slavery could only be successfully brought about with disregard to the maintenance of order and the well-being of the peoples concerned. This accounts for the use of the word "progressively" in paragraph (b), for it was recognized that in certain cases in the past the attempt to do away with slavery and other similar

The League of Nations and After

conditions in an abrupt manner, although noble in its inspiration, had resulted in unforeseen hardships for the individuals whose condition it was sought to alleviate and even in great social upheavals'.

Article 3 dealt with the slave trade, and contained an undertaking to negotiate another Convention for its suppression, to take the place of the Brussels Act of 1890. But this has remained a vain hope for thirty years. The British tried to get a stronger provision inserted, that 'the act of conveying slaves on the high seas shall be deemed an act of piracy, and the public ships of the signatory states shall have the same rights in relation to vessels and persons engaged in such an act as over vessels and persons engaged in piracy'. Such a provision had been recommended by the Temporary Slavery Commission, but it did not meet with the approval of the majority of the Committee.

Article 5 bound contracting parties to prevent forced labour from developing into conditions analogous to slavery, and an effort was made to put into the Convention all the provisions necessary to achieve this; but it was finally decided to let the matter be dealt with by another Convention. This was done later, by making the Forced Labour Convention of 1931.

Of the remaining six articles of the Convention five were procedural. Article 2, for instance, gave every state, whether a member-state of the League of Nations or not, the right to accede to the Convention; while Article 7 imposed on the contracting parties the obligation to communicate to the League any laws and regulations enacted by them to give effect to its provisions.

The Convention fell short by a long way of what was needed, and in spite of all that the Report of the Sixth Committee could do to strengthen it by suitable explanations and emphases, some of the signatories took full advantage of any loopholes, particularly with regard to debt-bondage, the sham adoption of children, and the sale of women into marriage without their consent. Viscount Cecil appropriately summed up the whole Convention thus:

'I would like to emphasize the fact that the Committee does not hold up this document as the ultimate aim to be achieved in the international effort to do away with such abuses as slavery, the slave trade and conditions analogous thereto. It represents what the Committee considers to be the highest minimum standard which can be set forth in formal international arrangements at the present time. It is recognized that the standard already existing in certain colonial areas is considerably higher, and it is hoped that no states will be satisfied with compliance with the minimum standard which is now proposed.'

The Convention, however, is still binding on the states that have

Slavery

ratified it; and it has been taken over by the United Nations. The Secretary-General of the League of Nations was specifically referred to in Articles 7, 10, 11 and 12, and the Permanent Court of International Justice in Article 8. Since both these offices had ceased to exist, the *ad hoc* Committee on Slavery of the United Nations recommended that the United Nations should take over their functions. The necessary protocol was therefore prepared, formally stating that the United Nations thereby assumed the powers and functions of the League of Nations under the Slavery Convention of 1926, and that it should come into operation when signed by twelve states. It was opened for signature in 1953 and came into operation on July 5, 1955.

With regard to the Permanent Court of International Justice referred to in Article 8 of the Convention, its function was taken over by the new International Court of Justice, under Article 37 of its statute. This states that 'Whenever a treaty or convention in force provides for reference of a matter to a tribunal to have been instituted by the League of Nations or to the Permanent Court of International Justice, the matter shall, as between the Parties to the present Statute, be referred to the International Court of Justice'.

The 1926 Convention of the League of Nations remained for some time a rather ineffectual document. Even information on the extent to which its provisions were carried out could not be guaranteed to be forthcoming. When the draft Convention was being discussed in 1925, a proposal was put forward that the contracting states should be asked to submit annual reports to the League on the measures they had taken to give effect to the provisions of the Convention. But this suggestion was not adopted. Instead the Assembly, in its resolution approving the draft Convention and recommending it for signature, expressed the hope that contracting states 'might be disposed spontaneously to furnish information with regard to measures taken by them' to give effect to the Convention. Another hope in place of an express undertaking. However, whatever information had been communicated to the League each year was thenceforward passed on by the Council in annual reports to the Assembly.

The League next considered slavery again in 1929, at its Tenth Assembly. In the view of abolitionists it was essential to establish some permanent international committee or commission on slavery, to secure further ratifications of the Slavery Convention of 1926, to gather all possible information on slavery, and to keep the aim of completing the abolition of the slave trade and slavery in all its forms constantly before the League. With this in mind Lord Cecil, of the British delegation, suggested reviving the Temporary Slavery Com-

The League of Nations and After

mission. But the Assembly postponed consideration of the proposal. Instead it made an urgent appeal to states which had not already done so to ratify the 1926 Convention, and instructed the Secretary General to request the fullest information on slavery from the contracting states, and to report on it. Once again the weaker alternative was adopted.

The Assembly's wishes were carried out, however. The Secretary General, on November 1, 1929, despatched letters to all the contracting states informing them that the Assembly would welcome any information, from official or private sources, which the different governments might be willing to give, and on August 11, 1930, he reported the results of his inquiries to the Council of the League.

The process was repeated in 1931. But at the meeting of the Assembly that year Lord Lytton, the British delegate, again proposed the reappointment of the Temporary Slavery Commission, to find out what progress had been made, and to advise on any necessary changes in the League's machinery for abolishing slavery. This time the Assembly was satisfied that further examination of the problem was due.

Accordingly, on September 25, 1931, it passed a resolution asking the Council to appoint a small committee of experts for one year, to examine all the material on slavery that had been supplied. In making up the committee the Council appointed the same people who had been members of the Temporary Slavery Commission, and instructed them to report on the extent to which the Slavery Convention of 1926 had been successful in ending slavery. They were also asked to study what obstacles to further progress remained, and to advise whether any modification of the League's existing machinery was desirable.

The Committee held two sessions in 1932, and produced a most valuable report. Its main recommendation was, yet again, the creation of a Standing Advisory Committee of Experts on Slavery to assist the Council of the League. The outstanding figures on the Committee were Dr Gohr of Belgium, the Chairman, and Lord Lugard. Lord Lugard was particularly outspoken on the ineffectiveness of the League to date. Commenting on the work of the Committee he wrote in January, 1933:

'The documents submitted to the Committee were practically valueless for the purpose of its terms of reference and it had no means of obtaining the data required. Its proceedings were saved from futility by its own recognition of the uselessness of such intermittent committees and its consequent unanimous recommendation that a permanent Committee of Experts should be established to

Slavery

which a small secretariat would be attached. A Permanent Bureau had been set up by the Brussels Act, and functioned until the outbreak of the First World War. It was abolished by the Convention of St Germain-en-Laye in so far as the signatories of that Convention were concerned. The Temporary Slavery Commission of 1925 had recommended its revival, but the draughtsmen of the Slavery Convention of 1926 had substituted Article VII, an injunction that participant states should communicate to the League laws and regulations they might enact regarding slavery. Few states had complied with this pledge, nor was it anyone's task to study and make practical use of such information as might be received.... The creation of the Committee of Experts might in the opinion of the Committee afford a more practical means of accomplishing the task to which the League has set its hand than the appointment of a temporary committee at intervals of several years with no means of obtaining the information necessary for its task or of following it up, and whose recommendations could be conveniently pigeon-holed. Such committees are mere waste of money and of the time and effort of the distinguished people who form them.'[1]

After all the years of effort the Assembly of the League was finally persuaded. It accepted the recommendations of the Committee and decided on October 12, 1932, that an Advisory Committee of Experts should be established. Anti-slavery endeavour was at last to have an international office from which to prosecute its efforts.

The Committee was to consist of seven members, chosen solely for their knowledge of slavery; and all were to be members of different nationalities. They were to be appointed for an undefined term, but the Council retained the right to renew the composition of the Committee every six years. Its functions were strictly advisory, and it was to have no power of supervision. It was instructed: (1) to study and examine the documents supplied or transmitted by Governments to the Secretariat; (2) to study, on the basis of such documents and of the special knowledge of its members, the facts and institutions mentioned in Article I of the Slavery Convention of 1926, and to examine their role in the social system; (3) to study the means of gradually abolishing these institutions or customs or of causing them to develop in such a way as to deprive them of any objectionable feature; and (4) if a country where slavery existed asked for financial assistance from the League of Nations in settling questions relating to the abolition of slavery, the Committee was, at the request of the Council, to examine the objects for which this

[1] Article on 'Slavery in all its Forms', in *Africa*, the journal of the International Institute of African Languages and Cultures, for January, 1933.

The League of Nations and After

financial assistance was requested, the minimum amount necessary, and the guarantees offered. It was expressly laid down that the Committee should not deal with the question of forced labour.

For five consecutive years, from 1934 to 1938, the Advisory Committee of Experts met annually in Geneva, and really came to grips with the detailed problems of slavery. Its yearly reports, published as League of Nations documents, shed valuable light on every aspect of slavery. Its work came to an end, not through any decision of the League, but solely because of the outbreak of war. The report of its last session, held in April 1938, indicated that there had been a considerable improvement in the main problems to which its attention had been drawn; but it contained nothing to suggest that the continuation of the Committee's work was unnecessary. Both in its observations and conclusions it assumed that the Committee's functions were abiding ones. As the result of its activities information concerning slavery was still being officially communicated to the League of Nations up till 1940.

Although the League was only with difficulty persuaded to adopt the necessary measures to check slavery, its efforts did meet with some success. As a result of its interest and pressure, the legal status of slavery was abolished by Afghanistan in 1923, Iraq in 1924, Nepal and Kelat in 1926, Transjordania and Persia in 1929, and Bahrein in 1937.

A matter in which the League became closely concerned was the investigation into the existence of slavery in Liberia. The Temporary Slavery Commission had cited Liberia as one of the countries where various forms of slavery were said to exist, and further evidence had come from private sources, especially from Dr Raymond L. Buell's investigations and Lady Simon's book on slavery. The question was first taken up, however, by the United States of America, whose traditional policy of friendliness towards the Republic of Liberia ever since its foundation in 1847 gave the Americans a peculiar interest in the country.

On June 8, 1929, the United States Department of State wrote to the Foreign Office of Liberia saying that it had received information from several reliable sources that the export of labour from Liberia to Fernando Po had resulted in the development of a system which seemed 'hardly distinguishable from an organized slave trade, and that in the enforcement of this system the services of the Liberian Frontier Force and the services and influence of certain high Government officials are constantly and systematically used'.

In replying to this letter the Liberian Government denied the charge of slave trading but expressed its willingness 'to have the

Slavery

question investigated by a competent, impartial and unprejudiced commission'. The Liberian Government then asked the League of Nations to take part in the investigation, and suggested that a commission of three be appointed of whom one member would be appointed by the League, another by the United States Government, and the third by the Liberian Government.

The League and the United States Government agreed to take part, and the Commission was appointed in April 1930. It was requested to ascertain: (a) whether slavery as defined in the Slavery Convention of 1926 in fact existed in Liberia; (b) whether this system was participated in or encouraged by the Government of Liberia; (c) whether and what leading citizens of Liberia participated in it; (d) to what extent did compulsory labour exist as a factor in the social and industrial economy of Liberia, if so, how were the labourers recruited; (e) whether shipment of contract labourers to Fernando Po under the terms of the agreement with Spain or shipment of such labour to the Congo or any other foreign country was associated with slavery, and whether the method employed in recruiting such labourers carried any compulsion; (f) whether the labour employed for private purposes on privately owned or leased plantations was recruited by voluntary enlistment or was forcibly impressed by the Liberian Government or by its authority; and (g) whether the Liberian Government had at any time given sanction or approval to the recruiting of labour with the aid of the Liberian Frontier Force or other persons holding official positions or in the Government employ or private individuals had been implicated in such recruiting with or without Government approval.

The Commission found that many of the charges were substantially true. Its Report,[1] published on January 10, 1931, found that while classic slavery no longer existed, inter-tribal slavery did exist and that the pawning of people was also practised. It found that forced labour had been used by the Government of Liberia for the construction of public works, and that some of the forced labour recuited for public works was diverted to private uses, and that none of this labour had been paid. It found that labour recruited for Fernando Po and French Gabon had been recruited under conditions scarcely distinguishable from slave-trading. It found that labour for private enterprise had been recruited involuntarily by high officials, but that the Firestone Co. employed only voluntary labour. Finally, it found that Vice-President Yancy and other officials had authorized the recruitment of forced labour.

[1] Document C.658.M.272, 1930 vi, published by the Printing Office of the United States Government.

The League of Nations and After

The Commission's Report went on to recommend various reforms, including the appointment of American and European advisers to Government departments. The Liberian Government accepted these in principle, and said that it would apply them so far as its resources would permit. To help her, financial assistance was provided through the League of Nations, and the necessary expert advisers on administration and finance were duly appointed from outside. The investigation thus had a successful outcome.

The League also helped to influence Ethiopia to take steps against slavery. When Ethiopia applied for admission to the League it was opposed on the ground that slavery existed in the country. Whereupon the Government of Ethiopia gave a pledge that slavery would be abolished within a definite time, and began to enact measures that would, after a transition period, lead to complete freedom.

One other particular matter in which the League was able to take effective action was mentioned in Chapter IV. This was the sale into slavery of servants and others who accompanied pilgrims to Mecca. When the League became aware of it, it was able to influence the relevant governments to institute stricter control over the departure and return of pilgrims, and of those who accompanied them, in order that any who did not return might be traced. As we have seen the Netherlands Government led the way with its thorough system of inspection of travel papers; but the British, French and Italians also established similar systems.

Considering all the difficulties the League had to face its anti-slavery record ended by being a good one. It had to be continually stirred before it would accept much responsibility for the matter, but after its Advisory Committee of Experts was established some really solid progress was made. It was a pity that its work, like so many other things, was brought to an end by the Second World War.

CHAPTER XVI

ACTION BY THE UNITED NATIONS

ಣಿ

WHEN the United Nations came into being in 1946 there was still less doubt about world sentiment on slavery than after the first war. Yet abolitionists had once again to begin the process of securing international interest in its detailed problems; for, like the Covenant of the League of Nations before it, the Charter of the United Nations contained no specific reference to slavery. That its abolition was envisaged could only be inferred from Article 1 (3) of its Charter, which defined the purposes of the United Nations as 'To achieve international co-operation . . . in promoting and encouraging respect for human rights and for fundamental freedoms for all without distinction as to race, sex, language or religion'.

This general statement of aim was amplified two years later, on December 10, 1948, when the General Assembly of the United Nations adopted its Universal Declaration on Human Rights. In it were the first references to slavery in the proceedings of the United Nations. Article 4 read: '1. No one shall be held in slavery; slavery and the slave trade shall be prohibited in all their forms. 2. No one shall be held in servitude.'

But although it was a categorical enough declaration, it was without force, for it was not binding on member states. A more effective document, therefore, the International Covenant on Human Rights, is now being prepared by the United Nations Commission on Human Rights. This too will contain references to slavery, but it will be binding only on those states which ratify it.

One of the first things the United Nations did when it came into existence was to take over some of the functions of the League, which naturally included some concerned with slavery, particularly in connection with the mandate system. This was done by a resolution[1] of the General Assembly of February 12, 1946, which read:

'Under certain of the instruments referred to at the beginning of this Resolution, the League of Nations has, for the convenience of the parties, undertaken to act as the custodian of the original signed

[1] No. 24 (i).

Action by the United Nations

texts of the instruments and to perform certain functions pertaining to a secretariat, which do not affect the operation of the instruments and do not relate to the substantive rights and obligations of the parties. These functions include: the receipt of additional signatures and of instruments of ratification, accession and denunciation; receipt of notice of extension of the instruments to colonies or possessions of a party or to protectorates or territories for which it holds a mandate; notification of such acts to other parties, and other interested states; the issue of certified copies; and the circulation of information or documents which the parties have undertaken to communicate to each other. Any interruption in the performance of these functions would be contrary to the interests of all the parties. It would be convenient for the United Nations to have the custody of these instruments which are connected with activities of the League of Nations and which the United Nations is likely to continue. Therefore the General Assembly declares that the United Nations is willing to undertake the custody of the instruments and to charge the Secretariat of the United Nations with the task of performing for the parties the functions pertaining to a secretariat, formerly entrusted to the League of Nations.'

When the League held its last meeting in 1946, its Assembly endorsed the United Nations Resolution, and the Secretary-General of the League was directed to transfer to the Secretariat of the United Nations the texts of treaties and conventions in his custody. The Slavery Convention of 1926, however, was not among them. It was only some years later that the United Nations, by a special Protocol, assumed the powers and functions of the League under this Convention.

The detailed anti-slavery work of the United Nations, like that of the League, did not begin until it appointed a special body to study the question. But unfortunately the body appointed, the *ad hoc* Committee of Experts on Slavery, was again only a temporary one. Its appointment was brought about, as before, largely through the efforts of the Anti-Slavery Society. The Society managed to win the support of the delegates of Belgium and France. Prof. Fernand de Housse and Prof. Rene Cassin; and at the Third Assembly of the United Nations in 1948, Prof. de Housse proposed a resolution,[1] which Prof. Cassin seconded, requesting the Economic and Social Council of the United Nations to study the problem of slavery. Their resolution was passed with a substantial majority.

The terms under which the United Nations *ad hoc* Committee of Experts on Slavery was eventually formed were contained in a reso-

[1] No. 278 (iii).

Slavery

lution adopted by the Economic and Social Council at its ninth session on July 20, 1949. This read:

'The Economic and Social Council instructs the Secretary-General, after consultation with the bodies having special competence, to appoint a small *ad hoc* committee of not more than five experts:

'1. To survey the field of slavery and other institutions or customs resembling slavery;

'2. To assess the nature and extent of these several problems at the present time;

'3. To suggest methods of attacking these problems;

'4. Having regard to the recognized fields of competence of the various bodies within the framework of the United Nations, to suggest an appropriate division of responsibility among those bodies;

'5. To report to the Council within twelve months of their appointment.'

On the authority of this resolution the Committee was appointed by the Secretary-General in December 1949. It consisted of Prof. Moises Poblete Troncoso (Chile), Madame Jane Vialle (France), Mr Bruno Lasker (United States), and myself of the United Kingdom, but we were not appointed as national representatives. An attempt was made to secure a fifth member from eastern Europe, but it proved unsuccessful. It was also to be regretted that the International Labour Office was not given full representation on the Committee from the beginning, as had been done with the Temporary Slavery Commission of the League of Nations. An observer from the ILO, Mr Robert Gavin, only attended the Committee's second session in 1951; but he did valuable work in suggesting compromises between the differing viewpoint of the members. Prof. Poblete Troncoso was elected Chairman of the Committee, Mr Edward Lawson of the UN Secretariat was appointed Secretary, and I was nominated its Rapporteur.

The Committee held its first session in the temporary headquarters of the United Nations at Lake Success during February and March 1950; and by a happy chance it began its session on the anniversary of the birthday of Abraham Lincoln, one of the great American abolitionists. Its preliminary task was to prepare a questionnaire on slavery for circulation to both member-states of the United Nations and to non-members. This was then submitted to the Economic and Social Council, which was also in session at the time, who approved it, subject to some amendments, and instructed the Committee to address it to all governments. The Committee also asked the Council to approve of its holding two more sessions, one in November 1950, to prepare requests for supplementary information from governments that replied to the questionnaire, and another,

Action by the United Nations

final session in the spring of 1951, to consider the replies and to prepare a report. This was also approved by the Economic and Social Council.

Thus far the *ad hoc* Committee had not met with any difficulties, but the completion of its work was greatly hampered by political action in the Economic and Social Council. Prof. Poblete Troncoso had prepared a memorandum for the *ad hoc* Committee on forms of servitude in Latin America, and had named Peru as being among the countries in which such practices still existed. When the Economic and Social Council met for its summer session in 1950, Prof. Poblete Troncoso's statements were challenged by the delegate from Peru, who went on to attack the whole procedure and programme of the *ad hoc* Committee. In the end he succeeded in getting a majority of the Council to agree to eliminate the November session of the Committee and to limit the remaining session to four weeks, and four weeks only.

Nor was this all. When the Committee met again in April 1951 it found that not only had its proposed programme been cut in half by the loss of a session, but that the one session left was further halved. This was due to the uncompleted state of the new headquarters building of the United Nations in New York, where the Committee was to hold its meetings. The electric equipment for simultaneous translation of what was said had not yet been installed, and since translation was rendered necessary through two members of the Committee speaking no English and one member speaking no French, consecutive translation had to be adopted. In effect this cut the four weeks allowed to the Committee by half. The working paper that formed the basis of the Committee's work during its final session was actually one I had prepared, at the request of the Secretariat of the United Nations, for the second session, which had been eliminated.

Hamstrung as it was the Committee could only submit a report, its majority report,[1] that was inevitably incomplete. The response to its questionnaire had been good, although Saudi-Arabia and the Yemen, two states in which slavery is believed to exist, did not reply; both of them have now ignored eight separate requests by the United Nations for information on slavery within their borders. The Committee was unable to attempt to act on the second of its terms of reference, however, 'to assess the nature and extent of these problems (i.e. slavery) at the present time'. I was fortunate in being able to remain in New York longer than my colleagues, and so was able to prepare a fuller report containing that information,

[1] No. E/1988.

Slavery

which I submitted as a minority report.[1] But both reports agreed in recommending almost the same methods for bringing about the abolition of slavery.

In compiling its questionnaire the Committee had had to consider whether forced labour and other forms of involuntary labour which are not actual slavery should be included in its inquiries. Some members of the Committee were in favour of this; but the Economic and Social Council rightly asked the Committee to confine itself to slavery. Forced labour is involuntary labour exacted by a government from a person whom it is desired to punish or discipline, whereas slavery is involuntary labour exacted from one individual by another by virtue of ownership. The two systems of involuntary labour must obviously be dealt with separately. Treating them as one and the same thing would inevitably lead to confusion.

The *ad hoc* Committee made three main proposals, two of which have been carried out. It found that the definitions of slavery and the slave trade in Article I of the Slavery Convention of 1926 were both accurate and adequate. It therefore recommended that the United Nations should assume the powers and functions of the League of Nations under this Convention by means of a protocol, which would be signed by the states that ratified the 1926 Convention. In addition, however, it recommended that a Supplementary Convention on Slavery should be made declaring that debt-bondage, the sale of women into marriage without their consent, and the sham adoption of children to exploit their labour, are also slavery, and prohibited. Its third main recommendation was one familiar from the days of the League, that a Standing Committee of Experts on Slavery should be set up by the United Nations to supervise the application of the Slavery Conventions and recommend measures to be taken to abolish slavery. But this has still not been done.

The Committee further recommended that serfdom should be defined and prohibited; that contracting states should undertake to transmit annual reports to the United Nations on the application of the Conventions on Slavery; that slave-trading on the high seas should be declared to be the same as piracy; that mutilation should be prohibited; that inchoate forms of enslavement should be prohibited; that a minimum age of consent to marriage of fourteen years should be fixed by law; and that registration of marriages should be encouraged.

The Committee's report was debated by the Economic and Social Council in September 1951. But no immediate action was taken. The Council decided to ask the Secretary-General of the United Nations

[1] No. E/AC.33.B.14.

Action by the United Nations

to collect more information on slavery, which proved to be of little value, and to report back to the Council on the whole subject.

He duly reported in January 1953, and in the spring session of the Economic and Social Council that year the matter was again debated. This time two decisions were taken. First, the Council decided to act on the *ad hoc* Committee's recommendation that the United Nations should assume the powers and functions of the League under the Convention of 1926. The Secretary-General was accordingly instructed to prepare the necessary protocol and to invite states to adhere to it. Secondly, the Council decided to find out whether member states considered the Supplementary Convention recommended by the *ad hoc* Committee was necessary and desirable. A draft convention embodying the Committee's suggestions was submitted at this session in a memorandum by the Anti-Slavery Society, which had been granted consultative status with the Council in category B.

The recommended protocol was soon executed, but the Supplementary Convention naturally required far more consideration. The next step was taken at the session of the Economic and Social Council in April 1954. The United Kingdom submitted a draft Convention on Slavery, and it was decided that this should be circulated to all states for their comments. A rapporteur was appointed, Mr Hans Engen, the leader of the Norwegian delegation to the United Nations, to present the comments, together with any other information available.

By the following year most of the necessary information, and more, had been gathered. Mr Hans Engen reported to the Economic and Social Council at its session in April 1955, and the results of the enquiry into the desirability of a further convention were also available. The consensus of opinion supported the idea, so the Economic and Social Council now proceeded to appoint a committee of the Council to draft it. The committee consisted of ten delegates, one from each of the following countries: Australia, Ecuador, Egypt, France, India, Netherlands, Turkey, USSR, the United Kingdom and Yugoslavia.

This drafting committee met in New York in January 1956, and used the British draft convention as the basis for its discussions. Only four of its articles, however, excited much controversy. The preliminary paragraph of Article 1 provided for the progressive abolition of slavery, but this was opposed by some members of the committee, who preferred immediate abolition. But in the end the original phrasing prevailed. Article 3 provoked rather more discussion. This provided a right of search and capture on the high

Slavery

seas of ships conveying slaves. But again the draft article which emerged left the principle intact. Almost the only article to be amended was Article 6, which provided that contracting parties should furnish information to each other on any measures they took to abolish slavery. The representative of India, supported by the representative of Egypt, moved that this information should be furnished not only to each other but also to the United Nations; and this was carried unanimously. The only other Article to give rise to much discussion was the draft Article 10, which gave to a metropolitan state the right to reserve any of its non-self-governing territories from the application of the Convention. But this right, too, was retained in the draft Article.

Having as it were internationalized the British draft Convention, the next stage was to get it considered by a full-scale conference, and, if possible, signed. In April 1956, the draft was submitted to the Economic and Social Council, and the Council decided to invite all member states, not only of the United Nations, but also of its specialized agencies, to a conference to be held in Geneva in August the same year.

The conference held its first meeting in Geneva on August 13, 1956, and forty-six states were represented at it. Eight further states and the International Labour Office were represented by observers, and the following non-governmental organizations in consultative status with the Economic and Social Council were also represented: the Anti-Slavery Society, St Joan's Social and Political Alliance, the Liaison Committee of Women's International Organizations, the Women's International League for Peace and Freedom, the Commission of the Churches on International Affairs, the Catholic International Union of Social Service, the International Alliance of Women, the International Committee of the Red Cross, the International Federation of University Women, the International Federation of Women Lawyers, and the World Union of Catholic Women's Organizations. The observers and the representatives of the non-governmental organizations were authorized by the conference to take part in the proceedings, but not to vote. The representatives of the first three organizations addressed the conference.

Discussion at the conference centred mainly on Articles 3, 9, and 10. Article 3 provided for the search and seizure of a ship flying the flag of a contracting state and reasonably suspected of conveying slaves on the high seas, in the Red Sea, the Indian Ocean, and the Persian Gulf, and its condemnation by a prescribed court. This was challenged on the ground that it would infringe sovereignty, the very ground on which a similar provision of the Congress of Vienna

Action by the United Nations

was attacked nearly one hundred and fifty years previously. Opposition to the Article again prevailed, however, and another was substituted for it. This imposed on contracting parties two obligations, to make conveyance of slaves by whatever means from one country to another a criminal offence, and to take effective measures to prevent ships and aircraft flying the flag of a contracting party, and their ports, coasts and airfields, from being used for conveying slaves. In addition, a new Article 4 was inserted giving freedom to any slave who takes refuge on a ship flying the flag of a contracting state. States that supported the original draft had been criticized for consenting to the change, but in fact the draft Article 3 could never have been effective, unless the countries in Arabia to which slaves were being conveyed adhered to the Convention; and that is a very remote possibility.

Article 9 also provoked a good deal of discussion. The draft Article provided that the Convention should be open to signature by any state, whether a member of the United Nations or not. But this was finally amended, limiting the right of signature to member states of the United Nations and to members of its specialized agencies. The article that dealt with this point, and was approved, is now Article 11 of the Convention.

Article 10, the third to excite much controversy, enabled a contracting party to reserve from the application of the Convention any of its non-self-governing territories. It was rightly criticized on the ground that it would be an 'escape clause'. But the United Kingdom pointed out that, since it had no constitutional power to initiate appropriate legislation in six of its non-self-governing territories, it would not be able to sign the Convention until it either got the consent of the six territories or was given the power to reserve them. The upshot of the discussion was that Article 10, which is now Article 12 of the Convention, was amended to give a contracting party a twelve-month period in which to obtain the necessary consent; but the principle of reserving territories was not accepted.

The Convention has now been signed by thirty-six states and ratified by three namely, the Soviet Union, the United Kingdom and Byelo-Russia. Since Article 13 provides that 'it shall enter into force on the rate on which two states have become parties hereto', it is now a Convention in operation.

It represents definite progress on the road to the abolition of slavery. Its definition of slavery (Article 1) firmly includes the analogous practices. It deals with the minimum age of consent to marriage, and the encouragement of marriage registration (Article 2); slave-trading (Articles 3 and 4); the mutilation of slaves (Article

Slavery

5); and inchoate acts of enslavement (Article 6). Article 8 obliges contracting parties to furnish each other and the United Nations with information on steps taken to abolish slavery; while Article 9 provides that the Convention must be adopted *in toto*. Other Articles define terms and procedures.[1]

Besides its main work of debating and signing the Supplementary Convention on Slavery the conference of 1956 also adopted two resolutions. The first called on all states that had not already acceded to the Slavery Convention of 1926, as amended by the Protocol of 1953, to do so, and the second recommended the Economic and Social Council to consider undertaking a study of the question of marriage, with the object of drawing attention to the desirability of free consent by both parties, and of establishing a minimum age of consent, preferably not less than fourteen years. The Supplementary Convention only obliged contracting states to define the age.

The conference was a great success. The fact that fifty-four states saw fit to send representatives to it was strong evidence of the widespread desire in the world to abolish slavery in all its forms. It was purely optional for them to be represented or not; they were not bound to be, as members of the United Nations. They elected to be represented solely because they wished to share in the world-wide endeavour finally to stamp out what is increasingly seen as an outrage on human morality.

Yet in spite of all this international interest and the good work that has been done, there is still a glaring omission which can prevent it from being consolidated. There is still no machinery to supervise the application of the two excellent Slavery Conventions. This is the greatest weakness of the Supplementary Convention of 1956, as it was of the Convention of 1926; and unless it is remedied the Conventions will almost certainly fail in their purpose.

Of the six hundred or so instruments to suppress slavery made in the past it was no accident that the General Act of Brussels of 1890 was the most successful; for it alone provided for the establishment of a permanent bureau. The only other convention to achieve much was the Convention of 1926; but it scarcely made any headway until a permanent committee was appointed. The Temporary Slavery Commission of 1922 recommended supervisory machinery, but no action was taken. Only after six barren years was the League persuaded, chiefly by the British delegation, Viscount Cecil, Lord Lytton and Mr Charles Roden Buxton, MP, and the outspokenness of Lord Lugard, to set up the necessary body.

The Standing Committee of Experts recommended by the Tem-

[1] The full text may be found in Appendix III.

Action by the United Nations

porary Slavery Commission was an admirably balanced one. It was not to exceed seven in number, and was to include a representative of the International Labour Office. Its members were all to be of different nationalities, chosen for their knowledge of slavery and appointed for an indefinite period, so as to maintain continuity of policy. Its role was to be purely advisory to the Council of the League. Lord Lugard pointed out the great value of such a committee. 'As a responsible and competent body it is probable that Governments and others would (under such stipulations regarding publicity as they might consider necessary) entrust to the Committee confidential reports from Consuls and other trustworthy sources, while scientific societies and others engaged in research would correspond with it regarding the existence of serfdom and the place of it in social organization, and on other forms of partial servitude.' Temporary committees Lord Lugard considered a complete waste of time and money.

As we have seen, when the League did set up its Permanent Committee of Experts on Slavery, it did valuable work, which was only ended by the Second World War. Today a similar body is just as necessary, and what Lord Lugard wrote in 1933 about the League applies equally to the United Nations. If a problem is to be solved, men and women with expert knowledge of it must apply themselves to it over a period of years.

In the case of the United Nations responsibility for suppressing slavery, in the absence of any committee, would rest solely with the Economic and Social Council, aided by the Secretariat of the United Nations. But there is no certainty that either the Council or the Secretariat would include experts, or even one expert, on slavery. As regards the Council the probability is the reverse; for delegates on the Council are national representatives usually chosen for their political eminence rather than for expert knowledge of any one subject. The Secretariat might overcome the difficulty by employing an expert consultant, but in that case the Council would get the advice of only one expert instead of that of several. Even this, however, would be better than no expert at all.

The danger is that if preparation of the groundwork for decision is entrusted by the Economic and Social Council to the Secretariat, the Council may find that it derives little or no assistance from their documents. The reconvened Slavery Committee of the League of 1925 found that the documents submitted to it, prepared presumably by the Secretariat of the League, were valueless. And this was also the complaint of the British delegate at the session of the Economic and Social Council in the spring of 1954. Supporting the resolution

Slavery

for the appointment of a Rapporteur, he said, 'All this additional information (two reports prepared by the Secretariat) which has become available since the report of the *ad hoc* Committee—however useful it may be—does not in fact make the picture any clearer. On the contrary, I would suggest that it rather adds to the confusion'.

Slavery cannot be suppressed without making unpleasant and unvarnished statements about territories in which it exists. Unfortunately these may be territories under the control of member-states of the United Nations, and international civil servants are naturally loath to say anything derogatory about their employers, and shirk doing so. But the battle against slavery cannot be fought in a vacuum. Unless people can be found sufficiently courageous to say that slavery exists wherever it does exist, the struggle might as well be abandoned. Such people are obviously far more likely to be found among the experts than among the international civil servants.

In all three main bodies have now studied this question, the Brussels Conference of 1890, the Temporary Slavery Commission of the League of Nations, in 1925 and again 1932, and the *ad hoc* Committee (1950-51) of the United Nations, and all three have arrived at the same conclusion: that an Advisory Committee of Experts is necessary to supervise the application of the Slavery Conventions. In the face of this unanimity how can it be doubted? And why has it not been done?

Opposition to the idea today comes mostly from some of the colonial powers, who argue that if such a Committee was set up by the United Nations it would constitute another forum for attacks on them by the anti-colonial powers. Anyone who has studied the proceedings of the various bodies of the United Nations can sympathize with this objection. There has been much unfounded criticism of their administration of non-self-governing territories, especially of those that are advancing to self-government as rapidly as their condition allows. At the same time the duty to abolish slavery as soon as possible surely transcends the less noble aim of sheltering from criticism, however unmerited it may be. It is to be hoped that the colonial powers will re-examine their policy on this issue, and with the example of the League of Nations before them, avoid wasting more time in the abolition of slavery.

The proposed Committee of Experts, it must be emphasized, would be advisory only. Decision would still rest with the Economic and Social Council. The Committee could be established easily enough, as under the League, by a resolution either of the Geneva Assembly of the United Nations, or of the Economic and Social Council.

CHAPTER XVII

WHAT REMAINS TO BE DONE

CHATTEL slavery still exists in Arabia, fed by a clandestine trade from Africa and from other neighbouring countries in Asia. This is the most important single fact that needs to be kept constantly before the eyes of the world. There is still an area of the world in which the outright ownership of one human being by another is openly accepted as part of the social structure. How can this be brought to an end?

The most hopeful approach is almost certainly through Moslem states and organizations. The patriarchal and heirarchical societies of Arabia are still highly suspicious of foreigners, especially of non-Moslem foreigners, who continue to be regarded as infidels. Only a few non-Moslems, who have lived long in Arabia, have succeeded in winning the confidence of Arabians. It is therefore far more likely that Arab rulers will pay attention to what Moslems say rather than to the exhortations of Christian westerners.

Slavery is condemned by the Koran on moral grounds, and the countries of Arabia profess to be ruled by the precepts of their holy Prophet. Yet they have not abolished slavery, as other Moslem countries have done. It was suggested by Eldon Rutter in 1933 that the League of Nations might persuade the rulers of Moslem states that have abolished slavery to use their influence on their fellow-Moslem rulers who have not to make them see the full iniquity of slavery and the urgent need to end it. This is an approach that the United Nations might fruitfully take up today.

The last time that any Moslem body discussed the abolition of slavery was more than thirty years ago, in 1926. On that occasion, a pan-Islamic conference in Mecca, a resolution was passed condemning slavery. The time has surely come for another Moslem body of equivalent, or even higher, authority to take up the problem afresh. It would be an encouraging sign if the Arab League, for instance, would put the abolition of slavery on its agenda in the near future, and impress on the slave-owning members of the League that only by ending slavery would they be conforming with their true

Slavery

religious faith. The main responsibility must in justice and expediency be placed on Moslems the world over.

If slavery in Arabia were abolished the trade would automatically cease. But until this occurs the most that the western world can do is to attempt once again to control it, and at least confine the evil of slavery within definite bounds. The best hope of achieving this undoubtedly lies in a revival of the Brussels Act.

The legal position of the Act is uncertain, but it would seem that the Convention of St Germain-en-Laye did not in fact abrogate it. There was no provision in the General Act of Brussels authorizing any contracting state to denounce it. The only way in which it could be abrogated therefore would be by securing the consent of all the states which signed and ratified it; at least, all those that are still sovereign states. But as only some of these states were party to the Convention of St Germain-en-Laye, it can be argued that the Brussels Act was not abrogated, but is still in force. To put the matter beyond doubt it would be of great value if one or more of the signatories to the Act, e.g. Britain and the United States of America, reconvened all the signatories and formally proposed that the machinery of the Act should be set going again. The main provision that needs reviving is the patrolling of the specified Maritime Zone, with the right to stop and search ships of under 500 tons.

While Arabia is the only remaining region in which the legal status of slavery has not been abolished, there is, unfortunately, strong evidence to suggest that slavery still exists in fact in Ethiopia, a country in which it is supposedly abolished. The Government of Ethiopia informed the United Nations that slavery and serfdom, the Gabar system, had been completely abolished throughout the country. But such a claim must inevitably be discounted by anyone who is familiar with the slow stages by which slavery is really brought to an end. In this process the legal abolition of the status is only the first step. Its execution requires never-ending vigilance and frank recognition of facts. The wide claim of Ethiopia does not therefore inspire confidence. There are, moreover, the well-authenticated stories of slaves escaping from the Province of Wallega in Ethiopia into the Sudan, pursued by their owners, as late as 1955.

When Ethiopia was admitted to the League of Nations in 1923, she gave a pledge that she would be willing 'now and hereafter to furnish the Council with all information desired' on the abolition of slavery. Will she not do so to the League's successor, the United Nations? The strongest proof of her good intentions would be for her to invite a mixed international committee, including Ethiopians,

What Remains to be Done

to tour the country and ascertain to what extent its anti-slavery laws have been effective. Until this is done the matter is bound to remain clouded in doubt and suspicion.

Apart from Arabia and Ethiopia slavery must be presumed to exist in Spanish Morocco, in the absence of any denial or information; and there is also no information available for Tibet, or Central Asia. There is evidence that there are still vestiges of slavery in Mauretania, French Equatorial Africa, Nigeria and Ghana. One can but hope that the day will come when all parts of the world are equally accessible and forthcoming on the subject of slavery.

Turning to practices analagous to slavery, debt-bondage remains a great economic and social problem, especially in India. The essential first step in tackling it, in countries where it is still impossible to prevent the pledging of services for credit, is to ensure that by law and vigilance the debtor may pledge only his own services and never those of a third person. The other important provisions are, to fix the value of the debt and services, to ensure that the value of the latter is applied to the extinction of the debt, and to set a time limit to the period of bondage. If these safeguards are placed on the practice it is at least robbed of its most pernicious features, and otherwise helpless individuals are prevented from being drawn into a state of unqualified slavery.

In combating serfdom, the key lies in land reform, and this cannot, of course, be imposed by international decree, though it can be speeded by pressure and serfdom ameliorated by technical aid. The debt-bondage element of the peonage practised in Latin America can be dealt with by legislation, though the value of such laws has always proved doubtful in the past. The whole evil of serfdom and peonage lies in the system of land tenure which conquerors are able to impose on a defeated people; in which huge estates are owned by a relatively small number of people. When these latifundia are broken up into smallholdings, or are turned into co-operative farms, serfdom ceases to exist. The co-operative system of agriculture has proved successful in Mexico and in Guatemala, and is now being tried in Bolivia. But it could be applied with great benefit in other countries of South America, such as Ecuador and Peru.

To prevent marriage in primitive societies from degenerating into a commercial transaction two points are essential, the consent of both parties, and a minimum age for marriage. Without these a wife tends to become a chattel, able to be sold by her husband to another man, or inherited among his effects. Fortunately the current of opinion in Africa is now set in favour of abolishing anything that tends to make a woman the property of her husband. In a great

Slavery

part of Africa administered by European nations, suitable laws have been enacted, and the all-African committee which studied the problem in Eastern Nigeria in 1955 was in favour of similar laws for Eastern Nigeria. It remains for this trend to be supported as actively as possible by any agencies able to do so.

Lastly, the most efficient system for protecting children has been proved to be one of registration of adopted children and their inspection by welfare officers. Only this ensures that a transferred child will not be unduly exploited or ill-treated; for the visiting officer is able to hear of any abuse and, if necessary, remove the child to an institution. Improved general economic conditions, again, usually help to check the whole practice of exploiting child labour by sham adoption. In China, it would seem from the accounts of travellers, the break-up of large estates which had previously been in the hand of landlords who exacted most of the produce of the soil from their tenants, has so improved the economic standing of the peasant that he is now better able to maintain a large family, and is no longer driven by poverty to part with one or more of his children. Similarly in South America, as standards of living among the Indian population rise as the result of agrarian reform, the need that drives some Indian families into giving children to European residents will vanish. But until it does much could still be done to regulate the practice of 'adoption' and safeguard its victims.

All these problems, however, and their possible solutions, are still floating unanchored in the sea of international schemes. There is still no single international body responsible for continuing interest in them. The United Nations has done a good deal to ventilate them, and individual nations have acted on suggestions and advice. But if further progress is to be made a specific agency of the United Nations must be established with the responsibility for gathering and collating all information, following up practical measures, and exerting an active vigilance in every part of the world. Even if chattel slavery itself were to be immediately abolished by some miracle, there would remain for many years to come the complex problems connected with the analagous practices, to study and seek to improve. The experience of the League of Nations showed what progress could be made once a permanent committee was set up. This is the greatest single need in the fight against slavery to-day.

APPENDIX I

GENERAL ACT FOR THE REPRESSION OF AFRICAN SLAVE TRADE

(Brussels, 2 July 1890)

[Translation]

IN THE NAME OF GOD ALMIGHTY ...
[*The list of the heads of the signatory States follows*]
Being equally actuated by the firm intention of puttng an end to the crimes and devastations engendered by the traffic in African slaves, of efficiently protecting the aboriginal population of Africa, and of securing for that vast continent the benefits of peace and civilization;

Wishing to give fresh sanction to the decisions already adopted in the same sense and at different times by the powers, to complete the results secured by them, and to draw up a body of measures guaranteeing the accomplishment of the work which is the object of their common solicitude;

Have resolved, in pursuance of the invitation addressed to them by the Government of His Majesty the King of the Belgians, in agreement with the Government of Her Majesty the Queen of Great Britain and Ireland, Empress of India, to convene for this purpose a conference at Brussels, and have named as their plenipotentiaries: . . .

[*The names and titles of the Plenipotentiaries follow*]
Who, being furnished with full powers, which have been found to be in good and due form, have adopted the following provisions:

CHAPTER I. SLAVE-TRADE COUNTRIES. — MEASURES TO BE TAKEN
IN THE PLACES OF ORIGIN

Article I

The powers declare that the most effective means of counteracting the slave-trade in the interior of Africa are the following:

1. Progressive organization of the administrative, judicial, religious, and military services in the African territories placed under the sovereignty or protectorate of civilized nations.

2. The gradual establishment in the interior, by the powers to which the territories are subject, of strongly occupied stations, in such a way as to make their protective or repressive action effectively felt in the territories devastated by slave hunting.

3. The construction of roads, and in particular of railways, connecting the advanced stations with the coast, and permitting easy access to the inland waters, and to such of the upper courses of the rivers and streams as are broken by rapids and cataracts, with a view to substituting economical and rapid means of transportation for the present system of carriage by men.

4. Establishment of steam-boats on the inland navigable waters and on the lakes, supported by fortified posts established on the banks.

5. Establishment of telegraphic lines, insuring the communication of the posts and stations with the coast and with the administrative centres.

Slavery

6. Organization of expeditions and flying columns, to keep up the communication of the stations with each other and with the coast to support repressive action, and to insure the security of high roads.

7. Restriction of the importation of fire-arms, at least of those of modern pattern, and of ammunition throughout the entire extent of the territory in which the slave-trade is carried on.

Article II

The stations, the inland cruisers organized by each power in its waters, and the posts which serve as ports of register for them shall, independently of their principal task, which is to prevent the capture of slaves and intercept the routes of the slave trade, have the following subsidiary duties:

1. To support and, if necessary, to serve as a refuge for the native population, whether placed under the sovereignty or the protectorate of the State to which the station is subject, or independent, and temporarily for all other natives in case of imminent danger; to place the population of the first of these categories in a position to co-operate for their own defence; to diminish intestine wars between tribes by means of arbitration; to initiate them in agricultural labour and in the industrial arts so as to increase their welfare; to raise them to civilization and bring about the extinction of barbarous customs, such as cannibalism, and human sacrifices.

2. To give aid and protection to commercial enterprises; to watch over their legality by especially controlling contracts for service with natives, and to prepare the way for the foundation of permanent centres of cultivation and of commercial settlements.

3. To protect, without distinction of creed, the missions which are already or that may hereafter be established.

4. To provide for the sanitary service and to extend hospitality and help to explorers and to all who take part in Africa in the work of repressing the slave-trade.

Article III

The powers exercising a sovereignty or a protectorate in Africa confirm and give precision to their former declarations, and engage to proceed gradually, as circumstances may permit, either by the means above indicated, or by any other means that they may consider suitable, with the repression of the slave-trade, each State in its respective possessions and under its own direction. Whenever they consider it possible, they shall lend their good offices to such powers as, with a purely humanitarian object, may be engaged in Africa in the fulfilment of a similar mission.

Article IV

The States exercising sovereign powers or protectorates in Africa may in all cases delegate to companies provided with charters all or a portion of the engagements which they assume in virtue of Article III. They remain, nevertheless, directly responsible for the engagements which they contract by the present act, and guarantee the execution thereof. The powers promise to encourage, aid and protect such national associations and enterprises due to private initiative as may wish to co-operate in their possessions in the repression of the slave-trade, subject to their receiving previous authorization, such authorization being revokable at any time, subject also to their being directed and controlled, and to the exclusion of the exercise of rights of sovereignty.

Appendix I

Article V

The contracting powers pledge themselves, unless this has already been provided for by laws in accordance with the spirit of the present article, to enact or propose to their respective legislative bodies, in the course of one year at the latest from the date of the signing of the present general act, a law rendering applicable, on the one hand, the provisions of their penal laws concerning grave offences against the person, to the organizers and abettors of slave-hunting, to those guilty of mutilating male adults and children, and to all persons taking part in the capture of slaves by violence; and, on the other hand, the provisions relating to offences against individual liberty, to carriers and transporters of, and to dealers in slaves.

The accessories and accomplices of the different categories of slave captors and dealers above specified shall be punished with penalties proportionate to those incurred by the principals.

Guilty persons who may have escaped from the jurisdiction of the authorities of the country where the crimes or offences have been committed shall be arrested either on communication of the incriminating evidence by the authorities who have ascertained the violation of the law, or on production of any other proof of guilt by the power in whose territory they may have been discovered, and shall be kept, without other formality, at the disposal of the tribunals competent to try them.

The powers shall communicate to one another, with the least possible delay, the laws or decrees existing or promulgated in execution of the present Article.

Article VI

Slaves liberated in consequence of the stoppage or dispersion of a convoy in the interior of the continent, shall be sent back, if circumstances permit, to their country of origin; if not, the local authorities shall facilitate, as much as possible, their means of living, and if they desire it, help them to settle on the spot.

Article VII

Any fugitive slave claiming, on the continent, the protection of the signatory powers, shall receive it, and shall be received in the camps and stations officially established by said powers, or on board of the vessels of the State plying on the lakes and rivers. Private stations and boats are only permitted to exercise the right of asylum subject to the previous consent of the State.

Article VIII

The experience of all nations that have intercourse with Africa having shown the pernicious and preponderating part played by fire-arms in operations connected with the slave-trade as well as internal wars between the native tribes; and this same experience having clearly proved that the preservation of the African population whose existence it is the express wish of the powers to protect, is a radical impossibility, if measures restricting the trade in fire-arms and ammunition are not adopted, the powers decide, so far as the present state of their frontiers permits, that the importation of fire-arms, and especially of rifles and improved weapons, as well as of powder, ball and cartridges, is, except in the cases and under the conditions provided for in the following Article, prohibited in the territories comprised between the 20th parallel of North latitude and the 22nd parallel of South latitude, and extending westward to the Atlantic Ocean and eastward to the Indian Ocean and its dependencies, including the islands adjacent to the coast within 100 nautical miles from the shore.

Slavery

Article IX

The introduction of fire-arms and ammunition, when there shall be occasion to authorize it in the possessions of the signatory powers that exercise rights of sovereignty or of protectorate in Africa, shall be regulated, unless identical or stricter regulations have already been enforced, in the following manner in the zone defined in Article VIII:

All imported fire-arms shall be deposited, at the cost, risk and peril of the importers, in a public warehouse under the supervision of the State government. No withdrawal of fire-arms or imported ammunition shall take place from such warehouses without the previous authorization of the said government. This authorization shall, except in the cases hereinafter specified, be refused for the withdrawal of all arms for accurate firing, such as rifles, magazine guns, or breech-loaders, whether whole or in detached pieces, their cartridges, caps, or other ammunition intended for them.

In seaports and under conditions affording the needful guarantees, the respective governments may permit private warehouses, but only for ordinary powder and for flint-lock muskets, and to the exclusion of improved arms and ammunition therefor.

Independently of the measures directly taken by governments for the arming of the public force and the organization of their defence, individual exceptions may be allowed in the case of persons furnishing sufficient guarantees that the weapon and ammunition delivered to them shall not be given, assigned or sold to third parties, and for travellers provided with a declaration of their government stating that the weapon and ammunition are intended for their personal defence exclusively.

All arms, in the cases provided for in the preceding paragraph, shall be registered and marked by the supervising authorities, who shall deliver to the persons in question permits to bear arms, stating the name of the bearer and showing the stamp with which the weapon is marked. These permits shall be revocable in case proof is furnished that they have been improperly used, and shall be issued for five years only, but may be renewed.

The above rule as to warehousing shall also apply to gunpowder.

Only flint-lock guns, with unrifled barrels, and common gunpowder known as trade powder, may be withdrawn from the warehouses for sale. At each withdrawal of arms and ammunition of this kind for sale, the local authorities shall determine the regions in which such arms and ammunition may be sold. The regions in which the slave-trade is carried on shall always be excluded. Persons authorized to take arms or powder out of the public warehouses, shall present to the State government, every six months, detailed lists indicating the destinations of the arms and powder sold, as well as the quantities still remaining in the warehouses.

Article X

The Governments shall take all such measures as they may deem necessary to insure as complete a fulfilment as possible of the provisions respecting the importation, sale and transportation of fire-arms and ammunition, as well as to prevent either the entry or exit thereof via their inland frontiers, or the passage thereof to regions where the slave-trade is rife.

The authorization of transit within the limits of the zone specified in Article VIII shall not be withheld when the arms and ammunition are to pass across the territory of the signatory or adherent power occupying the coast, towards inland territories under the sovereignty or protectorate of another signatory or adherent power, unless this latter power have direct access to

Appendix I

the sea through its own territory. If this access be wholly interrupted, the authorization of transit can not be withheld. Any application for transit must be accompanied by a declaration emanating from the government of the power having the inland possessions, and certifying that the said arms and ammunition are not intended for sale, but are for the use of the authorities of such power, or of the military forces necessary for the protection of the missionary or commercial stations, or of persons mentioned by name in the declaration. Nevertheless, the territorial power of the coast retains the right to stop, exceptionally and provisionally, the transit of improved arms and ammunition across its territory, if, in consequence of inland disturbances or other serious danger, there is ground for fearing lest the despatch of arms and ammunition may compromise its own safety.

Article XI

The powers shall communicate to one another information relating to the traffic in fire-arms and ammunition, the permits granted, and the measures of repression in force in their respective territories.

Article XII

The powers engage to adopt or to propose to their respective legislative bodies the measures necessary everywhere to secure the punishment of infringers of the prohibitions contained in Articles VIII and IX, and that of their accomplices, besides the seizure and confiscation of the prohibited arms and ammunition, either by fine or imprisonment, or by both of these penalties, in proportion to the importance of the infraction and in accordance with the gravity of each case.

Article XIII

The signatory powers that have possessions in Africa in contact with the zone specified in Article VIII, bind themselves to take the necessary measures for preventing the introduction of fire-arms and ammunition across their inland frontiers into the regions of said zone, at least that of improved arms and cartridges.

Article XIV

The system stipulated in Articles VIII and XIII, shall remain in force for twelve years. In case none of the contracting parties shall have given notice twelve months before the expiration of this period, of its intention to put an end to it, or shall have demanded its revision, it shall remain obligatory for two years longer, and shall thus continue in force from two years to two years.

CHAPTER II. CARAVAN ROUTES AND TRANSPORTATION OF SLAVES BY LAND

Article XV

Independently of the repressive or protective action which they exercise in the centres of the slave-trade, it shall be the duty of the stations, cruisers and posts, whose establishment is provided for in Article II, and of all other stations established or recognized by Article IV, by each government in its possessions, to watch, so far as circumstances shall permit, and in proportion to the progress of their administrative organization, the roads travelled in their territory by slave-dealers, to stop convoys on their march, or to pursue them wherever their action can be legally exercised.

Slavery

Article XVI

In the regions of the coast known to serve habitually as places of passage or terminal points for slave-traffic coming from the interior, as well as at the points of intersection of the principal caravan routes crossing the zone contiguous to the coast already subject to the control of the sovereign or protective powers, posts shall be established under the conditions and with the reservations mentioned in Article III, by the authorities to which the territories are subject, for the purpose of intercepting the convoys and liberating the slaves.

Article XVII

A strict watch shall be organized by the local authorities at the ports and places near the coast, with a view to preventing the sale and shipment of slaves brought from the interior, as well as the formation and departure landwards of bands of slave-hunters and dealers.

Caravans arriving at the coast or in its vicinity, as well as those arriving in the interior at a locality occupied by the territorial power, shall, on their arrival, be subjected to a minute inspection as to the persons composing them. Any such person being ascertained to have been captured or carried off by force, or mutilated, either in his native place or on the way, shall be set free.

Article XVIII

In the possessions of each of the contracting powers, it shall be the duty of the government to protect liberated slaves, to return them, if possible, to their country, to procure means of subsistence for them, and, in particular, to take charge of the education and subsequent employment of abandoned children.

Article XIX

The penal arrangements provided for by Article V shall be applicable to all offences committed in the course of operations connected with the transportation of and traffic in slaves on land whenever such offences may be ascertained to have been committed.

Any person having incurred a penalty in consequence of an offence provided for by the present general act, shall incur the obligation of furnishing security before being able to engage in any commercial transaction in countries where the slave-trade is carried on.

CHAPTER III. REPRESSION OF THE SLAVE-TRADE BY SEA
SECTION I. *General provisions*

Article XX

The signatory powers recognize the desirability of taking steps in common for the more effective repression of the slave-trade in the maritime zone in which it still exists.

Article XXI

This zone extends, on the one hand, between the coasts of the Indian Ocean (those of the Persian Gulf and of the Red Sea included), from Beloochistan to Cape Tangalane (Quilimane); and, on the other hand, a conventional line which first follows the meridian from Tangalane till it intersects the 26th degree of South lattitude; it is then merged in this parallel, then passes round the Island of Madagascar by the east, keeping 20 miles off the east and north shore, till it intersects the meridian at Cape Ambre. From this point the limit of the zone is determined by an oblique line, which extends to the coast of Beloochistan, passing 20 miles off Cape Ras-el-Had.

Appendix I

Article XXII

The signatory powers of the present general act,—among whom exist special conventions for the suppression of the slave-trade, have agreed to restrict the clauses of those conventions concerning the reciprocal right of visit, of search and of seizure of vessels at sea, to the above mentioned zone.

Article XXIII

The same powers also agree to limit the above mentioned right to vessels whose tonnage is less than 500 tons. This stipulation shall be revised as soon as experience shall have shown the necessity thereof.

Article XXIV

All other provisions of the conventions concluded for the suppression of the slave-trade between the aforesaid powers shall remain in force provided they are not modified by the present general act.

Article XXV

The signatory powers engage to adopt measures to prevent the unlawful use of their flag, and to prevent the transportation of slaves on vessels authorized to fly their colours.

Article XXVI

The signatory powers engage to adopt all measures necessary to facilitate the speedy exchange of information calculated to lead to the discovery of persons taking part in operations connected with the slave-trade.

Article XXVII

At least one international bureau shall be created; it shall be established at Zanzibar. The high contracting parties engage to forward to it all the documents specified in Article XLI, as well as all information of any kind likely to assist in the suppression of the slave-trade.

Article XXVIII

Any slave who has taken refuge on board a ship of war bearing the flag of one of the signatory powers, shall be immediately and definitively set free. Such freedom, however, shall not withdraw him from the competent jurisdiction if he has been guilty of any crime or offence at common law.

Article XXIX

Any slave detained against his will on board of a native vessel shall have the right to demand his liberty. His release may be ordered by any agent of any of the signatory powers on whom the present general act confers the right of ascertaining the status of persons on board of such vessels, although such release shall not withdraw him from the competent jurisdiction if he has committed any crime or offence at common law.

SECTION II. *Regulation concerning the use of the flag and supervision by cruisers*

1. RULES FOR GRANTING THE FLAG TO NATIVE VESSELS, AND AS TO CREW LISTS AND MANIFESTS OF BLACK PASSENGERS ON BOARD

Article XXX

The signatory powers engage to exercise a strict surveillance over native

Slavery

vessels authorized to carry their flag in the zone mentioned in Article XXI, and over the commercial operations carried on by such vessels.

Article XXXI
The term 'native vessel' applies to vessels fulfilling one of the following conditions:
1. It shall present the outward appearance of native build or rigging.
2. It shall be manned by a crew of whom the captain and a majority of the seamen belong by origin to one of the countries on the coast of the Indian Ocean, the Red Sea, or the Persian Gulf.

Article XXXII
The authorization to carry the flag of one of the said powers shall in future be granted only to such native vessels as shall satisfy at the same time the three following conditions:
1. Fitters-out or owners of ships must be either subjects of or persons protected by the power whose flag they ask to carry.
2. They shall be obliged to prove that they possess real estate situated in the district of the authority to whom their application is addressed, or to furnish *bona fide* security as a guarantee of the payment of such fines as may be incurred.
3. The above-named fitters-out or owners of ships, as well as the captain of the vessel, shall prove that they enjoy a good reputation, and that in particular they have never been sentenced to punishment for acts connected with the slave-trade.

Article XXXIII
This authorization granted shall be renewed every year. It may at any time be suspended or withdrawn by the authorities of the power whose colours the vessel carries.

Article XXXIV
The act of authorization shall contain the statements necessary to establish the identity of the vessel. The captain shall have the keeping thereof. The name of the native vessel and the amount of its tonnage shall be cut and painted in Latin characters on the stern, and the initial or initials of the name of the port of registry, as well as the registration number in the series of the numbers of that port, shall be printed in black on the sails.

Article XXXV
A list of the crew shall be issued to the captain of the vessel at the port of departure by the authorities of the power whose colours it carries. It shall be renewed at every fresh venture of the vessel, or, at the latest, at the end of a year, and in accordance with the following provisions:
1. The vessel shall be visaed at the departure of the vessel by the authority that has issued it.
2. No negro can be engaged as a seaman on a vessel without having previously been questioned by the authority of the power whose colours it carries, or, in default thereof, by the territorial authority, with a view to ascertaining the fact of his having contracted a free engagement.
3. This authority shall see that the proportion of seamen and boys is not out of proportion to the tonnage or rigging.
4. The authorities who shall have questioned the men before their departure shall enter them on the list of the crew in which they shall be

Appendix I

mentioned with a summary description of each of them alongside his name.

5. In order the more effectively to prevent any substitution, the seamen may, moreover, be provided with a distinctive mark.

Article XXXVI

When the captain of a vessel shall desire to take negro passengers on board, he shall make his declaration to that effect to the authority of the power whose colours he carries, or in default thereof, to the territorial authority. The passengers shall be questioned, and after it has been ascertained that they embarked of their own free will, they shall be entered in a special manifest, bearing the description of each of them alongside of his name, and specially sex and height. Negro children shall not be taken as passengers unless they are accompanied by their relations, or by persons whose respectability is well known. At the departure, the passenger-roll shall be visaed by the aforesaid authority after it has been called. If there are no passengers on board, this shall be specially mentioned in the crew-list.

Article XXXVII

At the arrival at any port of call or of destination, the captain of the vessel shall show to the authority of the power whose flag he carries, or, in default thereof, to the territorial authority, the crew-list, and, if need be, the passenger-roll previously delivered. The authority shall check the passengers who have reached their destination or who are stopping in a port of call, and shall mention their landing in the roll. At the departure of the vessel, the same authority shall affix a fresh visé to the list and roll, and call the roll of the passengers.

Article XXXVIII

On the African coast and on the adjacent islands, no negro passengers shall be taken on board of a native vessel, except in localities where there is a resident authority belonging to one of the signatory powers.

Throughout the extent of the zone mentioned in Article XXI, no negro passengers shall be landed from a native vessel except at a place in which there is a resident officer belonging to one of the high contracting powers, and unless such officer is present at the landing.

Cases of *vis major* that may have caused an infraction of these provisions shall be examined by the authority of the power whose colours the vessel carries, or, in default thereof, by the territorial authority of the port at which the vessel in question calls.

Article XXXIX

The provisions of Articles XXXV, XXXVI, XXXVII, and XXXVIII are not applicable to vessels only partially decked, having a crew not exceeding ten men, and fulfilling one of the two following conditions:

1. That it be exclusively used for fishing within the territorial waters.

2. That it be occupied in the petty coasting trade between the different ports of the same territorial power, without going further than five miles from the coast.

These different boats shall receive, as the case may be, a special licence from the territorial or consular authority, which shall be renewed every year, and subject to revocation as provided in Article XL, the uniform model of which licence is annexed to the present general act and shall be communicated to the international information office.

Slavery

Article XL

Any act or attempted act connected with the slave-trade that can be legally shown to have been committed by the captain, fitter-out, or owner of a ship authorized to carry the flag of one of the signatory powers, or having procured the licence provided for in Article XXXIX, shall entail the immediate withdrawal of the said authorization or licence. All violations of the provisions of Section 2 of Chapter III shall render the person guilty thereof liable to the penalties provided by the special laws and ordinances of each of the contracting parties.

Article XLI

The signatory powers engage to deposit at the international information office the specimen forms of the following documents:
1. Licence to carry the flag;
2. The crew-list;
3. The negro passenger list.

These documents, the tenor of which may vary according to the different regulations of each country, shall necessarily contain the following particulars, drawn up in one of the European languages:
1. As regards the authorization to carry the flag:
   (a) The name, tonnage, rig, and the principal dimensions of the vessel;
   (b) The register number and the signal letter of the port of registry;
   (c) The date of obtaining the licence, and the office held by the person who issued it.
2. As regards the list of the crew:
   (a) The name of the vessel, of the captain and the fitter-out or owner;
   (b) The tonnage of the vessel;
   (c) The register number and the port of registry, its destination, as well as the particulars specified in Article XXV.
3. As regards the list of negro passengers:
The name of the vessel which conveys them, and the particulars indicated in Article XXXVI, for the proper identification of the passengers.

The signatory powers shall take the necessary measures so that the territorial authorities or their consuls may send to the same office certified copies of all authorizations to carry their flag as soon as such authorizations shall have been granted, as well as notices of the withdrawal of any such authorization.

The provisions of the present article have reference only to papers intended for native vessels.

2. THE STOPPING OF SUSPECTED VESSELS

Article XLII

When the officers in command of war-vessels of any of the signatory powers have reason to believe that a vessel whose tonnage is less than 500 tons, and which is found navigating in the above-named zone, is engaged in the slave-trade or is guilty of the fraudulent use of a flag, they may examine the ship's papers.

The present article does not imply any change in the present state of things as regards jurisdiction in territorial waters.

Article XLIII

To this end, a boat commanded by a naval officer in uniform may be sent

Appendix I

to board the suspected vessel after it has been hailed and informed of this intention.

The officers sent on board of the vessel which has been stopped shall act with all possible consideration and moderation.

Article XLIV

The examination of the ship's papers shall consist of the examination of the following documents:

1. As regards native vessels, the papers mentioned in Article XLI.

2. As regards other vessels, the documents required by the different treaties or conventions that are in force.

The examination of the ship's papers only authorizes the calling of the roll of the crew and passengers in the cases and in accordance with the conditions provided for in the following article.

Article XLV

The examination of the cargo or the search can only take place in the case of vessels sailing under the flag of one of the powers that have concluded, or may hereafter conclude the special conventions provided for in Article XXII, and in accordance with the provisions of such conventions.

Article XLVI

Before leaving the detained vessel, the officer shall draw up a minute according to the forms and in the language in use in the country to which he belongs.

This minute shall be dated and signed by the officer, and shall recite the facts.

The captain of the detained vessel, as well as the witnesses, shall have the right to cause to be added to the minutes any explanations they may think expedient.

Article XLVII

The commander of a man-of-war who has detained a vessel under a foreign flag shall, in all cases, make a report thereof to his own government, and state the grounds upon which he has acted.

Article XLVIII

A summary of this report, as well as a copy of the minute drawn up by the officer on board of the detained vessel, shall be sent, as soon as possible, to the international information office, which shall communicate the same to the nearest consular or territorial authority of the power whose flag the vessel in question has shown. Duplicates of these documents shall be kept in the archives of the bureau.

Article XLIX

If, in performing the acts of supervision mentioned in the preceding articles, the officer in command of the cruiser is convinced that an act connected with the slave-trade has been committed on board during the passage, or that irrefutable proofs exist against the captain, or fitter-out, for accusing him of fraudulent use of the flag, or fraud, or participation in the slave-trade, he shall conduct the arrested vessel to the nearest port of the zone where there is a competent magistrate of the power whose flag has been used.

Each signatory power engages to appoint in the zone, and to make known to the international information office, the territorial or consular authorities

Slavery

or special delegates who are competent in the above mentioned cases.

A suspected vessel may also be turned over to a cruiser of its own nation, if the latter consents to take charge of it.

3. OF THE EXAMINATION AND TRIAL OF VESSELS SEIZED

Article L

The magistrate referred to in the preceding article, to whom the arrested vessel has been turned over, shall proceed to make a full investigation, according to the laws and rules of his country, in the presence of an officer belonging to the foreign cruiser.

Article LI

If it is proved by the inquiry that the flag has been fraudently used, the vessel shall remain at the disposal of its captor.

Article LII

If the examination shows an act connected with the slave-trade, proved by the presence on board of slaves destined for sale, or any other offence connected with the slave-trade for which provision is made by special convention, the vessel and cargo shall remain sequestrated in charge of the magistrate who shall have conducted the inquiry.

The captain and crew shall be turned over to the tribunals designated by Articles LIV and LVI. The slaves shall be set at liberty as soon as judgment has been pronounced.

In the cases provided for by this article, liberated slaves shall be disposed of in accordance with the special conventions concluded, or to be concluded, between the signatory powers. In default of such conventions, the said slaves shall be turned over to the local authority, to be sent back, if possible, to their country of origin; if not, this authority shall facilitate to them, in so far as may be in its power, the means of livelihood, and, if they desire it, of settling on the spot.

Article LIII

If it shall be proved by the inquiry that the vessel has been illegally arrested, there shall be clear title to an indemnity in proportion to the damages suffered by the vessel being taken out of its course.

The amount of this indemnity shall be fixed by the authority that has conducted the inquiry.

Article LIV

In case of the officer of the capturing vessel does not accept the conclusions of the inquiry held in his presence, the matter shall be turned over to the tribunal of the nation whose flag the captured vessel has borne.

No exception shall be made to this rule, unless the disagreement arises in respect of the amount of the indemnity stipulated in Article LIII, and this shall be fixed by arbitration, as specified in the following article.

Article LV

The capturing officer and the authority which has conducted the inquiry shall each appoint a referee within forty-eight hours, and the two arbitrators shall have twenty-four hours to choose an umpire. The arbitrators shall, as far as possible, be chosen from among the diplomatic, consular, or judicial officers of the signatory powers. Natives in the pay of the contracting Governments are formally excluded. The decision shall be by a majority of votes, and be considered as final.

Appendix I

If the court of arbitration is not constituted in the time indicated, the procedure in respect of the indemnity, as in that of damages, shall be in accordance with the provisions of Article LVIII, paragraph 2.

Article LVI

The cases shall be brought with the least possible delay before the tribunal of the nation whose flag has been used by the accused. However, the consuls or any other authority of the same nation as the accused, specially commissioned to this end, may be authorized by their Government to pronounce judgment instead of the tribunal.

Article LVII

The procedure and trial of violations of the provisions of Chapter III shall always be conducted in as summary a manner as is permitted by the laws and regulations in force in the territories subject to the authority of the signatory powers.

Article LVIII

Any decision of the national tribunal or authorities referred to in Article LVI, declaring that the seized vessel did not carry on the slave-trade, shall be immediately enforced, and the vessel shall be at perfect liberty to continue on its course.

In this case, the captain or owner of any vessel that has been seized without legitimate ground of suspicion, or subjected to annoyance, shall have the right of claiming damages, the amount of which shall be fixed by agreement between the Governments directly interested, or by arbitration, and shall be paid within a period of six months from the date of the judgment acquitting the captured vessel.

Article LIX

In the case of condemnation, the sequestered vessel shall be declared lawfully seized for the benefit of the captor.

The captain, crew, and all other persons found guilty shall be punished according to the gravity of the crimes or offences committed by them, and in accordance with Article V.

Article LX

The provisions of Articles L to LIX do not in any way affect the jurisdiction or procedure of existing special tribunals, or of such as may hereafter be formed to take cognizance of offences connected with the slave-trade.

Article LXI

The high contracting parties engage to make known to one another, reciprocally, the instructions which they shall give, for the execution of the provisions of Chapter III, to the commanders of their men-of-war navigating the seas of the zone referred to.

CHAPTER IV. COUNTRIES TO WHICH SLAVES ARE SENT, WHOSE INSTITUTIONS RECOGNIZE THE EXISTENCE OF DOMESTIC SLAVERY

Article LXII

The contracting powers whose institutions recognize the existence of domestic slavery, and whose possessions, in consequence thereof, in or out of Africa, serve, in spite of the vigilance of the authorities, as places of destination for African slaves, pledge themselves to prohibit their importation, transit and departure, as well as the trade in slaves. The most active and

Slavery

the strictest supervision shall be enforced at all places where the arrival, transit, and departure of African slaves take place.

Article LXIII
Slaves set free under the provisions of the preceding article shall, if circumstances permit, be sent back to the country from whence they came. In all cases they shall receive letters of liberation from the competent authorities, and shall be entitled to their protection and assistance for the purpose of obtaining means of subsistence.

Article LXIV
Any fugitive slave arriving at the frontier of any of the powers mentioned in Article LXII shall be considered free, and shall have the right to claim letters of release from the competent authorities.

Article LXV
Any sale or transaction to which the slaves referred to in Articles LXVIII and LXIV may have been subjected through circumstances of any kind whatsoever, shall be considered as null and void.

Article LXVI
Native vessels carrying the flag of one of the countries mentioned in Article LXVII, if there is any indication that they are employed in operations connected with the slave-trade, shall be subjected by the local authorities in the ports frequented by them to a strict examination of their crews and passengers both on arrival and departure. If African slaves are found on board, judicial proceedings shall be instituted against the vessel and against all persons who may be implicated. Slaves found on board shall receive letters of release through the authorities who have seized the vessels.

Article LXVII
Penal provisions similar to those provided for by Article V shall be enacted against persons importing, transporting, and trading in African slaves, against the mutilators of male children or adults, and those who traffic in them, as well as against their associates and accomplices.

Article LXVIII
The signatory powers recognize the great importance of the law respecting the prohibition of the slave-trade sanctioned by His Majesty the Emperor of the Ottomans on the 4th (16th) of December, 1889 (22 Rebi-ul-Akhir, 1307), and they are assured that an active surveillance will be organized by the Ottoman authorities, especially on the west coast of Arabia and on the routes which place that coast in communication with the other possessions of His Imperial Majesty in Asia.

Article LXIX
His Majesty the Shah of Persia consents to organize an active surveillance in the territorial waters and those off the coast of the Persian Gulf and Gulf of Oman which are under his sovereignty, and on the inland routes which serve for the transportation of slaves. The magistrates and other authorities shall, to this effect, receive the necessary powers.

Appendix I

Article LXX

His Highness the Sultan of Zanzibar consents to give his most effective support to the repression of crimes and offences committed by African slave-traders on land as well as at sea. The tribunals created for this purpose in the Sultanate of Zanzibar shall rigorously enforce the penal provisions mentioned in Article V. In order to render more secure the freedom of liberated slaves, both in virtue of the provisions of the present general act and of the decrees adopted in this matter by His Highness and his predecessors, a liberation office shall be established at Zanzibar.

Article LXXI

The diplomatic and consular agents and the naval officers of the contracting powers shall, within the limits of existing conventions, give their assistance to the local authorities in order to assist in repressing the slave-trade where it still exists. They shall be present at trials for slave-trading brought about at their instance, without, however, being entitled to take part in the deliberations.

Article LXXII

Liberation offices, or institutions in lieu thereof, shall be organized by the governments of the countries to which African slaves are sent, for the purposes specified by Article XVIII.

Article LXXIII

The signatory powers having undertaken to communicate to one another all information useful for the repression of the slave-trade, the Governments whom the present chapter concerns shall periodically exchange with the other Governments statistical data relating to slaves intercepted and liberated, and to the legislative and administrative measures which have been taken for suppressing the slave-trade.

CHAPTER V. INSTITUTIONS INTENDED TO INSURE THE EXECUTION OF THE GENERAL ACT

SECTION I. *Of the international maritime office*

Article LXXIV

In accordance with the provisions of Article XXVII, an international office shall be instituted at Zanzibar, in which each of the signatory powers may be represented by a delegate.

Article LXXIV

The office shall be constituted as soon as three powers have appointed their representatives.

It shall draw up regulations fixing the manner of exercising its functions. These regulations shall immediately be submitted to the approval of such signatory powers as shall have signified their intention of being represented in this office. They shall decide in this respect within the shortest possible time.

Article LXXVI

The expenses of this institution shall be divided in equal parts among the signatory powers mentioned in the preceding article.

Article LXXVII

The object of the office at Zanzibar shall be to centralize all documents

Slavery

and information of a nature to facilitate the repression of the slave-trade in the maritime zone. For this purpose the signatory powers engage to forward within the shortest time possible:

1. The documents specified in Article XLI;

2. Summaries of the reports and copies of the minutes referred to in Article XLVIII;

3. The list of the territorial or consular authorities and special delegates competent to take action as regards vessels seized according to the terms of Article XLIX;

4. Copies of judgments and condemnations in accordance with Article LVIII;

5. All information that may lead to the discovery of persons engaged in the slave-trade in the above mentioned zone.

Article LXXVIII

The archives of the office shall always be open to the naval officers of the signatory powers authorized to act within the limits of the zone defined by Article XXI, as well as to the territorial or judicial authorities, and to consuls specially designated by their Governments.

The office shall supply to foreign officers and agents authorized to consult its archives, translations into a European language of documents written in an oriental language.

It shall make the communications provided for in Article XLVIII.

Article LXXIX

Auxiliary offices in communication with the office at Zanzibar may be established in certain parts of the zone, in pursuance of a previous agreement between the interested powers.

They shall be composed of delegates of these powers, and established in accordance with Articles LXXV, LXXVI, and LXXVIII.

The documents and information specified in Article LXXVII, so far as they may relate to a part of the zone specially concerned, shall be sent to them directly by the territorial and consular authorities of the region in question, but this shall not exempt the latter from the duty of communicating the same to the office at Zanzibar, as provided by the same article.

Article LXXX

The office at Zanzibar shall prepare in the first two months of every year, a report of its own operations and of those of the auxiliary offices during the past twelve months.

SECTION II. *Of the exchange between the Governments of documents and information relating to the slave-trade*

Article LXXXI

The powers shall communicate to one another, to the fullest extent and with the least delay that they shall consider possible:

1. The text of the laws and administrative regulations, existing or enacted by application of the clauses of the present general act;

2. Statistical information concerning the slave-trade, slaves arrested and liberated, and the traffic in fire-arms, ammunition, and alcoholic liquors.

Appendix I

Article LXXXII
The exchange of these documents and information shall be centralized in a special office attached to the foreign office at Brussels.

Article LXXXIII
The office at Zanzibar shall forward to it every year the report mentioned in Article LXXX, concerning its operations during the past year, and concerning those of the auxiliary offices that may have been established in accordance with Article LXXIX.

Article LXXXIV
The documents and information shall be collected and published periodically, and addressed to all the signatory powers. This publication shall be accompanied every year by an analytical table of the legislative, administrative, and statistical documents mentioned in Articles LXXXI and LXXXIII.

Article LXXXV
The office expenses as well as those incurred in correspondence, translation, and printing, shall be shared by all the signatory powers, and shall be collected through the agency of the department of the foreign office at Brussels.

SECTION III. *Of the protection of liberated slaves*

Article LXXXVI
The signatory powers having recognized the duty of protecting liberated slaves in their respective possessions, engage to establish, if they do not already exist, in the ports of the zone determined by Article XXI, and in such parts of their said possessions as may be places for the capture, passage and arrival of African slaves, such offices and institutions as may be deemed sufficient by them, whose business shall specially consist in liberating and protecting them in accordance with the provisions of Articles VI, XVIII, LII, LXIII, and LXVI.

Article LXXXVII
The liberation offices or the authorities charged with this service shall deliver letters of release and shall keep a register thereof.

In case of the denunciation of an act connected with the slave-trade, or one of illegal detention, or on application to the slaves themselves, the said offices or authorities shall exercise all necessary diligence to insure the release of the slaves and the punishment of the offenders.

The delivery of letters of release shall in no case be delayed, if the slave be accused of a crime or offence against the common law. But after the delivery of the said letters an investigation shall be proceeded with in the form established by the ordinary procedure.

Article LXXXVIII
The signatory powers shall favour, in their possessions, the foundation of establishments of refuge for women and of education for liberated children.

Article LXXXIX
Freed slaves may always apply to the offices for protection in the enjoyment of their freedom

Whoever shall have used fraudulent or violent means to deprive a freed

Slavery

slave of his letters of release or of his liberty, shall be considered as a slave-dealer.

CHAPTER VI. MEASURES TO RESTRICT THE TRAFFIC IN SPIRITUOUS LIQUORS

Article XC

Being justly anxious concerning the moral and material consequences to which the abuse of spirituous liquors subjects the native population, the signatory powers have agreed to enforce the provisions of Articles XCI, XCII and XCIII within a zone extending from the 20th degree of North latitude to the 22nd degree of South latitude, and bounded on the west by the Atlantic Ocean and on the east by the Indian Ocean and its dependencies, including the islands adjacent to the mainland within 100 nautical miles from the coast.

Article XCI

In the districts of this zone where it shall be ascertained that, either on account of religious belief or from some other causes, the use of distilled liquors does not exist or has not been developed, the powers shall prohibit their importation. The manufacture of distilled liquors shall be likewise prohibited there.

Each power shall determine the limits of the zone of prohibition of alcoholic liquors in its possessions or protectorates, and shall be bound to make known the limits thereof to the other powers within the space of six months.

The above prohibition can only be suspended in the case of limited quantities intended for the consumption of the non-native population and imported under the regime and conditions determined by each Government.

Article XCII

The powers having possessions or exercising protectorates in those regions of the zone which are not subjected to the regime of the prohibition, and into which alcoholic liquors are at present either freely imported or pay an import duty of less than 15 francs per hectolitre at 50 degrees centigrade, engage to levy on such alcoholic liquors an import duty of 15 francs per hectolitre at 50 degrees centigrade, for three years after the present general act comes into force. At the expiration of this period the duty may be increased to 25 francs during a fresh period of three years. At the end of the sixth year it shall be submitted to revision, the average results produced by these tariffs being taken as a basis, for the purpose of then fixing, if possible, a minimum duty throughout the whole extent of the zone where the prohibition referred to in Article XCI is not in force.

The powers retain the right of maintaining and increasing the duties beyond the minimum fixed by the present article in those regions where they already possess that right.

Article XCIII

Distilled liquors manufactured in the regions referred to in Article XCII, and intended for inland consumption, shall be subject to an excise duty.

This excise duty, the collection of which the powers engage to secure, as far as possible, shall not be less than the minimum import duty fixed by Article XCII.

Article XCIV

The signatory powers having possessions in Africa contiguous to the zone

Appendix I

specified in Article XC engage to adopt the necessary measures for preventing the introduction of spirituous liquors within the territories of the said zone via their inland frontiers.

Article XCV

The powers shall communicate to one another, through the office at Brussels, and according to the terms of Chapter V, information relating to the traffic in alcoholic liquors within their respective territories.

CHAPTER VII. FINAL PROVISIONS

Article XCVI

The present general act repeals all contrary stipulations of conventions previously concluded between the signatory powers.

Article XCVII

The signatory powers, without prejudice to the stipulations contained in Articles XIV, XXIII and XCII, reserve the right of introducing into the present general act, hereafter and by common consent, such modifications or improvements as experience may prove to be useful.

Article XCVIII

Powers who have not signed the present general act shall be allowed to adhere to it.

The signatory powers reserve the right to impose such conditions as they may deem necessary to their adhesion.

If no conditions shall be stipulated, adhesion implies acceptance of all the obligations and admission to all the advantages stipulated by the present general act.

The powers shall agree among themselves as to the steps to be taken to secure the adhesion of states whose co-operation may be necessary or useful in order to insure complete execution of the general act.

Adhesion shall be effected by a separate act. Notice thereof shall be given through the diplomatic channel to the Government of the King of the Belgians, and by that Government to all the signatory and adherent states.

Article XCIX

The present general act shall be ratified within the shortest possible period, which shall not in any case exceed one year.

Each power shall address its ratification to the Government of the King of the Belgians, which shall give notice thereof to all the other powers that have signed the present general act.

The ratification of all the powers shall remain deposited in the archives of the Kingdom of Belgium.

As soon as all the ratifications shall have been furnished, or at the latest one year after the signature of the present general act, their delivery shall be recorded in a protocol which shall be signed by the representatives of all the powers that have ratified.

A certified copy of this protocol shall be forwarded to all the powers interested.

Article C

The present general act shall come into force in all the possessions of the contracting powers on the sixtieth day, reckoned from the day on which the protocol provided for in the preceding article shall have been drawn up.

APPENDIX II

THE SLAVERY CONVENTION OF THE LEAGUE OF NATIONS, 1926

Whereas the signatories of the General Act of the Brussels Conference of 1889-90 declared that they were equally animated by the firm intention of putting an end to the traffic in African slaves;

Whereas the signatories of the Convention of Saint Germain-en-Laye of 1919 to revise the General Act of Berlin of 1885 and the General Act and Declaration of Brussels of 1890 affirmed their intention of securing the complete suppression of slavery in all its forms and of the slave trade by land and sea;

Taking into consideration the report of the Temporary Slavery Commission appointed by the Council of the League of Nations on June 12th, 1924;

Desiring to complete and extend the work accomplished under the Brussels Act and to find a means of giving practical effect throughout the world to such intentions as were expressed in regard to slave trade and slavery by the signatories of the Convention of Saint Germain-en-Laye, and recognizing that it is necessary to conclude to that end more detailed arrangements than are contained in that Convention;

Considering, moreover, that it is necessary to prevent forced labour from devoloping into conditions analogous to slavery;

Have decided to conclude a Convention and have accordingly appointed as their Plenipotentiaries:

Who, having communicated their full powers, have agreed as follows:

Article 1

For the purpose of the present Convention, the following definitions are agreed upon:

1. Slavery is the status or condition of a person over whom any or all the powers attaching to the right of ownership are exercised.

2. The slave trade includes all acts involved in the capture, acquisition or disposal of a person with intent to reduce him to slavery; all acts involved in the acquisition of a slave with a view to selling or exchanging him; all acts of disposal by sale or exchange of a slave acquired with a view to being sold or exchanged, and, in general, every act of trade or transport in slaves.

Article 2

The High Contracting Parties undertake, each in respect of the territories placed under its sovereignty, jurisdiction, protection, suzerainty or tutelage, so far as they have not already taken the necessary steps:

(a) To prevent and suppress the slave trade;

(b) To bring about, progressively and as soon as possible, the complete abolition of slavery in all its forms.

Article 3

The High Contracting Parties undertake to adopt all appropriate measures

Appendix II

with a view to preventing and suppressing the embarkation, disembarkation and transport of slaves in their territorial waters and upon all vessels flying their respective flags.

The High Contracting Parties undertake to negotiate as soon as possible a general Convention with regard to the slave trade which will give them rights and impose upon them duties of the same nature as those provided for in the Convention of June 17th, 1925, relative to the International Trade in Arms (Articles 12, 20, 21, 22, 23, 24, and paragraphs 3, 4 and 5 of Section II of Annex II) with the necessary adaptations, it being understood that this general Convention will not place the ships (even of small tonnage) of any High Contracting Parties in a position different from that of the other High Contracting Parties.

It is also understood that, before or after the coming into force of this general Convention, the High Contracting Parties are entirely free to conclude between themselves, without, however, derogating from the principles laid down in the preceding article, such special agreements as, by reason of their peculiar situation, might appear to be suitable in order to bring about as soon as possible the complete disappearance of the slave trade.

Article 4

The High Contracting Parties shall give to one another every assistance with the object of securing the abolition of slavery and the slave trade.

Article 5

The High Contracting Parties recognize that recourse to compulsory or forced labour may have grave consequences and undertake, each in respect of the territories placed under its sovereignty, jurisdiction, protection, suzerainty or tutelage, to take all necessary measures to prevent compulsory or forced labour from developing into conditions analogous to slavery.

It is agreed that:

(1) Subject to the transitional provisions laid down in paragraph (2) below, compulsory or forced labour may only be extracted for public purposes.

(2) In territories in which compulsory or forced labour for other than public purposes still survives, the High Contracting Parties shall endeavour progressively and as soon as possible to put an end to the practice. So long as such forced or compulsory labour exists, this labour shall invariably be of an exceptional character, shall always receive adequate remuneration, and shall not involve the removal of the labourers from their usual place of residence.

(3) In all cases, the responsibility for any recourse to compulsory or forced labour shall rest with the competent central authorities of the territory concerned.

Article 6

Those of the High Contracting Parties whose laws do not at present make adequate provision for the punishment of infractions of laws and regulations enacted with a view to giving effect to the purposes of the present Convention undertake to adopt the necessary measures in order that severe penalties may be imposed in respect of such infractions.

Article 7

The High Contracting Parties undertake to communicate to each other and to the Secretary-General of the League of Nations any laws and regulations

Slavery

which they may enact with a view to the application of the provisions of the present Convention.

Article 8

The High Contracting Parties agree that disputes arising between them relating to the interpretation or application of this Convention shall, if they cannot be settled by direct negotiation, be referred for decision to the Permanent Court of International Justice. In case either or both of the States Parties to such a dispute should not be parties to the Protocol of December 16th, 1920, relating to the Permanent Court of International Justice, the dispute shall be referred, at the choice of the Parties and in accordance with the constitutional procedure of each State, either to the Permanent Court of International Justice or to a court of arbitration constituted in accordance with the Convention of October 18th, 1907, for the Pacific Settlement of International Disputes, or to some other court of arbitration.

Article 9

At the time of signature or of ratification or of accession, any High Contracting Party may declare that its acceptance of the present Convention does not bind some or all of the territories placed under its sovereignty, jurisdiction, protection, suzerainty or tutelage in respect of all or any provisions of the Convention; it may subsequently accede separately on behalf of any one of them or in respect of any provision to which any one of them is not a party.

Article 10

In the event of a High Contracting Party wishing to denounce the present Convention, the denunciation shall be notified in writing to the Secretary-General of the League of Nations, who will at once communicate a certified true copy of the notification to all other High Contracting Parties informing them of the date on which it was received.

The denunciation shall only have effect in regard to the notifying State, and one year after the notification has reached the Secretary-General of the League of Nations.

Denunciation may also be made separately in respect of any territory placed under its sovereignty, jurisdiction, protection, suzerainty or tutelage.

Article 11

The present Convention, which will bear this day's date and of which the French and English texts are both authentic, will remain open for signature by the States Members of the League of Nations until April 1st, 1927.

The Secretary-General of the League of Nations will subsequently bring the present Convention to the notice of States which have not signed it, including States which are not Members of the League of Nations, and invite them to accede thereto.

A State desiring to accede to the Convention shall notify its intention in writing to the Secretary-General of the League of Nations and transmit to him the instrument of accession, which shall be deposited in the archives of the League.

The Secretary-General shall immediately transmit to all the other High Contracting Parties a certified true copy of the notification and of the instrument of accession, informing them of the date on which he received them.

Article 12

The present Convention will be ratified and the instruments of ratification

Appendix II

shall be deposited in the office of the Secretary-General of the League of Nations. The Secretary-General will inform all the High Contracting Parties of such deposit.

The Convention will come into operation for each State on the date of the deposit of its ratification or of its accession.

In faith whereof the Plenipotentiaries have signed the present Convention.

DONE at Geneva the twenty-fifth day of September, one thousand nine hundred and twenty-six, in one copy, which will be deposited in the archives of the League of Nations. A certified copy shall be forwarded to each signatory State.

APPENDIX III

SUPPLEMENTARY CONVENTION ON THE ABOLITION OF SLAVERY, THE SLAVE TRADE, AND INSTITUTIONS AND PRACTICES SIMILAR TO SLAVERY

PREAMBLE

The States Parties to the present Convention
Considering that freedom is the birthright of every human being;
Mindful that the peoples of the United Nations reaffirmed in their Charter their faith in the dignity and worth of the human person;
Considering that the Universal Declaration of Human Rights, proclaimed by the General Assembly of the United Nations as a common standard of achievement for all peoples and all nations, states that no one shall be held in slavery or servitude and that slavery and the slave trade shall be prohibited in all their forms;
Recognizing that, since the conclusion of the Slavery Convention signed at Geneva on 25th September, 1926, which was designed to secure the abolition of slavery and of the slave trade, further progress has been made towards this end;
Having regard to the Forced Labour Convention of 1930 and to subsequent action by the International Labour Organization in regard to forced or compulsory labour;
Being aware, however, that slavery, the slave trade and institutions and practices similar to slavery have not yet been eliminated in all parts of the world;
Having decided, therefore, the Convention of 1926, which remains operative, should now be augmented by the conclusion of a supplementary convention designed to intensify national as well as international efforts towards the abolition of slavery, the slave trade and institutions and practices similar to slavery.
Have agreed as follows:

SECTION I
INSTITUTIONS AND PRACTICES SIMILAR TO SLAVERY

Article 1

Each of the States Parties to this Convention shall take all practicable and necessary legislative and other measures to bring about progressively and as soon as possible the complete abolition or abandonment of the following institutions and practices, where they still exist and whether or not they are covered by the definition of slavery contained in Article 1 of the Slavery Convention signed at Geneva on 25th September, 1926:

(a) debt bondage, that is to say, the status or condition arising from a pledge by a debtor of his personal services or of those of a person under his control as security for a debt, if the value of those services as reasonably assessed is not applied towards the liquidation of the debt or the length and nature of those services are not respectively limited and defined;

(b) serfdom, that is to say, the condition or status of a tenant who is by

Appendix III

law, custom or agreement bound to live and labour on land belonging to another person and to render some determinate service to such other person, whether for reward or not, and is not free to change his status;
(c) any institution or practice whereby:
   (i) a woman, without the right to refuse, is promised or given in marriage on payment of a consideration in money or in kind to her parents, guardian, family or any other person or group; or
   (ii) the husband of a woman, his family, or his clan, has the right to transfer her to another person for value received or otherwise; or
   (iii) a woman on the death of her husband is liable to be inherited by another person;
(d) any institution or practice whereby a child of young person under the age of eighteen years is delivered by either or both of his natural parents or by his guardian to another person, whether for reward or not, with a view to the exploitation of the child or young person or of his labour.

Article 2

With a view to bringing to an end the institutions and practices mentioned in article 1(c) of this Convention, the States Parties undertake to prescribe, where appropriate, suitable minimum ages of marriage, to encourage the use of facilities whereby the consent of both parties to a marriage may be freely expressed in the presence of a competent civil or religious authority, and to encourage the registration of marriages.

SECTION II
THE SLAVE TRADE

Article 3

1. The act of conveying or attempting to convey slaves from one country to another by whatever means of transport, or of being accessory thereto, shall be a criminal offence under the laws of the States Parties to this Convention and persons convicted thereof shall be liable to very severe penalties.

2. (a) The States Parties shall take all effective measures to prevent ships and aircraft authorized to fly their flags from conveying slaves and to punish persons guilty of such acts or of using national flags for that purpose.

(b) The States Parties shall take all effective measures to ensure that their ports, airfields and coasts are not used for the conveyance of slaves.

3. The States Parties to this Convention shall exchange information in order to ensure the practical co-ordination of the measures taken by them in combating the slave trade and shall inform each other of every case of the slave trade, and of every attempt to commit this criminal offence, which comes to their notice.

Article 4

Any slave who takes refuge on board any vessel of a State Party to this Convention shall *ipso facto* be free.

SECTION III
SLAVERY AND INSTITUTIONS AND PRACTICES SIMILAR TO SLAVERY

Article 5

In a country where the abolition or abandonment of slavery, or of the institutions or practices mentioned in article 1 of this Convention, is not yet complete, the act of mutilating, branding or otherwise marking a slave or a person of servile status in order to indicate his status, or as a punishment, or

Slavery

for any other reason, or of being accessory thereto, shall be a criminal offence under the laws of the States Parties to this Convention and persons convicted thereof shall be liable to punishment.

Article 6

1. The act of enslaving another person or of inducing another person to give himself or a person dependent upon him into slavery, or of attempting these acts, or being accessory thereto, or being a party to a conspiracy to accomplish any such acts, shall be a criminal offence under the laws of the States Parties to this Convention and persons convicted thereof shall be liable to punishment.

2. Subject to the provisions of the introductory paragraph of article 1 of this Convention, the provisions of paragraph 1 of the present article shall also apply to the act of inducing another person to place himself or a person dependent upon him into the servile status resulting from any of the institutions or practices mentioned in article 1, to any attempt to perform such acts, to being accessory thereto, and to being a party to a conspiracy to accomplish any such acts.

SECTION IV
DEFINITIONS

Article 7

For the purposes of the present Convention:
(a) 'slavery' means, as defined in the Slavery Convention of 1926, the status or condition of a person over whom any or all of the powers attaching to the right of ownership are exercised, and 'slave' means a person in such condition or status;
(b) 'a person of servile status' means a person in the condition or status resulting from any of the institutions or practices mentioned in article 1 of this Convention;
(c) 'slave trade' means and includes all acts involved in the capture, acquisition or disposal of a person with intent to reduce him to slavery; all acts involved in the acquisition of a slave with a view to selling or exchanging him; all acts of disposal by sale or exchange of a person acquired with a view to being sold or exchanged; and, in general, every act of trade or transport in slaves by whatever means of conveyance.

SECTION V
CO-OPERATION BETWEEN STATES PARTIES AND COMMUNICATION OF INFORMATION

Article 8

1. The States Parties to this Convention undertake to co-operate with each other and with the United Nations to give effect to the foregoing provisions.

2. The Parties undertake to communicate to the Secretary-General of the United Nations copies of any laws, regulations and administrative measures enacted or put into effect to implement the provisions of this Convention.

3. The Secretary-General shall communicate the information received under paragraph 2 of this article to the other Parties and to the Economic and Social Council as part of the documentation for any discussion which the Council might undertake with a view to making further recommendations for the abolition of slavery, the slave trade or the institutions and practices which are the subject of this Convention.

Appendix III

Section VI
FINAL CLAUSES

Article 9
No reservations may be made to this Convention.

Article 10
Any dispute between States Parties to this Convention relating to its interpretation or application, which is not settled by negotiation, shall be referred to the International Court of Justice at the request of any one of the parties to the dispute, unless the parties concerned agree on another mode of settlement.

Article 11
1. This Convention shall be open until 1st July, 1957 for signatures by any State Member of the United Nations or of a specialized agency. It shall be subject to ratification by the signatory States, and the instruments of ratification shall be deposited with the Secretary-General of the United Nations, who shall inform each signatory and acceding State.

2. After 1st July, 1957 this Convention shall be open for accession by any State Member of the United Nations or of a specialized agency, or by any other State to which an invitation to accede has been addressed by the General Assembly of the United Nations. Accession shall be effected by the deposit of a formal instrument with the Secretary-General of the United Nations, who shall inform each signatory and acceding State.

Article 12
1. This Convention shall apply to all non-self-governing, trust, colonial and other non-metropolitan territories for the international relations of which any State Party is responsible; the Party concerned shall, subject to the provisions of paragraph 2 of this article, at the time of signature, ratification or accession declare the non-metropolitan territory or territories to which the Convention shall apply *ipso facto* as a result of such signature, ratification or accession.

2. In any case in which the previous consent of a non-metropolitan territory is required by the constitutional laws or practices of the Party or of the non-metropolitan territory, the Party concerned shall endeavour to secure the needed consent of the non-metropolitan territory within the period of twelve months from the date of signature of the Convention by the metropolitan State, and when such consent has been obtained the Party shall notify the Secretary-General. This Convention shall apply to the territory or territories named in such notification from the date of its receipt by the Secretary-General.

3. After the expiry of the twelve-month period mentioned in the preceding paragraph, the States Parties concerned shall inform the Secretary-General of the results of the consultations with those non-metropolitan territories for whose international relations they are responsible and whose consent to the application of this Convention may have been withheld.

Article 13
This Convention shall enter into force on the date on which two States have become Parties thereto. It thereafter shall enter into force with respect to each State and territory on the date of deposit of the instrument of ratifi-

Slavery

cation or accession of that State or notification of application to that territory.

Article 14

1. The application of this Convention shall be divided into successive periods of three years, of which the first shall begin on the date of entry into force of the Convention in accordance with the first part of article 13.

2. Any State Party may denounce this Convention by a notice addressed by that State to the Secretary-General not less than six months before the expiration of the current three-year period. The Secretary-General shall notify all other Parties of each such notice and the date of the receipt thereof.

3. Denunciations shall take effect at the expiration of the current three-year period.

4. In cases where, in accordance with the provisions of article 12, this Convention has become applicable to a non-metropolitan territory of a Party, that Party may at any time thereafter, with the consent of the territory concerned, give notice to the Secretary-General of the United Nations denouncing this Convention separately in respect of that territory. The denunciation shall take effect one year after the date of the receipt of such notice by the Secretary-General, who shall notify all other Parties of such notice and the date of the receipt thereof.

Article 15

This Convention, of which the Chinese, English, French, Russian and Spanish texts are equally authentic, shall be deposited in the archives of the United Nations Secretariat. The Secretary-General shall prepare a certified copy thereof for Communication to States Parties to this Convention, as well as to all other States Members of the United Nations and of the specialized agencies.

IN WITNESS WHEREOF the undersigned, being duly authorized thereto by their respective Governments, have signed this Convention on the date appearing opposite their respective signatures.

DONE at the European Office of the United Nations at Geneva, this......... day of September, 1956.

NOTE: The Member States that are known to have signed the Supplementary Convention up to the end of 1956 are: Australia, Belgium, Byelorussia, Canada, Czechoslovakia, El Salvador, France, Federal Republic of Germany, Greece, Guatemala, Haiti, Hungary, India, Iraq, Israel, Liberia, Luxembourg, Mexico, Netherlands, Norway, Pakistan, Peru, Poland, Portugal, Roumania, San Marino, Sudan, Ukraine, U.S.S.R., U.K., Viet Nam and Yugoslavia.

INDEX

Abolition of slavery by various States, 37, 187
ad hoc Committee on Slavery of the UN, 191 *et seq.*, 194
African slave trade, origin of, 17
African debt-bondage, 70
Allen, Beatrice, bequest to Anti-Slavery Society, 169
American abolition of the slave trade, 154
American emancipation, 154 *et seq.*
American abolitionists, 152
André, Sister Marie, on African tribal marriage, 99
Anti-slavery Conventions, 148, 149, 152
Anti-Slavery Society, origin of, 145, 161
Anti-Slavery Reporter, 161
Anti-Slavery treaty, first, 18
Apprenticeship system, 149
Arabian slave trade, 141
Arabia, slavery in, 38 *et seq.*
Aristotle, acceptance of slavery, 15

Barbados, slave rising in, 144
Barbarossa, 18
Barbary piracy, 18
Barbary piracy, end of, 119
Berlin Act of 1885, 174
Betton's Charity, 122
Bolivia, sham-adoption of children in, 115
Brooks family in anti-slavery endeavour, 168
Brussels Conference of 1890, 175
Brussels Act of 1890, 29, 49, 141, 163, 176, 179, 202
Buxton, Fowell, 145, 146
Buxton, Sydney (later Earl), 162, 175
Buxton, Charles Roden, 166
Buxton, Travers, 164

Canning denounced slavery, 146

Cape Colony, effects of slavery in, 151
Cassin, René, supports slavery resolution at the UN, 191
Castration of slaves, 27
Ceylon, quasi-adoption in, 115
China, slavery in, 47
Clapham Sect, 133
Clarkson, Thomas, 131, 152, 160
Coates, C.H., on Chinese slavery, 35
Contract labour, 150
Congo, atrocities in, 163
Cruelty to child slaves in China, 35
Cy-Près Doctrine in law of trusts, 119

Debt-bondsman, Nieboer's definition of, 71
Debt-bondage, remedial measures, 71 *et seq.*
Declaration of Congress of Vienna, 1815, 172
Definitions of slavery, 21
de Gaury, Gerald, on slavery in Arabia, 51
de House, Prof Fernand, moves resolution on slavery at UN, 169
Dolben's Bill on loading of slave ships, 134
Drafting Committee of ECOSOC, 195

Eastern Nigeria, Committee on tribal marriage, 102
Eitel, Dr E. J., on sham-adoption of children, 106
Ejido system of land holding in Mexico, 85
Emancipation Bill, 149
Encyc. of Islam, on Islam on marriage, 62
Engen, Hans, Rapporteur to ECOSOC on slavery, 195
Epictetus, slave origin of, 16
Ethiopia, slavery in, 46, 202
Ethiopia, pledge to abolish slavery, 189, 202

Slavery

Experts on Slavery, Standing Advisory Committee of, 185

Forced Labour, 24, 26, 194
Fox, Charles James, 137
French anti-slavery activities, 135
French emancipation, 153

Gabars in Ethiopia, 91
Geneva Conference on Slavery, 1956, 196
Gold Coast (Ghana) cocoa profits, disposal of, 168
Grenville, Lord, introduced Abolition Bill, 138
Grimshaw, H. A., on tribal marriage, 96

Harris, Sir John and Lady, 164, 167
Harrison, Dr Paul, on Arabian slavery, 34
Headley, Lord, on Islam on slavery, 59
Hebrew Debt-bondage, 66
Hejaz, Treaty of 1927 with, 54
Holwood Park, Wilberforce Oak at, 133
Hurgronje, Snouk, on Islam on slavery, 61
Human Rights, Declaration of, on Slavery, 190
Hussey, Rebecca, Charity, 120

Ibn Saud's, King, Decree of 1936 on Slavery, 34, 56
India, debt-bondage in, 67, 203
International Slavery Bureau at Brussels, 177, 185 et seq.
Iraq, conviction of slave-trader in, 51

Jewish freeing of slaves in year of Jubilee, 31
Japan, sale of children in, 113

Kirk, Sir John, in Zanzibar, 173
Kedah, Debt-bondage Enactment in, 72

La Graviere, E., on slave trade into Arabia, 50, 153
Lasker, B., on Indian debt-bondage, 67
Lavigerie, Cardinal, on mutilation, 28
League of Nations Covenant, 180
League's Temporary Slavery Commission on marriage, 94

League of Nations on where slavery exists, 36
Liberia, Slavery Commission to, 188

Macaulay, Zachary, 161
Mandel Decree on marriage, 102
Mansfield's, Lord, judgment on slavery in Britain, 20
Mauritius, effects of slavery in, 151
Maxwell, Sir G., on Islam on slavery, 59
Maxwell, Sir G., on sham-adoption of children, 107
Mico, Lady, Charity, 120
Moslem States, duty of to Arabia, 65
Mutilation, 29

Napoleon, reintroduced slavery, 139
Nigeria, Govt. of, on marriage, 103
Noel-Buxton, Lord, mission to Ethiopia, 167

Omán, Treaty of 1822 with Sultan of, 173

Peonage, definition of, 76
Peonage, what it is, 75
Peonage in Latin-America, 78 et seq.
Peonage, remedies for, 85
Peru, hampered ad hoc Committee of the UN, 193
Peru, sham-adoption of children in, 115
Pilgrims to Mecca sold, 53
Pilgrims to Mecca, inspection of travel papers of, 189
Poblete, M. Troncoso, chairman of ad hoc Committee of UN, 192
Portuguese law on Debt-bondage, 78
Protocol re Slavery Convention of 1926, 195
Putumayo atrocities, 165

Quaker anti-slavery endeavour, 128, 146

Ramsay, James, 131
Roberts, Charles, attacked Putumayo atrocities, 165
Roman freeing of slaves, 31
Rutter, Eldon, on Arabian slavery, 33
Rutter, Eldon, suggestion on abolition of slavery in Arabia, 20

Index

Saudi-Arabia, slavery in, 37
Saudi-Arabia, treaty of 1927 with, 55
Search for slaves, right of, 197
Secretary-General of the UN reports on slavery, 195
Serfdom, 24
Serfdom in Bechuanaland, 89
Sham-adoption of children, where found, 105
Sharp, Granville, 129
Shoelcher, Victor, 152
Shrewsbury, W., forced to leave Barbados, 147
Simon, Lady Kathleen, 167, 187
Simon, First Viscount, leads deputation on slave charities, 125, 166
Slav, origin of slave, 16
Slavery, origin of, 15
Slavery in the UK, 17
Slave trade, British abolition, 49
Slavery in Ghana, 90
Slavery Convention of 1926, 181 et seq.
Slave risings, 144, 147
Smith Charity, 123
Smith, John, conviction and death of, 147
Society for the Abolition of the Slave Trade, 132
Somaliland, marriage in, 102
Stephen, James, introduces registration of slaves, 144

St. Germain-en-Laye, Convention of, 178
Supervisory Machinery, 198
Supplementary Convention on marriage, 104
Supplementary Convention on Slavery of 1956, 198, 251, App. III
Syed Ameer Ali on Islam on slavery, slavery, 62

Tapscott, Henry, J., Chairman of Committee of Anti-Slavery Soc., 16
Terence, slave origin of, 16

UN-ILO Mission in Bolivia, 86

Vialle, Jane, on African tribal marriage, 98
Victims of African slave trade, 18
Vienna, Congress of, 139

Wades Mill, monument to Clarkson at, 132
Wilberforce, Richard, Counsel for Anti-Slavery Society, 125
Wilberforce, William, 132, 142, 149

Yemen, slave trade through, 51
Yemen, slavery in, 40 et seq.
Yemen, Treaty of 1934 with, 56

Zanzibar, Treaty of 1845 with Sultan of, 173

For Product Safety Concerns and Information please contact our EU
representative GPSR@taylorandfrancis.com
Taylor & Francis Verlag GmbH, Kaufingerstraße 24, 80331 München, Germany

www.ingramcontent.com/pod-product-compliance
Lightning Source LLC
Chambersburg PA
CBHW070604300426
44113CB00010B/1390